The Complete RFID Handbook

A Manual and DVD
for Assessing, Implementing,
and Managing Radio Frequency
Identification Technologies
in Libraries

Diane Marie Ward

Neal-Schuman Publishers, Inc.

New York

London

Published by Neal-Schuman Publishers, Inc.
100 William St., Suite 2004
New York, NY 10038

Printed and bound in the United States of America.

The paper used in this publication meets the minimum requirements of American National Standard for Information Sciences—Permanence of Paper for Printed Library Materials, ANSI Z39.48-1992. ∞

Library of Congress Cataloging-in-Publication Data

Ward, Diane Marie, 1971-
    The complete RFID handbook : a manual and DVD for assessing, implementing, and managing radio frequency identification technologies in libraries / Diane Marie Ward.
        p. cm.
    Includes bibliographical references and index.
    ISBN 978-1-55570-602-9
    1. Libraries—Inventory control. 2. Radio frequency identification systems. I. Title.
Z699.75.W37 2007
025.00285—dc22

2007007651

To all the librarians

who strive to provide

the best access

to the information

they house and preserve,

and to the

patrons they shepherd.

Contents

List of Figures

Preface

If your library is considering adopting radio frequency identification (RFID), you may hear some heated opinions about this new technology. Patrons who hear that your library is considering a new system may go home and search on Google, only to find articles comparing it to a spy chip. Stories in the popular media have sensationalized radio frequency identification for shock value. When interviewing librarians about RFID, I have heard statements such as

- "Our patrons will worry about their privacy being compromised by a new Orwellian system that is going to monitor the books they read."
- "We don't have the money to afford a tag for each book, let alone all the other associated costs."
- "We don't have the staff to support implementing such a new system."

But when I speak to vendors, they say:

- "If only people understood that the system is not like Orwell's Big Brother from "1984". It actually helps to ensure patron satisfaction."
- "RFID might seem expensive, but it is the technology of the future and it is worthwhile to work with us *now* on pricing and get in on the ground floor. In the long run, it will pay off for the institution which implements early."
- "We can work with the library from selection to implementation and offer it support for the life of the system. We aren't going to just walk away after they sign the check."

What's the truth about RFID? Objective information can be difficult to find. Other than vendor Web sites and personal blogs, there is little information on RFID specifically for library applications. How can librarians make clear, informed decisions without an unbiased guide to explain this technology as it applies to them?

In the articles and white papers I have published and in the university courses I teach, I have tried to explore the real benefits of this emerging technology as well as strongly caution people about its limitations. *The Complete RFID Handbook* is the first book designed to help librarians decide whether or not to adopt this technology. It addresses the applications available for libraries, provides real-world examples, and offers sound suggestions for the best way to select and implement. I seek to provide information to all staff members who are involved in making the decision, implementing the equipment, or educating patrons about new procedures. I also include other librarians' RFID experiences: their concerns and questions as well as their success stories and problems they had to overcome.

In addition, this book seeks to arm the librarian against popular misconceptions about this technology. It is crucial for librarians to educate themselves about RFID's limitations in library settings, and to stay vocal in protecting patron privacy. Library applications are not the same as the more dynamic applications used by adopters such as Wal-Mart and the Department of Defense. When you thoroughly understand the difference, you will be able to calm patron's fears that the library's new system may compromise their privacy by explaining to them that it is not able to track or trace patrons, and there is no linkage between patron and item on the tag.

Benefits

In the simplest terms, RFID employs radio frequency to automatically identify and transmit data. Researchers have succeeded in utilizing radio frequency as a basis for the transmission of serialized identity information between an object, a reader, and a computer network system.

Automatic identification of items has several benefits for libraries. Perhaps the most obvious benefit is that it can provide a reliable self-checkout technique that discharges and deactivates items in just one step. Staff can free their time from routine library tasks to spend more time offering value-added patron-centric interactions. *The Complete RFID Handbook* seeks to demonstrate through research, interviews, and scientific data the many ways in which libraries can benefit from this technology. Using RFID, libraries can:

- reduce costs
- decrease repetitive stress injuries among staff
- empower patrons
- increase the ease and frequency of doing a complete stack inventory
- manage print material and audiovisual materials more efficiently
- locate missing items

- replace magnetic theft detection systems
- maximize productivity

Organization

The Complete RFID Handbook is organized with the busy librarian in mind. Chapters 1–4 explain the basics.

- Chapter 1, "RFID: An Innovative Technology in Libraries," defines terminology and gives examples of common applications. All involved parties should read this chapter.
- Chapter 2, "Understanding RFID Systems and Standards," describes a typical system's technical details.
- Chapter 3, "RFID Library Applications," describes applications and includes statistical information from my surveys.
- Chapter 4, "Determining the Return on Investment (ROI) of RFID," highlights some installations case studies, and also provides interviews with adopters on their experiences.

Chapters 5–8 are designed specifically for the library's adoption committee.

- Chapter 5, "Deciding to Put RFID into Operation," shares the experiences of early adopting libraries and lists important questions to ask your colleagues before you choose to buy.
- Chapter 6, "Designing Your RFID Solution: RFP," provides RFP guidelines and sample questions.
- Chapter 7, "Selecting Vendors," offers detailed information about the major library-specific vendors.
- Chapter 8, "Installing and Maintaining the Complete RFID System," focuses on integrated library systems.

The main part of the book concludes with information geared toward systems and public relations librarians.

- Chapter 9, "Protecting Staff and Patron Privacy within an RFID System," addresses the social issues and public relations aspects of adoption. The current opinions of privacy-rights advocates are included in order to give a balanced view of the issue.
- Chapter 10, "Public Relations and Patron Education," offers suggestions on managing a public relations campaign to teach the public about this technology.

The final part of the book, the RFID Pocket Guides, includes sections on RFID acronyms, the Library of Congress subject headings for RFID, and summarizes my library and vendor surveys conducted in the late winter and spring of 2006.

About the Accompanying DVD

On the DVD, I demonstrate how RFID self-check works; show tags on books and audiovisual materials; show the conversion process; illustrate what happens during inventory and searching for a missing item; and discuss the motivations for implementation and some of the results. This presentation will show RFID in live action. I visited Waterloo Public Library in Waterloo, Ontario, Canada, and interviewed Systems Manager Ellen Jones and Manager of Technical Services Sheila Mehes during their RFP (Request for Proposal) process. I filmed portions of an RFID demonstration by Shai Robkin, Chief Executive Officer of library RFID vendor, ITG, and I also filmed at Northland Public Library in Pittsburgh, Pennsylvania. I interviewed Executive Director Sandra Collins and Manager of Technical Services Edith Sutterlin. Their time and comments are greatly appreciated. All are excellent examples of librarians and technology enthusiasts. I thank them all for appearing in my first-ever DVD.

Acknowledgments

I would like to thank my mom for her love and encouragement and for taking me to a library soon after I could walk, for buying me a date stamp so I could properly due-date my homemade patron slips at age four, for remembering that I would line up my books and use them as a bridge for my Barbie; and thanks to my dad for not suggesting therapy at the age of five when he caught me scolding my Ernie and Bert dolls for having overdue books; to my brother for being the "cool" one in the family and taking that weight off of my shoulders so I could spend my summers working in libraries; to my mentor Serafino Porcari for hiring me 14 years ago and sharing his skills of cataloging; and to my loving husband, Jay Bartelo, who patiently listened to my incessant ramblings about this book for the last two years, and who never walks away from me when I start to ogle security gates and RFID labels on wooden pallets in stores.

Thanks also to my editors at Neal-Schuman for support and encouragement. I would especially like to thank all the librarians who graciously welcomed me into their libraries and took time to share their experiences implementing an RFID system. I wish to voice my appreciation to the hundred or so North American and international librarians, administrators, project managers, circulation librarians and systems administrators, and vendors of RFID systems and ILS's that were more than generous with their time. All were eager to help their colleagues make good decisions about RFID for libraries.

I hope my scholarly research presented here is in some humble way helpful to all who use it.

1

RFID: An Innovative
Technology in Libraries

Introduction

Radio Frequency Identification (RFID) is proving itself to be a viable technology to conduct routine library tasks and free up valuable staff time. It allows librarians and public services staff to move toward offering more value-added patron-centric interaction. Library administration, staff, patrons, and the collection as a whole benefit from RFID. This chapter gives the reader a historical and contextual grounding of RFID. For public service staff that may encounter a public only familiar with RFID from sensationalized media reports likening it to surveillance technology, this chapter highlights some current, everyday RFID applications that readers may find familiar. Chapter 1 provides an overview of RFID before we delve into the library-specific applications in the following chapters.

Defining RFID

RFID is the acronym for "Radio Frequency Identification." It is pronounced as it is spelled: R-F-I-D. RFID technology focuses on the automatic identification of objects. The basic function of an RFID system is to automatically transmit data from a uniquely identified item to a reader operating on a common radio frequency wavelength. Information is routed to a database in real time so staff can use data to more efficiently conduct business. It is essentially a bar code that can talk via radio frequency waves as it passes near a reader operating on the same frequency. This smart, conversant tag has a serialized identity, data storage memory, may be rewritten, and does not require line of sight to be read. Therefore, routine tasks that require human intervention can be automated through the use of these smart tags, relieving workers from mundane tasks to accomplish value-added services.

> A bar code is a set of lines that can be read via line-of-sight by an optical laser reader. It is used by many libraries as a means of item management for the circulation process. Each bar code is unique and is linked to an item record in the database. A book has to be physically handled and properly aligned in order to read the bar code.

RFID was viewed as a way to streamline the data flow using automatic identification and thus freeing up workers from mundane tasks associated with warehouses and product receiving which involved having to use a laser reader to read bar codes, or physically count merchandise to be unloaded. For retailers, RFID allows real-time data to be shared among retailer, Consumer Packaged Goods (CPG), and third-party logistics companies. At any point in time, authenticated network users would know exactly where products are in the supply chain using software developed for specific RFID applications.

During this time, some saw a comparable usage for these tags in libraries, archives, and museums. Librarians need to have control over the organization of the materials that their physical space houses and preserves. The physical space of a distribution center is similar to that of a library: objects are stored in a finite amount of space and, at any instance, an item may need to be located using an organization system that is dependent upon humans, and subsequently, possible human error, rooted in accomplishing mundane, routine tasks, may occur.

Adopting Technology in Libraries

Librarians are proud to be early adopters of new technology as evidenced by the early use of computers and bar code technology. In the 1950s, Henriette D. Avram and her colleagues created the computerized metadata framework, Machine Readable Cataloging (MARC), to share bibliographic and holdings information between libraries. In the 1970s, Fred Kilgour constructed what would become the Online Computer Library Center (OCLC), a cooperative online union catalog capitalizing on the technical functionality of MARC. Gradually, online library catalogs replaced the paper-based card catalog system and the 1980s witnessed the development of integrated library management systems. A library would contract with a single vendor to supply all the hardware, software, and technical support it needed, and the online public access catalog (OPAC) became ubiquitous. The circulation process was automated, borrowing the bar code technology that retailers introduced to improve their logistics and point-of-sale operations. The introduction of electronic article surveillance systems (EAS) protected each item from theft through the use of a electromagnetic and acoustomagnetic security system tags and security gates. The 1990s saw the emergence of client-server applications for library systems: staff used personal computers with graphical user interfaces tied into the library's server to perform tasks related to cataloging, acquisitions, and circulation. Today, patrons can search a library's catalog holdings 24 hours a day, 7 days a week via the library's Web site.

All of these innovations that improved service and access to information that patrons appreciate today are a result of the library profession's demonstrated eagerness to experiment with technology. RFID is the next in this list of technological enhancements. RFID systems capitalize upon the client-server arrangement to improve efficiency, reduce repetitive tasks, empower the patron, and allow staff to interact more with patrons. In 2003, Dr. Christopher Brown-Syed, editor of *Library & Archival Security*, wrote that perhaps RFID will be the bar code replacement since RFID: "does away with the need to handle materials when performing inventories, facilitates self-service for patrons, can replace magnetic theft detection systems, and can even facilitate reader's advisory . . . RFID seems an attractive long-term solution for large libraries and archives." (Brown-Syed, 2003: 2)

RFID-IN-ACTION INTERVIEW: USING WIRELESS TECHNOLOGY

As evidenced by the growing number of libraries adopting RFID, the trend toward using this wireless technology as a means of item management and security is legitimate, yet still at it genesis point. I asked the recent president of the American Library Association, Dr. Michael Gorman, his opinion:

Q: What are your thoughts on RFID?

A: I believe that, if librarians pay attention to the privacy and confidentiality rights of library users and if they employ the technology judiciously with due regard for those rights, RFID can be a very effective tool in library management, collection maintenance, etc. (Ward-Gorman interview, 2006)

Addressing the Image of "Big Brother"

What does RFID mean to patrons that hear it mentioned as a new technology for the community library and go home to search on Google, only to find articles comparing it to a spy chip? How do these Web-based media stories tarnish the library's image in the mind of its patrons? This book is designed to provide the librarian with information on RFID to drive home that a library's RFID system is not tied to any type of governmental scheme to monitor the reading habits of patrons. It is important to understand that RFID used in libraries is not linked to a Global Positioning System (GPS) and that it is not able to track or trace patrons, and that there is no linkage between patron and item on the RFID tag, as there is in the ILS. Citizens value privacy, and this is especially a factor for library patrons—where privacy is considered a paramount aspect of the library-patron relationship.

The potential for RFID to stretch beyond its closed-system use in libraries alarms some futurists and civil libertarians that feel RFID will bring about a society devoid of privacy. Some early articles on RFID painted a future society where ubiquitous RFID readers detect who an individual is based on embedded RFID tags in the consumer's clothing, shoes, handbags, books. Some patrons may associate a library's new RFID system with movies and books such as Steven Spielberg's *Minority Report*, George Orwell's *1984*, and Aldous Huxley's *Brave New World*. It is crucial for librarians to understand other applications that exist in order to speak informatively about the limitations of RFID in library settings so as not to confuse the library application with other applications which might have more dynamic features.

> For an early example of such an article comparing RFID to these fictionalized works, see Declan McCullagh's January 13, 2003 article on C/Net, "RFID Tags: Big Brother in Small Packages," available at: http://news.com.com/2102-1069-980325.html

Exploring the Beginning of a New Technology

Many important inventions, patents, and outside-the-box papers contributed to the development of RFID. Christopher Coleman wrote in his textbook, *An Introduction to Radio Frequency Engineering:* "Broadly speaking, radio frequency (RF) technology, or wireless as it is sometimes known, is the exploitation of electromagnetic wave phenomena in that part of the spectrum between 3 Hz and 300 GHz. It is arguably one of the most important technologies in modern society. The possibility of electromagnetic waves was first postulated by James Maxwell in 1864 and their existence was verified by Heinrich Hertz in 1887. By 1895, Guglielmo Marconi had demonstrated radio as an effective communications technology." (Coleman, 2004: 1)

In 1948, Harry Stockman wrote a paper titled "Communication by Means of Reflected Power," which some view as the beginning of using Marconi, Hertz, and Michael Faraday's discoveries for automatic identification. RFID has been used since the World War II era to identify aircraft in a friend or foe system. A signal was sent to a transponder to energize and reflect a signal to indicate if the craft was from a friendly country of origin, or if it was an enemy.

In 1969, Mario Cardullo sketched a drawing for an RFID passive tag while on a plane: " . . . I started to sketch in my notebook the idea for the RFID tag with a changeable memory. The original sketch showed a device with a transmitter, receiver, internal memory, and a power source." (Cardullo, 2002) Cardullo and William Parks were the principal forces at ComServ that sought out a patent for a passive, read/write RFID tag. U.S. Patent number 3,713,148 for "Transponder Apparatus and System," issued January 23, 1973, was approved for a transponder operating on internal power that had the means to transmit data stored on memory via radio frequency waves. This patent (and those of other inventors) provided for the automated toll collection systems that we use today.

California inventor Charles Walton holds ten RFID patents that have been referenced repeatedly in the development of current RFID applications. Walton held one of the first RFID-specific patents for a "Portable Radio Frequency Emitting Identifier," which used "an electrical current from a radio transceiver, or reader, to activate a key card when the two are within six inches of each other." (MIT's Inventor of the Week Archive, 2005) In 1973, Walton's company Proximity Devices created a passive transponder used as a keyless method of unlocking a door.

> For more on Charles Walton, please see Dean Takahashi's article on the inventor, "The Father of RFID," in the June 7, 2004 *Mercury News*.

For the next 30 years, RFID was studied by engineers. The Massachusetts-based Auto-ID Center was one of several global Auto-ID Centers that sought to expand upon Walton's RFID patent to automatically identify and transmit data between an object and a database using radio frequency waves. Led by a research and development group composed of Daniel W. Engels, Sanjay Sarma, and David L. Brock, MIT scientists tried to develop applications. When it was apparent that RFID could be scaled down to a size and cost that would make it usable to identify merchandise, the Auto-ID Center started to attract attention.

With the addition of Procter & Gamble's Kevin Ashton, the Auto-ID Center captured the financial support (estimated to be $20 million) of many consumer packaged goods manufacturers (CPG) and retailers. Research and development at the Auto-ID Center was supported by those who would benefit the most from an efficient logistics operation such as Wal-Mart, the United States Department of Defense, Gillette, Target, Home Depot, Coca-Cola, etc. In October 2003, when a shift in focus to marketing the RFID tag as an Electronic Product Code seemed natural, the Auto-ID Center's functions moved away from RFID, and "EAN International and the Uniform Code Council assumed the administrative functions of the Auto-ID Center to support the development and deployment of the Electronic Product Code (EPC) network. At the very heart of the network was to be the 96-bit EPC, using a string of numbers to identify an item's manufacturer and product category." (Poirier and McCollum, 2006: 4)

> The Center produced several white papers and research findings describing how data would be routed, shared, and mined in a networked physical world. See Sanjay Sarma, David L. Brock, and Kevin Ashton's white paper "The Networked Physical World: Proposals for Engineering the Next Generation of Computing, Commerce & Automatic-Identification."

Emergence of the Electronic Product Code (EPC)

EPCglobal, an international nonprofit consortium of governing boards was established to work cooperatively to create a seamless commercialized network of EPC tags and data. EPCglobal is interested in creating standards such as the RFID tags used in the marketplace especially for supply chain applications. Retailers saw RFID and hoped to reduce the need for back-room staff to manually count and scan the contents of each case and pallet shipment that arrives at the dock. With RFID dock portal readers, unloaded product is automatically read and the data uploaded in real time via EPCglobal's Object Name Service which allows both retailer and manufacturer cooperatively to track the movement of products from point A to B.

> Two good resources on RFID's history and applications are: Claus Heinrich's *RFID and Beyond* published by Wiley, and Steven Shepard's *RFID: Radio Frequency Identification,* published by McGraw-Hill.

**Figure 1.1:   Electronic Product Code Label Example
(Photo by Diane Ward)**

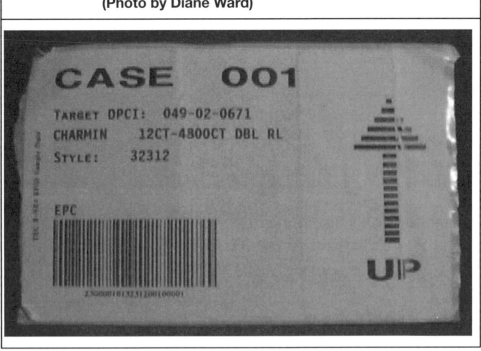

Adoption by Wal-Mart

Supply chain experts regard Wal-Mart as the model of supply chain efficiency and its former Chief Information Officer, Linda Dillman, has been credited with leading the drive to an RFID-enabled supply chain. In 2003, Wal-Mart issued a "mandate" to its top three tiers of large suppliers that they needed to affix RFID tags to each case and pallet shipped to Wal-Mart. Since Wal-Mart was adopting RFID for their supply chain, suppliers and manufacturers had to follow their RFID guidelines in order to sell their product. Soon other retailers and the U.S. Department of Defense issued similar supply chain RFID directives. However these case-and-pallet-level tagging mandates caught many suppliers off guard and they had to scramble to get up to speed on what RFID is, and how to implement it to meet mandates.

As a result, many problems with technical compliance and hardware reliability and tag interoperability ensued with the glut of new RFID-products entering the market trying to fill the demand. Conferences, blogs, online journals strove to disseminate information and pushed the vendors to a standard-based RFID market and *RFID Journal* emerged as a leader to report on and test the reliability of the RFID equipment produced by startup companies that were trying to fill the void in the industry created by the rush to mandate compliance.

Many academic centers and reliability labs started up to test the operability of RFID tags and hardware. They tested the claims of the RFID product and ensured that they adhered to ISO standards governing tag construction and operation. See RFID Journal's 2004 article, "RFID Alliance Lab to Test RFID Products," available at: http://rfidjournal.com/article/articleprint/1129/–1/1/

It is common at RFID conferences to hear how organizations have implemented RFID and claim that it improves logistics omniscience, increases accuracy, reduces out-of-stocks, reduces repetitive stress injuries, eliminates stock shrinkage, and enhances the cost-effectiveness and productivity of staff involved with supply chain procedures. The tightrope walk is to introduce a new system without totally reengineering an existing or legacy system.

A DECADE OF RESEARCH AND DEVELOPMENT SUCCESS

- Unique serialized item identification.
- Automatic transmission of data from object to reader on same radio frequency.
- Transmission of data in real time.
- Event data storage available via a server.
- Does not require line-of-sight to be read.
- Multiple tags can be read simultaneously without data collision.
- Location of items through read-event tracking.
- Ability to generate reports using RFID event data.
- Ability to couple tag with Electronic Article Surveillance (EAS).
- Security of data using encryption or authentication.
- Ability to couple tag with sensors to gauge environment conditions such as temperature and humidity.

Integrating RFID into Consumer Culture

Stories that shock the public garner more attention than technical stories about the true limitations of an emerging technology. There are reports of people being implanted, in some cases as techno-centric publicity stunts, in others it is for research-oriented experimental RFID applications. For example, library patrons and staff may be familiar with the hyped Robyn Curnow's 2004 CNN-reported story "The Price to

Pay for VIP Status." Curnow wrote she was implanted with an RFID chip at a Barcelona nightclub as a form of cashless payment that identified her as a club VIP. When she wanted it removed, the chip had moved a centimeter from its original point of insertion and was hard to locate, and had to be removed by a surgeon. Libraries are not implanting patrons with RFID chips; however, during my research, this story was often referenced by patrons I informally surveyed about RFID. The amount of time spent disqualifying a sensational report of an RFID application is often far greater than the time spent explaining the common and beneficial applications of the technology.

The following list is a compilation of some of the more common popular applications of RFID technology that staff and patrons might find familiar. The applications do not necessarily use the same type of RFID technology that the library application uses. For example, a military use of RFID would need a strong tag that could broadcast for meters and is expensive, and the tag used by libraries is inexpensive (in comparison) and cannot accomplish this. A caveat: Different tags can do different things. We will look at tag architecture in detail in Chapter 2.

Some popular applications include:

- Some may associate RFID with tagging their family pet with a unique identification chip. The RFID chip contains relevant data about the pet and its owner such as name, address, and contact information. The chip serves as an identifiable element to any animal rescue agency or veterinarian that has RFID readers.
- RFID is used by major retailers to gain efficiency and supply chain omniscience.
- RFID-enabled proximity smart cards are used to authenticate card-carrying individuals for entry into restricted areas.
- The United States Department of Defense (DOD) is requiring suppliers to include an active RFID tag on each pallet destined for DOD locations. The return on investment (ROI) is in knowing the exact contents of containers that are shipped to a war theater. During the Persian Gulf War, many containers with perishable food lay unopened and unrecognized in the hot desert sun because they were not labeled and therefore unidentifiable.
- RFID is a part of battlefield operations to authenticate government transport vehicles and their contents. The return on investment is improved safety of troops and increased gathering of battlefield intelligence without the unnecessary risk of life. High-end RFID tags can be customized with sensors that can gather valuable information about surroundings and movements and relay this information back to command posts.
- U.S. passports will contain RFID chips also in an attempt to avert terrorists from crossing borders with bogus passports.

- Exxon Mobil SpeedPass key fob contains an radio frequency microchip which enables gas station customers to wave the fob near the Exxon Mobil corporate logo on the pump to process their transaction on their account on record with the company.
- Contactless payment systems, popular in Asia, are used to pay for services and products, such as movie tickets or transportation.
- Contactless credit cards are emerging: American Express® Blue card has an RFID chip, as does the MasterCard PayPass®. For example, an RFID-enabled credit card reader requires an RFID-enabled credit or debit card to be held four inches above the terminal: No swiping is necessary, and no signatures are required for purchases under a certain amount.

This translates for the consumer to be able to use contactless payment cards at a point-of-sale device. Standards and interoperability of RFID systems are crucial to the success of RFID. An important factor in utilizing RFID technology for contactless payment systems is interoperability of the cards through strict adherence to mutually agreed upon standards ISO/IEC 14443. More information can be found at the Smart Card Alliance's home page:
www.smartcardalliance.org/pdf/about_alliance/
Final_Contactless_Payment_Backgrounder.pdf

- Automatic toll collection devices are used by drivers in some U.S. states and Canadian provinces. These RFID-driven toll collection devices are placed on a car window and enable a quick, cashless transaction without stopping at a staffed toll collection booth. The device is tied to a payment account, and tolls are deducted automatically.
- RFID is used to track and trace North American cattle and livestock from birth to slaughterhouse in order to control disease, provide safety for consumers, and enable efficient recalls of problems in the food supply.
- Loss prevention of children in amusement parks is in the application developed by Guest Technologies' SafeTzone Technologies Corporation. Family members wear RFID-enabled bracelets and use park terminals located to read the bracelet and find the whereabouts of other members displayed in real time on the screen.
- RFID has been incorporated into loss prevention applications involving seniors and Alzheimer patients in nursing homes. VeriChip™ has developed applications for wearable medical assistance in patient-wander prevention and to protect patients and infants in hospitals, assist in emergency man-

agement and help in asset location. RFID tags in healthcare can result in reduced costs associated with replacing lost or misplaced medical items and equipment.

- RFID can authenticate pharmaceuticals. Anticounterfeiting efforts are important since it has been reported that a small, but increasing, percentage of drugs are counterfeit. The United States Food and Drug Administration set up guidelines for its usage with "Radiofrequency Identification Feasibility Studies and Pilot Programs for Drugs."

> The United States Food and Drug Administration set up guidelines for its usage with "Radiofrequency Identification Feasibility Studies and Pilot Programs for Drugs," available at: www.fda.gov/oc/initiatives/counterfeit/rfid_cpg.html

- The concept of loss prevention extends to clothing and objects with RFID being sewn into uniforms, casino chips, and medical tools.
- At the Buffalo Enterprise Charter School, an RFID attendance system was instituted to increase efficiency in morning attendance by David Straitiff's Intuitek Company in 2004. A supervising teacher monitors students who hold a card six inches above an RFID reader while the RFID network marks the attendance via the RFID card automatically. A similar implementation by another company in Sutter, California, met with protests regarding privacy and was abandoned.

> Julia Scheeres' article in the October 24, 2003 *Wired* discusses the RFID badges used in this Buffalo school: "Three R's: Reading, Writing, RFID." It is available at: www.wired.com/news/technology/1,60898-1.html

- Automakers use RFID chips in their key-based security systems: "The keys in these systems include a transceiver, a transponder containing a unique identification encryption algorithm, and battery working together to immobilize a car until the owner wants to drive away." (Gould, 2000)
- RFID tags can be applied to high value items to authenticate their place of origin authenticity.
- CHEP, the largest producer of wooden pallets, embeds RFID tags into their product so that manufacturers and third-party logistics agencies can access information about the pallet's contents from portable readers, forklifts, trucks, and mounted dock readers. This helps to cut down on shrinkage (or theft) in the supply chain.

The corporation leading the market in implantable RFIDs is VeriChip Corporation, a subsidiary of Applied Digital: www.verichipcorp.com

- McCarran International Airport is one of the first airports to use RFID tags to prevent baggage loss. It is believed that RFID could exercise a dramatic improvement upon the monthly statistic of 100,000 people reporting missing bags and the $125 return cost that airlines pay to reunite a bag with its owner. The installation is an improvement over the bar code system that had a 70 percent accuracy read rate; RFID is providing 98–99 percent accuracy. (Roberti, 2006)
- Boeing and Airbus have issued a mandate that component suppliers should affix an RFID tag to shipments. With this system in place, it is estimated that the total time required to build a plane will decrease.
- The United States Food and Drug Administration approved RFID tags for medical use. In October 2004, the FDA approved an RFID chip implant the size of a grain of rice in humans, the VeriChip™. (Sullivan, 2004) The application was designed to help communicate the medical records of individuals when they cannot communicate this information themselves, for example after an accident, prior to surgery, and to avoid drug allergies/interaction. Contrary to what many might suspect, the VeriChip™ is not a Global Positioning System tracking device as it contains only a 16-digit unique identifier.

For more detailed information on current applications and pilot projects of RFID, please see *RFID Applications: Security and Privacy* by Simson Garfinkel and Beth Rosenberg, Addison-Wesley, 2006. This book features 32 chapters written by scores of leading theorists and practitioners in the field of radio frequency identification.

A complete list of RFID-related sources is provided in the RFID Pocket Guide D.
RFID Gazette, www.rfidgazette.org
RFID Journal, www.rfidjournal.com
RFID Update, www.rfidupdate.com
LITA Blog, http://litablog.org/
RFID in Libraries Blog, www.libraryrfid.net/wordpress

RFID-IN-ACTION INTERVIEW: BLOG AND DISCUSSION LIST

The online blog *RFID in Libraries* was started by Laura Smart currently at California State Polytechnic University. Smart was the chairperson of her library's RFID investigation team, but her library, Pomona, did not end up going with RFID.

Q: What role does the blog play for librarians?

A: I started the blog to teach myself how to blog. My interest in RFID was predicated by my appointment as chair of our library's RFID investigation team. I didn't find much information out there pertaining to libraries specifically, so I figured other librarians would be in the same boat. Thus, the blog was born.

Q: What role do you feel the blog "RFID in Libraries" had/will have for librarians trying to find information about RFID?

A: There's a big difference between how I envisioned the blog and how it ended up. I had hoped that the blog would become the go-to site for any librarian interested in RFID and that it would be written by multiple authors. It was to be newsy. That is: current; timely; informative; and well written in a journalistic style. Now there is much more information available to librarians interested in RFID. The blog is one of many ways that a librarian can get information. That's ok. With the new editor in charge I'm sure the blog will be the place to go for consolidated information about RFID in libraries.

Q: Do you have any advice?

A: Do your homework. Our library decided not to go with RFID after evaluating our options. (Ward-Smart interview, 2006)

The *RFID in Libraries* blog is now administrated by Principal Librarian for Technology at Eugene Public Library, Margaret Hazel. Hazel's library converted its 350,000 item collection to RFID and has automated material handling with RFID-enabled circulation. In 2004, she also began RFID_LIB, an electronic discussion list devoted to RFID library applications and troubleshooting.

Q: What role can the blog "RFID in Libraries" play for librarians trying to find information about RFID?

A: While the blog is not very active at the moment, there is very good information in the archives. I'd like to get it integrated with my e-mail list, RFID_LIB, which does have regular traffic, so that postings show up both places. These venues both have a wide readership, from what I can tell, including libraries of every stripe, vendors, and many folks in countries other than the U.S., as well as students and the merely curious. I would like to think that these two resources can provide a place to ask questions of experienced users and developers of RFID, as well as policymakers. Information on both ranges from quite technical to quite basic, and from policy-oriented to theoretical, and even covers alarmist media." (Ward-Hazel interview, 2006)

Enhancing Library Technology with RFID

Executive conferences draw thousands of CEOs, CIOs, and people involved in R&D (research and development). RFID Journal Live has routinely seen double digit percentage growth in attendance with each annual conference. There are also academic research labs that sponsor consortiums which draw the leading RFID researchers and inventors such as MIT's Auto-ID Center, and UCLA's WINMEC RFID Center, which is administrated by Rajit Gadh. There are a few online and print journals that have been created to disseminate the daily news from vendors and clients. The first of its kind is RFID Journal created by Mark Roberti. Much has been written about RFID usage in libraries in the RFID Journal as well as peer-reviewed library print journals and online publications.

> To join the electronic discussion list RFID_LIB, see http://
> slisweb.sjsu.edu/ecommunication/list subscriptions.html or send an
> email to listproc@ listproc.sjsu.edu. In the body, type: subscribe
> RFID_LIB firstname lastname

References

Brown-Syed, Christopher. 2003. "Editor's Introduction." *Library & Archival Security* 18, no. 2: 1–2.

Cardullo, Mario. 2002. "Genesis of the Versatile RFID Tag." *RFID Journal.* Available: www.rfidjournal.com/article/articleprint/392/–1/1/

Coleman, Christopher. 2004. *An Introduction to Radio Frequency Engineering.* Cambridge, UK: Cambridge University Press.

Gould, Lawrence S. 2000. "What You Need to Know About RFID." *Automotive Design and Production.* Available: www.autofieldguide.com/articles/020003.html

Greene, Thomas C. 2004. "Feds Approve Human RFID Implants." *The Register* (October 14). Available: www.theregister.co.uk/2004/10/14/human_rfid_implants/

Massachusetts Institute of Technology. Inventor of the Week Archive. Lemelson MIT Program. May 2005. Available: http://web.mit.edu/invent/iow/waltonc.html

Poirier, Charles, and Duncan McCollum. 2006. *RFID: Strategic Implementation and ROI: A Practical Roadmap to Success.* Fort Lauderdale, FL: J. Ross.

Roberti, Mark. 2006. "RFID Facilitates Remote Baggage Check-In." *RFID Journal* (February 28). Available: www.rfidjournal.com/article/articleprint/2174/–1/1

Sullivan, Laurie. 2004. "FDA Approves RFID Tags for Humans." *Information Week* (October 14). Available: http://informationweek.com/story/showArticle.jhtml?articleID=49901698

Ward, Diane Marie, and Michael Gorman, e-mail interview, August 20, 2006.

Ward, Diane Marie, and Margaret Hazel, e-mail interview, August 30, 2006.

Ward, Diane Marie, and Laura Smart, e-mail interview, August 23, 2006.

Additional Resources

Curnow, Robyn. 2004. "The Price to Pay for VIP Status: Settling the Bill the High-Tech Way." Atlanta, GA: CNN (October 6). Available: http://edition.cnn.com/2004/TECH/10/05/spark.bajabeach/

Heinrich, Claus. 2005. *RFID and Beyond.* Indianapolis, IN: Wiley.

McCullagh, Declan. 2003. "RFID Tags: Big Brother in Small Packages." *C/Net News.com* (January 13). Available: http://news.com.com/2102–1069–980325.html

RFID Journal. 2004. "RFID Alliance Lab to Test RFID Products." *RFID Journal* (September 22). Available: http://rfidjournal.com/article/articleprint/1129/–1/1/

Sarma, Sanjay, David L. Brock, and Kevin Ashton. 2000. "The Networked Physical World: Proposals for Engineering the Next Generation of Computing, Commerce & Automatic-Identification." Cambridge, MA: MIT. Available: http://64.233.161.104/search?q=cache:hiKO3TEk7lUJ:autoid.mit.edu/whitepapers/MIT-AUTOID-WH–001.PDF+kevin+ashton+proctor&hl=en&gl=us&ct= clnk&cd=1&client= safari

Scheeres, Julia. 2003. "Three R's: Reading, Writing, RFID." *Wired News* (October 24). Available: www.wired.com/news/technology/1,60898–1.html

Shepard, Steven. 2005. *RFID: Radio Frequency Identification.* New York: McGraw-Hill.

Takahashi, Dean. 2004. "The Father of RFID." *Mercury News* (June 7).

United States Food and Drug Administration. "Radio Frequency Identification Feasibility Studies and Pilot Programs for Drugs." Available: www.fda.gov/oc/initiatives/counterfeit/rfid_cpg.html

2

Understanding RFID Systems
and Standards

Introduction

For libraries, RFID applications have been designed at the item level. Everything is focused on item shelf management and the circulation lifecycle. Unlike supply chain applications, the library application truly makes dynamic and repeated use of the data storage functionality of the RFID tag creating a positive cost-benefit. Library RFID tags are designed to last the lifetime of the object to which it is affixed, so libraries have only a one-time cost associated with applying a tag to an item.

An RFID system is comprised of tags, readers, server, standard protocol, database, middleware. The transmission of data is dependent upon these components operating at the same frequency and using the same protocols and standards. In technical terms, the chip, antenna, and label create a transponder, and the reader (or interrogator) is the transceiver able to power the tag and receive its transmitted data and route it to the database.

RFID systems for libraries operate via wireless communication using near-field inductive coupling. Radio waves operating at 13.56 MHz emanate from a coupler's antenna, awakening a tag to send its unique data through its coiled antenna back to the reader. Therefore, a coupler (for example, one present in a self-checkout reader) emits radio frequency (RF) energy and interrogates and receives an RFID tag's unique data. RF is the conduit for the transmittal of information in two readable directions.

It is important to note that not all systems or their component parts are created equal: some have features that another vendor's wares might lack at the moment. RFID components are constantly being improved upon to offer new features and to troubleshoot problems. At the RFP (request for proposal) stage, it is advisable to ask vendors to be specific about the functionality of their current equipment.

The Power Source

Each integrated circuit needs a power source. It is beyond the scope of the book's focus to go into detail about all types of tags, since libraries exclusively use passive tags that operate on 13.56 MHz. However, it is crucial for librarians to understand the different types of tags in order to educate the public about the technical limitations of the library RFID tag.

RFID tags may be classed as active, passive or (seldom-used) semi-passive. Generally, applications that require a tag to transmit data far (up to 300 feet/100 meters) or relay sensory information (like temperature) will employ an active tag. The power source for data transmission is a battery, which, although not replaceable, lasts a long time. Active tags can cost several dollars a piece and are found on items used in government applications or maritime shipping containers. Active tags are never turned off.

Library-specific passive tags use induction to receive the energy to power up the tag and transmit data. Passive tags for library applications do not have a battery as an internal power source so they are dead or asleep until the RF of a reader operating at 13.56 MHz reaches a tag's antenna. The RF is converted to electricity and becomes the recipient tag's power source. The tag's coiled antenna wakes up inside this signal field and couples with the reader's antenna to form a magnetic transferal field. The RF tag answers the RF reader's interrogation by transmitting its unique chip data via 13.56 MHz. After the reading event occurs and it is out of a reader's RF range, the tag's circuitry loses energy and it falls back to sleep. Since the reader's RF-emitting antenna is the coupling agent, passive RFID tags on library shelves cannot couple each other.

This call and response is what makes each RFID tag work: the coupler in the handheld reader or desktop reader powers the tag via RF operating at 13.56 MHz. The range for a reader and tag antenna in a library setting is designed to be under a foot so a tag needs to be close enough to the reader's antenna to couple power to wake up the tag. Passive tags are not powered by a battery and therefore do not constantly broadcast unique data. Because of its architecture and power source, a passive RFID tag has a long shelf life and should be expected to last the life of the item to which it is attached.

Radio Frequency

It is important to understand the importance of radio frequency: high frequency (HF 3–30 MHz range), ultra high frequency (UHF 300–3000 MHz range), or low frequency (LF 30–300 KHz range). Libraries use the high frequency tags at 13.56 MHz. This tag has a read range usually of up to three feet or one meter. This makes it particularly attractive for a library. The read range can be modified so that tags can be read from under a distance of one foot (usually eight inches) rather than three feet.

The 13.56 MHz tag has been used in the past for retail implementations of RFID, but the testing of the tag did not prove to bring the results that retail research and development teams were looking for. The high frequency range provides for paper thin construction and a simple coiled antenna design which allows for fast data transfer of a small amount of unique data encoded on the microchip.

Interference results in inaccurate reads. For instance, have you ever been on a cordless 2.4 GHz phone and found your laptop's wireless connection fails you? It is this type of competition and interference that can negate benefits in some RFID supply chain; libraries do not seem to experience this problem that often. A wireless site survey of your library by the vendor can alleviate some of these problems.

In the United States, the FCC does not require people to get a license to operate RFID tags on 13.56 MHz. Operating on this frequency means that library tags should not interfere with wireless hotspots (802.11 abg), pacemakers, cell phones, or other security mechanisms. Other RFID applications call for a different set of elements thus requiring a different frequency to suit the data transmission or in order for optimum operation in a harsh environment like a warehouse.

The radio frequency tag used to meet the mandate requirements set forth by Wal-Mart and the Department of Defense is an UHF tag which operates around 915MHz (see "EPC Gen What?" later in this chapter). This tag works well for logistics usage, although it can suffer from interference in a dirty warehouse environment which includes high power electrical wires, metal forklifts, 2.4 GHz phones, and walkie-talkies. Even item and tag orientation sometimes played havoc with early warehouse installations. Slowing down a conveyor belt from a standard six miles per hour just to have item tags read seemed unacceptable and counterproductive to many in the industry; thus, scientists responded by architecting a tag that could be properly read from different angles.

Library tags cannot be read by readers when used in warehouse applications that operate on other frequencies. And if the data is encrypted, it will not be able to be properly read by an unauthorized/unauthenticated reader. The small amount of data that is passed between transceiver and transponder takes milliseconds; however, if the goal is to transmit more data at 13.56MHz, one would need a faster RFID system with a longer expected time to transmit the data, perhaps seconds. Therefore it is in the interests of efficiency to keep the amount of data transmitted very small. The main manufacturers of RFID chips and tags are: Tagsys, Texas Instruments, Philips Semiconductors, and UPM Rafsec/UPM Raflatec.

> For a general introduction to the components of RFID, please see: Patrick J. Sweeney II, *RFID for Dummies*, published by Wiley in 2005. Sweeney is a highly respected RFID researcher, developer, and entrepreneur who trained at MIT. He is the CEO of ODIN Technologies, one of the earliest RFID companies. This book offers an approachable and thorough look at many aspects of RFID.

Smart Tags

The composition of an RFID smart tag is fairly straightforward. A microchip is the brains of the tag and has an integrated circuit. This chip contains the memory bits—an amount which varies depending upon the amount of information a library wants stored on a chip. Usually, a library simply wants an item identification and perhaps some space to write and rewrite data, that is, physical library branch or collection location which may change over time. In order for this information to be utilized or "read," the chip needs to be connected to an antenna. The antenna is coiled around the chip. It might be aluminum or copper, the latter of which is better for conductivity but is costly to manufacture. These two elements are housed in a protective substrate. This substrate has an adhesive backing on one side in order to adhere to an item. It may or may not have an eye-readable area with identifying printing on the non-adhesive side. The tag becomes a label which can be affixed to a book or a wooden pallet.

Chips and Data Programming

Each RFID tag is unique and may be programmed by the manufacturer or left to be programmed by a library. The quality of uniqueness stems from the multi-bit number associated with each tag. Memory storage varies on chips but is measured in bits. Library chips might have 256 to 2,048 bits of data, but they can be considerably higher or lower depending upon vendor and library application. The larger the amount of bits, the more expensive the tag and the more data that can be stored; however, most libraries want only a minimal amount of data on the tag. Libraries might want to select a tag (as well as a system) that allows for scalability and future applications such as sorting. Vendors will work with your team so you do not select a tag that does

Figure 2.1:   RFID Book Tag from Bibliotheca
(Supplied by Bibliotheca, photographed by Diane Ward)

Figure 2.2:   RFID D8 Book Tag from 3M™
(Photo courtesy of 3M™)

not have enough memory to expand to put a physical location or code for sorting, in case your library someday wants to buy a sorter for automated material handling.

The chip's data affords serialization with an impressive amount of non-repeating numbers. Data is separated into four or five areas, either lockable (not able to be changed) or unlockable (able to be rewritten). Vendors and tags vary in their amount of locked and unlocked fields. Furthermore, another number sequence delineates a unique product and then serializes that down to the level of unique object. My 2006 survey of library vendors showed a range of bits of memory on the tags, but 256 bits was very common.

The RFID tag is applied to each individual item that an agent (in our case, a library) wants to manage. For a library, item management means that each book or media object is defined with a unique identifier to the database so that it can properly circulate, be secured against theft, and can be located on the shelf. Theoretically, it is the same practice as with the common bar code management system, but this bar code can automatically communicate to you via an RFID reader.

> For more detailed engineering information on RFID components, please see Klaus Finkenzeller's textbook: *RFID Handbook: Fundamentals and Applications in Contacless Smart Cards and Identification*, 2nd ed., published by Wiley in 2003 and translated by Rachel Waddington. This work features detailed engineering information about frequency, read range, and so on. It is a popular text for students of RFID and is regarded as the authority on constructing RFID system components and networks.

Data is housed on bits of memory on the microchip. Most of the tags offered to libraries contain 256 to 2,048 bits of information. The RF emanating from the reader's antenna signals the RF antenna in the tag to wake up and transmit its data. The call and response is initiated by the reader. The data packet containing the item's unique identifier (bar code) is then sent to the ILS using a protocol that interfaces with the RFID system. Improvements have been made on the early RFID systems so that data packet collision is rare. The fields on the tag that hold the information are usually limited to the item's unique identifying number such as the bar code number and, perhaps, the physical library location of the book, if more than one branch is involved. Data is written in blocks at the point of manufacture which can be locked or unlocked. It is advisable to lock the item's unique identification field block.

As Bruce Potter of Booz Allen Hamilton, a New York City-based consulting firm specializing in risk assessment, succinctly points out in "RFID: Misunderstood or Untrustworthy": "RFID tags typically only contain a unique number that is useless on its own. The idea is that the reader interfaces with some backend systems and databases for all transactions. The database stores the information that ties the unique

ID to something of interest." (Potter, 2005) Data is transferred in milliseconds. Data is secured by either data encryption or authentication between RFID reader and tag.

Tags can be designed in a number of ways:

- Read only, which can come preprogrammed with a serialized identifier;
- Write once read many (WORM), which can come preprogrammed but has some space for unique data, but it cannot be changed dynamically in the future;
- Read/write, which has some portion of data that is locked but also has some space to write or update information. Libraries can program the tag to match an item's bar code and reprogram it again and again. This is the standard design for library tags.

Although most tags in use today are rewritable to take advantage of being able to change data in the future (like an item location, or limitations on usage or reproduction), they are not rewritten at the point of borrowing to include the patron's identification. There is no link on the RFID tag between the book and the patron's identification.

It is advisable to lock certain sections of memory to prevent them from being accidentally overwritten. Lockable memory usually comprises only a portion of the total number of memory bits available. Early RFID tags contained 96 to 256 bits of memory and cost nearly $1.00 each. In 2006, the price averages around 53 cents and a library can store much more data on the tag; however, most libraries choose only to place the item's original eye-readable barcode identifier or a random RFID tag number in a locked memory area to link the item with its OPAC record.

> Tag price has decreased by 50 percent in the last five years from a high of $1.00 (U.S.) to just over 50 cents on average.

The ability to rewrite data may prove a benefit for libraries for future projects like sorting materials destined for disparate physical branch locations. If a library wants to house certain items in a storage facility, an area of memory can be used to write to and add a physical location (such as "Storage"). The capabilities and uses of the rewritable aspect of the tag have not been realized yet as we are early on in library RFID installations.

Anti-collision algorithms allow for more than one tag to send its data to a reader in the same RF field without interference or confusion. Anti-collision allows more than one tag to be read at once. This is why library patrons are able to place a stack of materials on a reader pad for self-checkout, and why inventorying a collection is feasible using RFID. The multiple tags are read in real time at what appears to be simultaneous transactions. Anti-collision does not reflect on the way data is sent into the ILS: data enters the library's ILS one at a time via the unique identifier. Patents for new developments relating RFID functionality abound, but the patents for the anti-collision algorithms were crucial because they enable multiple tags to be read in the same RF reader field. (RFID Journal, 2002)

Figure 2.3: RFID Read and Write Characteristics		
Read Only	The tag is preprogrammed with data. It can be read numerous times.	Tag is already programmed and you can never change the data on the tag.
Write Once, Read Many (WORM)	You can encode the tag with data only once. It can be read numerous times.	You program it once, perhaps using the item's bar code during conversion, but then you cannot change the data later.
Read/Write	You can write data and choose to lock the fields or not. An unlocked field can be rewritten. It can be read numerous times.	You can program the tag with data at conversion. Then if you want to change the data, you can reprogram the tag with new information. This is useful if you want to reuse a tag for a different item and you need to change the bar code, or you want to change data, such as a location code.

Security Bits

Libraries can choose to keep their legacy security system or to purchase an RFID tag that has a security bit on it. With this option, the library receives a benefit by removing an additional step in the circulation process which makes discharging materials faster for patrons.

Traditional EAS is a one bit system because the bit answers yes (1) or no (0) to a question and can be part of an electromagnetic or acoustomagnetic tag system. 3M's RFID solution offers an opportunity for libraries that do not want to give up their existing EAS (Electronic Article Surveillance) system to benefit from RFID's item management capabilities.

RFID systems use a variety of systems to accomplish EAS. 3M's system offers two options: One Tag™ which has item management and security on one tag, or a system that allows the library to keep its original EAS system, in many cases the 3M™

Tattle Tape™ magnetic strip system. At this point in time, Checkpoint Systems do not have a security bit on the tag for their system. Instead, the gates query the file on the server to see if the tag has been checked out in order to determine if the item should set off an alarm. Other systems, Bibliotheca-RFID, Integrated Technology Group, Library Automation Technologies, Libramation, Tech Logic, and VTLS offer tags that have item management and the EAS bit on the chip.

Putting a security bit on the chip makes the chip more expensive, but the cost may be worth it if one considers the convenience of having one tag perform two functions using automatic identification. The EAS is designed as a single bit that switches on or off to signal to the gate if the book has been properly checked out. The security gates in an RFID system read the tag to see if it has been deactivated.

Of course, any security system can be foiled if someone is determined. RFID can literally be foiled by aluminum foil when placed over an RFID tag. The readability of tags can also be negatively affected by Mylar. If a thief does not have foil handy, he/she could just look on the cover for a plain label that has a raised bump. These older, thicker tags are easy to spot and thus easier for thieves to peel off and walk through the gates undetected. Some RFID tags do not have a raised center and bear the library's logo and therefore appear to be a simple book label to the thief. We must all remember that even with electromagnetic strips, a thief might rip off the cover and the security device and again, succeed at stealing the object. Karen Coyle notes that often security gates function as "a social deterrent" more so than actual prevention (Coyle, 2005). It is best to discuss your vision for a security system with your RFID vendors and in your RFP.

Label Application

When the microprocessing chip is linked to the antenna and applied to a substrate, the next step is to fashion it into a label with an adhesive backing. Most tags created for libraries are 2" x 2" or 2" x 3" and are fairly thin and may be peeled off of a backing. As with a bar code or EAS label, an RFID label is affixed to a book cover or dust jacket. Labels have a reliable adhesive on the back. For a few extra cents, eye-readable printing can appear on the tag which could bear the name of your library and any identifying information that your library wants such as a Web site or physical address. RFID labels are less susceptible than a bar code to damage from dirt, grease, or other physical treatment because the eye-readable part of the label is not the mechanism to convey data to an optical reader.

Audiovisual Material Tags

Bar codes are usually affixed to a cover of a book, or on the container of an audiovisual item, since affixing it to certain audiovisual materials will impact the playability of the audiovisual item. As the impact of multimedia materials was fully realized, more companies developed cases and kits to house CDs, DVDs, audiocassettes, and videocassettes.

> The RFID Alliance Lab seated at the University of Kansas in Lawrence specializes in testing RFID equipment for interoperability and adherence to approved standards. It provides RFID customers with a sense of certainty that the product delivers its advertised functionality and is within the parameters of ISO standards.

With early installations of RFID, there was a problem using the tags on media materials, especially CDs and DVDs as they have metal content which impedes the easy readability of a tag. The tags for objects that need to slide into disc readers need to be small and thin, but if your traditional book label is affixed directly to the metal CD or DVD, you will not have a good read rate because of the way metal affects RF. If you apply what has been learned in supply chain implementations, such as creating a buffer between the RFID tag and the metal, you run into the problem of space. A CD has to fit into a narrow slot of a CD player and there is no allowance for a buffer zone for the RFID tag. Researchers worked to try and establish some type of tag that would respect the architecture of disc players and allow for the proper transmission of RF between tagged object and RF reader.

In my RFID Journal article "Tags for CDs Get a Boost," I included information about the new (at the time) development for tagging audiovisual discs which was created by Bibliotheca and manufactured by UPM Rafsec during an installation in the Mastics-Moriches-Shirley Community Library in Long Island, New York. The BiblioChip Secure-it label system consisted of a hub label (about the size of a quarter), which sat on the disc's clear plastic center, and a booster label covering the top surface of the disc with an aluminum ring circling the disc's outer edge to amplify the signal of the hub. The hub cost .99 cents and the booster $1.49 and both were ISO 15693 compliant. It was said this tag combination boosted the read accuracy from 70 percent to near 100 percent (Ward, 2004).

> The names of the labels associated with audiovisual equipment are called hubs, donuts, or boosters.

Figure 2.4:   RFID Donut Tag for Audiovisuals from Bibliotheca
(Supplied by Bibliotheca, photographed by Diane Ward)

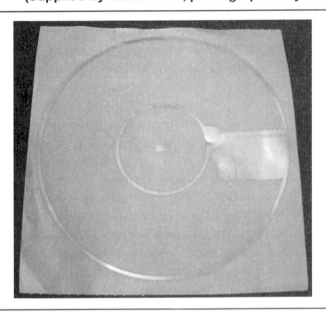

Figure 2.5:   RFID Hub Tag for Audiovisuals from Bibliotheca
(Supplied by Bibliotheca, photographed by Diane Ward)

Electronic Production Code (EPC)

When investigating RFID tags, librarians may notice many references to EPC Gen 2, Class 1 and ISO 18000–6. This is due to the movement for standardization and interoperability for tags used by retailers operating within the EPCglobal network. Early in the rush to meet Wal-Mart and U.S. DOD mandates, many R&D departments put forward new products (RFID readers, tags, and so on) but products from different companies were inoperable. IBM's Chen Junwei succinctly states in "Lightweight RFID Framework" that it was "a cacophony of incompatible RFID standards. Most of the major RFID vendors present proprietary systems with differing frequencies and protocol. This lack of open systems standardization could partly be responsible for the slow commercial growth of RFID and also impeded the price reductions that occur when a technology enjoys broad-based consumer use" (Junwei, 2004). EPCglobal seeks to have a standard air interface protocol so that true interoperability is possible no matter what vendor a company buys products from. Tags for case and pallet level implementations are known technically as EPC Gen 2 Class 1 ISO 18000–6C.

These EPC tags can range from 32 to 256 bits in data length and identify the product on a serial level, as well as the product family type, and the manufacturer. Although they are passive tags like those used in libraries, they operate on a different frequency, the Ultra High Frequency (860–960 MHz). Wal-Mart supported the work of EPCglobal and RFID manufacturers and encouraged them to hone standards and strive for interoperability of RFID tags, readers, and middleware.

EPCglobal does not regulate the tags used by libraries; however, it regulates the use of the codes by retailers. One hopes that the NISO RFID standards committee working with the Book Industry Studies Group will consider the positive implications for libraries of using the 13.56 MHz tag for use in materials supplied from the book publishing industry. If the EPC UHF tag is used, library readers will not be able to take advantage of the data transmission, and another HF tag will have to be applied.

In July 2006, the International Standards Organization (ISO) approved the EPC Gen 2 Class 1 UHF standards as 18000–6C, an add-on to the ISO 18600 standard for RFID air interface (O'Connor, 2006b).

Figure 2.6: Typical 96-Bit Electronic Product Code™ (EPC) Data Structure			
Header	EPC Manager	Object Class	Serial Number
12345678	123456789	1234567890123	123456789012345678901234567
Reserved 8 bits of memory	28 bits of memory (company)	24 bits of memory (product type)	36 bits of memory (unique for each product)

For more information on the EPCglobal tag standard, please see:
www.epcglobalinc.org/standards

Integration Standards

The major consideration with most library technology purchases is "How might this work with our existing integrated library system?" In order for data to be successfully exchanged between the RFID network and the library database, there needs to be a common protocol. The SIP2 protocol accomplishes this for RFID vendors, but there were problems with some ILS's and vendors had to tweak the SIP2 protocol in order to exchange the data and update the circulation records in real time. Without a real-time update of circulation information, the value of the RFID system is in question. Most RFID vendors will be able to integrate their RFID software with your library's legacy integrated library system through SIP2-protocol, unless their system does not need SIP.

A nonproprietary tag which adheres to an ISO standard is important since it guarantees chips can be supplied from various makers and will be compatible. Emmett Erwin and Christian Kern wrote about nonproprietary solutions as a "requirement for modern libraries today, since they make long-term investments and cannot afford to be dependent on one company for their lifeline. In a worst case scenario, all the labels in a library of 100,000 books would have to be ripped out and replaced by a new version of chips." (Erwin and Kern, 2003: 34)

Data Models

The Danish National Library Association has worked on a thorough data model for RFID tag construction. Its suggestions are found in an intensive study on the needs of data for library applications including self-check, sorting, and inventory. The group forwarded a data model for RFID before any other large library group did and thus they are looked to as an example of diligent and thoughtful work in terms of what type of data should be stored and transmitted on a library RFID tag. Leif Andresen is one of the architects of the data model and has delivered at conferences and shared his group's work on RFID_LIB. Their informational page is available at: www.bs.dk/standards/rfid

The Dutch and Finnish followed suit and issued their own data model based on the Danish findings. The Danish data model has caught the attention of American NISO RFID committee and Australian librarians that consider it a viable way to model an RFID tag's data structure: what fields carry what types of information, are fields locked or unlocked? Currently, group work is taking place to create an international standard with participation from some of the Danish, Dutch, and Finnish data model veterans. There are also representatives from the U.S., U.K., Australia, Germany, and Sweden. The models are very technical in nature, but are listed here for those interested:

- Danish Data Model: www.bs.dk/standards/RFID%20Data%20Model%20for%20Libraries.pdf
- Finnish Data Model: www.lib.helsinki.fi/katve/toiminta/docs/RFID-DataModel-FI–20051124.pdf
- Dutch Data Model: Generic Set of Requirements RFID Netherlands: www.debibliotheken.nl/content.jsp?objectid=5179

An excellent resource for technical specifications about RFID tags created for libraries is the "RFID Data Model for Libraries: Proposal for a Data Model," which was proposed by the RFID Data Model for Libraries Working Group, affiliated with Danish Standard S24/u4. The final version of the document from July 2005 is available at www.bs.dk/standards/RFID%20Data%20Model%20for%20Libraries.pdf. The Danish National Library Association is committed to creating standards. Their Web site is www.bs.dk/standards/rfid.

NISO RFID Committee

In 2002, NISO (National Information Standards Organization) gave the green light to the National Circulation Interchange Protocol (NCIP). The movement toward NISO standards should help to improve the adoption rate. NISO organized a standards group to work through this problem of interfacing the ILS and the RFID system and also for hardware interoperability. It is hoped that the group, the NISO RFID Committee, will draft a best practices document leading toward a standard data model for tag information encoding and researching interoperability. Privacy will be an issue addressed by the Committee working in concert with the American Library Association and the Books Industry Study Group. The Committee is composed of librarians using RFID, vendors, book jobbers, hardware, software and integration professionals, and is led by Dr. Vinod Chachra, CEO of VTLS. Chachra has been very influential in promoting standardization of RFID technology and has written extensively on the topic. Other members include: Livia Bitner of Baker and Taylor, Jim Lichtenberg of BISG, Michael Guillory of Philips, Corrie Marsh of University of North Texas, Alistair McArthur of Tagsys, Allan McWilliams of BCPL.net, Louis Schaper of Fayetteville Public Library, Paul Sevcik of 3M, Rick Weingarten of ALA, and Marty Withrow of OCLC. Minutes from the March 6, 2006 meeting indicate the urgency to develop a data model, and the use the Danish Model as an example of what the committee would like to produce, but tailored to the needs of American libraries. In a presentation for ALA's 2006 LITA session on RFID, Vinod Chachra gave a presentation titled: "A Report on NISO's Work on RFID Standards in Libraries."

For more on this group, please see Vinod Chachra's 2006 ALA/LITA presentation "A Report on NISO's Work on RFID Standards in Libraries," available at www.niso.org/committees/RFID/RFIDLITAALApresentation.pdf

RFID-IN-ACTION INTERVIEW: NISO'S WORK ON RFID STANDARDS IN LIBRARIES

I interviewed Vinod Chachra on this topic:

Q: How would you explain important differences between the ISO 18000 and ISO 15693 to a librarian interested in an RFID solution in easy-to-understand terms?

A: In order to understand the relationship between ISO 18000 and ISO 15693 standards for RFID applications in libraries we must, for a moment, look at the broader picture.

- ISO 18000–3 (Part 3 of the ISO 18000 standard) addresses itself to the frequency of 13.56 MHz. Other parts deal with other frequencies. So, when librarians talk about ISO 18000 they are really referring to ISO 18000–3.
- ISO 18000–3 is an air interface communications protocol and governs how an RFID chip communicates with an RFID antenna over the air. In that sense it represents a physical layer protocol. It also provides for a collision management system.
- In social environments, when two individuals start to speak at the same time, then good manners (human behavior protocol) dictate that one stops and tells the other to go ahead. The collision management system governs the behavior of the RFID chips.
- The chips have no power. They are energized by the electromagnetic waves from the antenna. When more than one chip is energized by the presence of energy from an antenna they all begin to "speak." The collision management system determines the order in which they "speak."
- The ISO 15693 standard was originally defined for contact-less smart cards but now it is used for many applications including libraries.
- These RFID systems can be classified into three types depending on the operating range (distance between transponder—RFID chip—and antenna. The three types are
  1. close coupled systems
  2. proximity systems
  3. vicinity systems

Q: How are they classified?

A: These RFID systems can be classified into three types. The ISO 15693 standard is applicable only to vicinity systems. The ISO 15693 standard is written in three main sections dealing with
  1. physical characteristics
  2. air interface (also called signal interface)
  3. anti-collision and transmission protocol

Q: What are the physical characteristics of the standards?

A: They specify the environmental conditions under which the tags must operate. This includes temperatures, magnetic fields, and physical distortions that the tags must tolerate.

Q: Will you explain the air interface and anti-collision and transmission protocol?

A: The air interface and anti-collision specifications are exactly the topic of ISO 18000–3 mentioned above.

Q: Why are there two similar standards?

A: The difference is this—the ISO 18000 has two modes of operations designed for different RFID applications.

- In Mode 1, ISO 18000 is compatible with ISO 15693.
- In Mode 2, ISO 18000 is not compatible with ISO 15693.
- Mode 2 works at higher speeds and supports more memory.

The two modes of ISO 18000 do not interoperate. Simply stated, if a library application is ISO 15693 compliant then it is also ISO 18000 compliant. However, if an application is ISO 18000 compliant then it may or may not be ISO 15693 compliant.

Q: What is your role in the NISO committee that seeks to create standards?

A: Before I talk about my role in the NISO Committee it is important to state NISO's goal in creating the NISO RFID for Library Applications Working Group.

The chief goal is interoperability of RFID tags, hardware and software. The objectives are to insure:

- tags from one supplier can work with hardware and software from other suppliers;
- new generation of tags are backwards compatible (interoperate) with standards-based older generation of tags;
- books and materials with RFID tags from one library fully function at another library with RFID systems from the same or different vendors; and
- books with RFID tags do not interfere with operations of RFID systems in other industries like grocery stores and retail chains.

Q: What other issues concern the committee?

A: In addition to interoperability the committee is concerned with four issues:

1. privacy concerns
2. support of functional capabilities
3. performance issues
4. cost considerations

I serve as the chairman of the NISO RFID Committee. As chairman, it is my responsibility to insure that the new standards or recommendations meet the interoperability requirements stated above. There are several stakeholders in this project. The chief stakeholders are libraries, RFID tag and hardware manufacturers, RFID software developers, book jobbers, and other service providers. We wish to have a standard that is broad enough, useful enough, and solid enough to encourage voluntary compliance by all stakeholders. To this end, it is important to understand each group's perspective and weigh all available solutions before making any recommendations. My role as chairman is to facilitate this objective.

Q: Do you feel that this committee's work will help to increase the adoption rate of RFID by libraries?

A: Yes, I feel certain that the committee's work will increase the adoption rate of RFID by libraries. Clearly, the cost of this technology is declining quarter to quarter. As the technology becomes more affordable, adoption rates will increase with or without standards. The standards work, which focuses on interoperability, will help protect the investment against premature obsolescence and help create a more competitive environment reducing costs for all stakeholders. (Ward-Chachra interview, 2006)

For years, there were different ISO standards for RFID tags. ISO 15693 is the standard that many libraries followed at the genesis of the library application of RFID. In August 2004, ISO 18000–3 "Parameters for Air Interface Communications at 13.56 MHz" was passed and quickly championed by vendors because of its ability to offer more security during data transfer between the tag and the reader.

Nonproprietary tags open up the RFID library market for true price competition, which many feel will drive more libraries to adopt the technology. Otherwise, proprietary or non-ISO standard tags could lock a library to a specific vendor or a sole source of tags and equipment for the lifetime of their RFID system.

More on SIP2 and NCIP

An ILS operates in a closed system which allows only authenticated library staff to hop on the network and access data. Circulation data is kept under very tight security and is limited to only circulation staff that cannot misuse this data or go on witch-hunts to see what a patron has checked out. A library should not need to purchase an additional server as the RFID software interfaces with the ILS via the following protocols.

Most ILS vendors charge for the installation and maintenance of a protocol. SIP is Standard Interchange Protocol. SIP or SIP2 (meaning second generation) is involved in each charging transaction. 3M developed SIP to enable self-checkout of materials. In 2002, the National Information Standards Organization (NISO) gave the green light to the National Circulation Interchange Protocol, referred to as NCIP. Vendors have been slow to fully implement NCIP as SIP is more prevalent. API (Applications Programming Interface) is also a method of information exchange that is available for use.

RFID-IN-ACTION INTERVIEW: ILS'S AND RFID INSTALLATION

I asked Brent Jensen, SirsiDynix's Senior Software Engineer and SIP/NCIP Manager, about his experience with ILS's and RFID installation using SIP and NCIP.

Q: RFID systems communicate with the ILS's circulation system usually through SIP, SIP2 or NCIP protocol. Could you explain in layman's terms SIP and SIP2?

A: SIP stands for Standard Interchange Protocol. It is a standard way in which to exchange necessary data between the vendor application, such as an inventory wand or self-check machine. SIP was developed by 3M and freely released to the library industry.

SIP is now in its second iteration, or SIP2, with many enhancements that provide for greater functionality from the vendor application. SIP and SIP2 use ASCII or optionally UNICODE characters transmitted over Telnet or TCP/IP. SIP messaging happens in pairs, a "request" message is sent from the application, and a "response" message is returned by the ILS.

Q: What is NCIP protocol?

A: NCIP is the NISO Circulation Interchange Protocol, ANSI/NISO Z39.83–2002. As such it is governed by the ANSI/NISO standards committee. It is targeted to be the replacement for the aging SIP2 standard.

NCIP provides far more options to application vendors, especially in the interlibrary loan (ILL) areas. NCIP also sends and receives messages in pairs. NCIP messages are XML. XML offers a lot of advantages over the free-text format of SIP. NCIP is still rather young and has been widely adopted for ILL purposes, but has been slow to catch on with the self-service vendors.

Q: If a library does not have SIP, how much does it cost to get the library ready to install an RFID system?

A: SIP and NCIP prices vary among the various ILS vendors. Most vendors charge a licensing fee that is based on library size and may also be tied to other factors. Typically, an annual maintenance fee is also required for ongoing support. More about NCIP can be found at the NCIP Implementers Group Web site: www.cde.state.co.us/NCIP/NCIP-IG.htm.

Q: What do librarians interested in bringing RFID to their library need to understand about SIP, SIP2, and NCIP?

A: Typically, librarians only need to know that one of these methods is required to have the RFID vendor application "talk" with their ILS. Which one is required will usually be dictated by what both the vendor and the ILS mutually support.

Librarians will also be interested in the total cost to their particular libraries. Most librarians don't need to know any details about SIP, SIP2, or NCIP. Installation and maintenance are handled by the vendor and the ILS. Some libraries have staff members that are very knowledgeable of the standards. For example, one of SirsiDynix's customers, Seattle Public Library, has a staff that can hold its own in conversations with any SIP2 vendor. This is helpful for them since they have a large automated check-in machine and they use SIP2 staff machines on all of the circulation desks in every branch. All of these technologies depend on the RFID systems that drive them. (Ward-Jensen interview, 2006)

Readers

Readers interrogate a tag and therefore are often referred to as "interrogators." Read rate is a crucial topic for librarians to understand when considering an RFID solution as a replacement of its current item management and security systems. Readers are constructed of a hard case housing the electronics and a power supply, usually in the form of a battery with about a four-hour lifespan. The reader also possesses an antenna that is powerful enough to arouse a tag to send its data back to it. Vendors offer libraries three types of readers:

- *Handheld reader.* The earliest readers had designs that appear clunky in comparison to currently available models. The read range is usually about one foot. Readers are becoming more ergonomic and stylish. Some readers have a small screen on them; some do not. Some have an internal data storage capacity; some do not. They usually weigh about three pounds and have some type of internal rechargeable battery or electrical power source.
- *Stationary reader that is mounted to a circulation desk.* The reader has a coupling antenna in the bed on which staff lay materials. The read range is usually under one foot, and is most common in the six-to-eight-inch range. It has an electrical power source. The flat bed reader is integrated into the circulation desk architecture as have been screens, computers, and EAS deactivation devices.
- *Stationary reader that is part of a self-check unit.* This reader usually lies in the flat bed upon which a patron places materials to borrow. The reader has a coupling antenna in the bed on which patrons lay their materials. The read range is usually under one foot, and is most common in the six-to-eight-inch range. It has an electrical power source.

Readers need to have good construction and be durable. This is especially true for handheld readers. It is advisable to ask your vendor about the durability of the handheld reader and what damage might occur if it is dropped.

RFID Journal has a thorough "Glossary of RFID Terms" available at www.rfidjournal.com/article/glossary/

**Figure 2.7: 3M™ Digital Library Assistant™
(Photo of reader courtesy of 3M™)**

**Figure 2.8: The Symbol MC9060-G RFID HandHeld Reader
(Photo courtesy of Motorola)**

Software and Servers

Software or middleware is the heart of RFID transactions and is loaded by the RFID vendor onto the library server. It is unlikely that most libraries will need to purchase an additional server for RFID and its related software applications, but committees investigating RFID should ask vendors their opinions and requirements on servers. Most libraries will already employ at least one server which handles the transactions of the integrated library system. Although the RFID system's software captures the data for all tags in its read range at one time, it conveys them in a form that the ILS will understand: one item identification bar code at a time.

The software supporting the graphical user interface (GUI) allows staff to utilize data from the RFID events for circulation, inventory, and so on. It is provided by the vendor and is proprietary so the GUI appearance will vary based on vendor. For most circulation desk purposes, the item management software interface will not deviate from your current ILS screen that you see when a patron checks out. For many RFID vendors, they only interject a small box in the window which appears to let you know the tag has been read and the security bit is deactivated. There is no need to switch between ILS and RFID vendor screens. The systems should not compete, but complement in the same way a traditional bar code scanner would interact with the ILS in the circulation module. With the standards for communication between ILS and RFID systems, NCIP and SIP provide for communication between the two systems.

Network Security

Tag data may be encrypted during transfer. Readers may also be prompted to authenticate themselves to the tags before the transmission of data occurs. The 13.56MHz passive tags that will be delivered to Jefferson County Public Library in Colorado are manufactured by Philips with encryption that can only be read by readers linked to the library's network. (O'Connor, 2006a)

> Tag data may be encrypted during transfer. Readers may also be prompted to authenticate themselves to the tags before the transmission of data occurs.

In a 2006 IEEE presentation paper "Is Your Cat Infected with a Computer Virus?" by Melanie R. Rieback, Bruno Crispo, and Andrew S. Tanenbaum, the authors explain how RFID tags could be manipulated with a virus and infect back-end software systems and databases. Much of the article was refuted by Larry Loeb of PBC Enterprises in "Roaming Charges: Pet-Embedded RFID Chips Bring Down Las Vegas: News Flash: The Old Software-Virus Scam Strikes Again." Loeb explains how the authors are also the creators of RFID Guardian, a tool to protect RFID tags and systems from such malware.

RFID-IN-ACTION INTERVIEW: SECURE RFID TAGS

I asked Lee Tien, a lawyer specializing in RFID for the privacy rights advocacy group Electronic Frontier Foundation, about this area.

Q: Do you believe the RFID tag can be engineered to make it impervious to attack, hacking, or unauthorized third-party intrusion?

A: RFID should be engineered to protect against unauthorized reading. This makes absolute sense: within the closed system of a library ILS, a patron should feel confident that the tag can only be read by authorized readers, used by authorized library staff during the charging process, and with their knowledge and consent. This is why the use of wall-mounted readers found in many RFID warehouse-applications is an unpopular option for libraries. (Ward-Tiem interview, 2006)

Figure 2.9:   Definitions of RFID Terms

Term	Definition
Label or Tag	Small (2" x 2" or 2" x 3") label consisting of a microchip, coiled antenna, substrate, adhesive backing, and optional eye-readable face. Uses RF 13.56 MHz to communicate serialized data written on the chip. Passive power source which is read using RF and is either ISO 18000–3 or ISO 15693
Chip	Microchip
Interrogator	RFID reader. Data transmission can be encrypted or authenticated
SIP/SIP2	Standard Interchange Protocol 2
NCIP	National Circulation Interchange Protocol
Event	Instance of an RFID tag being read via radio waves by the reader and data being transmitted back to the library's database

References

Coyle, Karen. 2005. "Management of RFID in Libraries." *Journal of Academic Librarianship* 31, no. 5 (September): 486–489.

Erwin, Emmett, and Christian Kern. 2003. "Radio Frequency-Identification for Security and Media Circulation in Libraries." *Library & Archival Security* 18, no. 2: 23–38.

Junwei, Chen. 2004. "Lightweight RFID Framework." IBM (November). Available: www–128.ibm.com/developerworks/wireless/library/wi-rfid/

Loeb, Larry. 2006. "Roaming Charges: Pet-Embedded RFID Chips Bring Down Las Vegas: News Flash: The Old Software-Virus Scam Strikes Again." IBM (April 18). Available: www–128.ibm.com/developerworks/library/wi-roam45.html

O'Connor, Mary Catherine. 2006a. "Colorado Library Checks Out RFID." *RFID Journal* (July 6) Available: www.rfidjournal.com/article/articleprinte/2475/–1/1/

O'Connor, Mary Catherine. 2006b. "Gen 2 EPC Protocol Approved as ISO 18000–6C." *RFID Journal* (July 11) www.rfidjournal.com/article/articleprint/2481/–1/1/

Potter, Bruce. 2005. "RFID: Misunderstood or Untrustworthy." *Network Security* 4 (April 1): 17–18.

RFID Journal. 2002. New Anti-Collision Protocol Patent. *RFID Journal* (July 25). Available: www.rfidjournal.com/article/articleview/31/1/1/

Rieback, Melanie R., Bruno Crispo, and Andrew S. Tanenbaum. 2006. "Is Your Cat Infected with a Computer Virus?" IEEE PerCom 2006 conference presentation. Available: www.rfidvirus.org/papers/percom.06.pdf

Ward, Diane Marie. 2004. "Tags for CDs Get a Boost." *RFID Journal* (August 6). Available: www.rfidjournal.com/article/articleprint/1075/–1/1/

Ward, Diane Marie, and Vinod Chachra, e-mail interview, August 26, 2006.

Ward, Diane Marie, and Brent Jensen, e-mail interview, August 18, 2006.

Ward, Diane Marie, and Lee Tien, e-mail interview, July 10, 2006.

Additional Resources

Bhuptani, Manish, and Shahram Moradpour. 2005. *RFID Field Guide: Deploying Radio Frequency Identification Systems.* Upper Saddle River, NJ: Sun Microsystems Press, Prentice Hall Professional Technical Reference.

Chachra, Vinod. "A Report on NISO's Work on RFID Standards in Libraries." ALA/LITA 2006 Conference presentation. Available: www.niso.org/committees/RFID/RFIDLITAALApresentation.pdf

Coleman, Christopher. 2004. *An Introduction to Radio Frequency Engineering.* Cambridge, UK: Cambridge University Press.

Eskelinen, Pekka. 2004. *Introduction to RF Equipment and System Design.* Boston: Artech House.

Finkenzeller, Klaus. 2003. *RFID Handbook: Fundamentals and Applications in Contactless Smart Cards and Identification.* 2nd ed. Translated by Rachel Waddington. West Sussex, UK: John Wiley & Sons.

Hawkes, P. L., D. W. Davies, and W. L. Price. 1990. *Integrated Circuit Cards, Tags and Tokens: New Technology and Applications.* Oxford: BSP Professional Books.

Kleist, Robert A. et al. 2004. *RFID Labeling: Smart Labeling Concepts & Applications for the Consumer Packaged Goods Supply Chain.* Irvine, CA: Printronix.

Kleist, Robert A. et al. 2005. *RFID Labeling: Smart Labeling Concepts & Applications for the Consumer Packaged Goods Supply Chain.* 2nd ed. Irvine, CA: Printronix.

Paret, Dominique. 2005. *RFID and Contactless Smart Card Applications.* Translated by Roderick Riesco. West Sussex, UK: John Wiley & Sons.

Sweeney, Patrick J. II. 2005. *RFID for Dummies.* Hoboken, NJ: Wiley.

3

RFID Library Applications

Introduction

In Chapter 1, we learned how RFID works and in Chapter 2 we explored the technical side of RFID. Chapter 3 explores the library applications of RFID. Librarians and researchers have created innovative ways to weave RFID into the library environment. For library purposes, RFID offers item management and security benefits that in some ways supersede the benefits of traditional bar codes and electronic article surveillance systems. Price compatibility is a crucial element that currently prevents many libraries from converting to RFID; however, for the early adopters who took the leap to RFID, they have realized value-added services from automatic identification technology.

The workflow of a library is reliant upon many separate pieces working well to ensure service excellence. The library's collection is organic: its size fluctuates due to acquisitions and weeding. Subsequently, patrons need the wisdom of librarians to enhance their library experience, but so often our reference and circulation librarians are over-taxed and understaffed. In a "perfect-RFID-library" scenario, circulation staff members could be reallocated to duties that require judgment and analytical thinking to help patrons and liberated from borrowing duties. RFID does not eliminate the role of librarians. RFID increases the granularity of locating information, and empowers the patron, and liberates the staff from purely borrowing-related functions to more meaningful contact with patrons.

RFID labels provide the same type of serialized identification that one-dimensional bar codes offer. The promise of RFID for libraries includes the ability for the RFID tag to identify itself automatically and transmit its information to an RFID reader from its location inside the item on the shelf. The automatic identification of RFID enables the automation of routine library tasks that would otherwise require staff.

Current applications of RFID in library settings include:

- Item Management
- Item Security
- Circulation
  Staffed Circulation Desk
  Patron Self-Checkout
  Patron Self-Checkin
- Shelf Management Functions
  Inventory Control
  Weeding
  Location of Missing Items
- Automated Material Handling
- Sorting
- Audiovisual Materials
- Patron Cards

Item Management Security

Bar codes have a near 100 percent read rate accuracy when in good physical condition and therefore have come to be relied upon as a legitimate and necessary technology for libraries to use on all items. Thousands of librarians have participated in efforts to bar code each volume a library holds. The bar code provides a unique identifier that links the physical item to the bibliographic record in the online catalog record, and facilitates work for both cataloging and circulation staff. However, in order for the data to link a bar code to an OPAC bibliographic record, a staff member needs to orient the bar code on the item so that it can be read by a reader's beam using line of sight. The average price for a basic RFID tag to use in a book that has EAS on it is 53 cents based on my survey of vendors. The range was 30 to 72 cents for all tags (some of those inexpensive tags may intentionally lack the EAS bit). Keep in mind that printing text on the label will add to the base cost. Of course, if you buy 5 million tags, you could surmise that the vendor might cut you a deal.

Across the board, RFID tags are not yet at 100 percent read rate accuracy. Libraries I surveyed indicated privately to me that there are items that cause the security gates to trigger improperly, which is a serious drawback; however, there is continual research and development in the RFID field ensuring improvements upon the readability and functionality of tags within the reader field.

RFID systems interact with your library's circulation system, and if that system goes down, most RFID systems have a back-up to automatically store the item numbers in a file that can be uploaded when the system or server comes back up.

> A good article on RFID applications is Jay Singh, Navjit Brar, and Carmen Fong's "The State of RFID Applications in Libraries" published in *Information Technology and Libraries.*

When an item's circulation information is updated in the circulation system, the staff member also needs to deactivate the security component of the item. Some early adopting RFID libraries chose to remain with their legacy security system and opted only for RFID to accomplish item identification. Recently, the trend is moving toward libraries choosing tags with both components on one tag.

Some libraries still rely upon physically checking the bags of exiting patrons, which many feel is intrusive and unwarranted. However, if a library does not have an electronic security system in place, how does one protect its materials? 3M makes a very popular product, Tattle Tape™, which can be inserted into the book by a library book vendor or by a technical services or circulation staff member. Checkpoint also makes a popular EAS system for libraries, as well as retail. Some libraries feel comfortable with their legacy EAS and want an RFID solution that allows them to rely upon their security system. Hence, many vendors provide a tag with just item information so customers can continue to use their EAS. The price for a tag without EAS is modestly less expensive.

The RFID security bit has depth that other types of security, which rely upon electromagnetism, lack. The computer screen at a circulation desk informs the staff member of exactly what item triggered the alarm. Gone are the days of peering through book bags and guessing why any number of items may have been improperly desensitized. RFID tags provide specific data.

For some libraries, the performance of current security systems is wanting, even after tweaking the system. Who is to say why technology sometimes behaves strangely at one location and fine at the next; however, it can be a frustrating and expensive exercise that sometimes results in libraries shutting off the system they pay for and benefiting from the psychological deterrent that the gates offer. I have heard this scenario from more than one library—that the gates sometimes offer a deterrent simply by their presence.

RFID-IN-ACTION INTERVIEW: ELECTROMAGNETIC SECURITY SYSTEMS

Early in 2006, I interviewed Maureen Karl, Materials and Technology Management Division Chief at Arlington County Department of Libraries in Arlington, Virginia.

Q: Is there any dissatisfaction with the existing electromagnetic security system that made the library think RFID would be better?

A: Arlington has not been successful in adjusting its electromagnetic security gates to perform accurately and eliminate consistent false alarms. . . . Staff frustration grew to such a level that we recently disconnected the alarms on the electromagnetic system gates at Central Library. Though our security gates remain in place, they serve a deterrent role only. We certainly are counting on better performance from the RFID security system but improvements in customer self-check functionality (Arlington's in-progress new branch buildings will both rely almost exclusively on RFID self-checkout) were a very big factor in our decision. (Ward-Karl interview, 2006)

This situation is more common than many librarians would like to admit. Therefore, the physical presence of security gates serves a great psychological deterrent to thieves who would expect the security system to acutely sense theft. No system is 100 percent perfect and librarians should expect to have some adjustment to a new RFID system; however, many libraries adopting RFID for both item management and security are looking for the next generation of security and item location technology.

Modify Circulation Desk Tasks

Since traditional bar codes require line-of-sight in order to read and transmit data to the ILS, staff members need to adjust books in order to line up the bar code with the laser beam. This process can sometimes prove to be cumbersome and uncomfortable for staff if the item is large or heavy. Many libraries use bar codes and a security system that require circulation staff to handle each item a patron wants to borrow twice:

- For each item, the staff member has to locate and then read each item's bar code via a line-of-sight laser beam using a handheld or desk-mounted reader. This may take several adjustments of the way the item is positioned or the bar code reader is moved in order to get a successful read, usually verified by an audible signal or a visual alert.
- The staff member also needs to deactivate the electronic article surveillance system by passing it over a deactivating bed (or via other method). If this is

not done properly, the item will trigger the gates to sound an alarm. It is easy to see why patrons become frustrated at the time and steps necessary to check-out items.

The RFID tag can be constructed to contain both of these components. RFID does not require the repetitive movements of lining up a bar code with a laser beam as RFID relies upon radio waves and this mean that the staff member does not need to open the book in order for it to be read. The RFID reader automatically reads the identity of the tag, therefore simplifying the two-step process. A staff member needs simply to place the stack of materials to be borrowed on the stationary checkout reader to update its circulation status in the catalog and to deactivate its security bit. This allows staff to participate in more value-added patron-centric work and alleviates stress for the employee who feels pressured to hurry through each patron in order to avoid long lines of people waiting to be checked out. Ninety-one percent of the libraries I surveyed chose a tag that had both identification for circulation applications and a security bit.

It is beneficial to free up the staff member to concentrate on longer procedures, such as handling unlinked item records, suggesting other materials to read or view, setting up a person's patron privileges, squaring a patron's library fines. All of these activities that are now interspersed with straightforward borrowing lengthen a patron's wait and may cause frustration and dissatisfaction with the operation of a library for the patron who is pressed for time. The RFID tag and reader work in concert through radio frequency waves to bring irregularities to the staff member's attention. Thus, the staff member becomes a problem solver, while the technology does the routine work.

Install Self-Checkout Stations

The RFID self-checkout machine operates as a stand-alone borrowing center for patrons to use instead of waiting in line to be serviced by a circulation clerk. The patron is empowered to manage his or her borrowing, freeing up the circulation staff from clerical duties related to the borrowing routine. Trusting the patron and trusting RFID to automate borrowing is a solution that has proven in libraries to shorten the patron queues and allow those opting for self-checkout to be able to do just that.

Self-checkout stations vary in shape and size. Some will have cabinetry that blends in with the décor of the library; most have a very state-of-the art look and have a space to place books to borrow. The flat touch screen with its GUI is the link for the patron as to how to use the machine. All come with software that guides the user through the process of self-check, and will alert a staff member if assistance is needed. If the library's tag contains both item identification information (usually the bar code

Figure 3.1: Ward's Survey Results: Libraries with RFID	
Q: What sort of tag did you select?	
A tag with both item identification for circulation and security bit on one chip. A tag with only item identification for circulation. Other	91% 6% 3%
Q: Did you install self-checkout?	
Yes No	80% 20%
Q: Did your public library install self-checkout?	
Yes No	84% (21 libraries) 16% (4 libraries)
Q: Did your academic library install self-checkout?	
Yes No	67% (6 libraries) 33% (3 libraries)
Q: Have you used the handheld RFID reader to inventory your collection?	
Yes No	17% 83%
Q: Have you used the handheld RFID reader to locate misplaced items in the stacks?	
Yes No	12% 88%
Q: Do you offer patron cards with an RFID chip?	
Yes No Planning on this	11% (4 libraries) 86% (30 libraries) 3% (1 library)
Q: Did you install RFID-enabled sorters and sorting bins for checked-in materials?	
Yes No Planning on this	23% (8 libraries) 68% (24 libraries) 9% (3 libraries)

number) and a security bit, the patron need only place the books on the reader bed once: the item record is marked as circulating and the security bit is switched to the off position so that the gate does not sound. According to research by Richard W. Boss: "A patron self-charging station can handle up to 20,000 transactions per month." (Boss, 2006) These kiosks or stations provide privacy to patrons through self-check units.

In my research, libraries that have installed self-check machines find them to be quite popular with patrons, but this is an expensive investment that might be cost-prohibitive to some libraries. In my survey of major North American vendors of RFID equipment to libraries, the average price for self-check readers was $14,300, with a range of $9,000 to $25,000 depending upon what type of machine was purchased and if cabinetry was included.

Streamline Shelf Management with Handheld RFID Readers

The invention of the handheld reader is essential in differentiating the functionality of RFID from that of its predecessor bar code. As a result of RFID tags not needing optical reading, the handheld reader becomes an assistant in shelf management in a way that would have been unimaginable ten years ago. This section will examine some uses of the handheld reader for inventory control, weeding, and locating misplaced items in the stacks.

> For a demonstration of using a handheld reader, please see the DVD that accompanies this book. ITG's Shai Robkin demonstrates this.

It is important to explain at the outset that vendors have widely differing handheld readers, and depending upon your ILS software set-up, you may not immediately be ready to capitalize on the functionality of the handheld reader. Library systems professionals and RFID vendors should discuss the parameters for effective usage.

The first prototyped handheld readers were bulky. Currently, models vary in size, shape, and functionality, but are generally under three pounds in weight, with constant efforts to reduce the size. Vendor handhelds differ in shape, but all try to produce an ergonomic reader. Some need to be used in conjunction with a laptop (perhaps placed on a book cart), while others house data in the handheld for download at a later point. The overall battery life is improving on the handhelds also.

RFID-IN-ACTION INTERVIEW: HANDHELD READERS

I asked Susan O'Neal, Director of Middletown Township Public Library in Middletown, New Jersey:
  Q: What was your experience with the RFID handheld readers?
  A: Our only disappointment thus far has been the slow development of a manageable handheld scanner. We are anxious for this product." (Ward-O'Neal interview, 2006)

I asked William Marsterson, Pro Vice Chancellor, Head of Learning Resources and University Librarian at Middlesex University in the United Kingdom:
  Q: What is your experience with the handhelds your staff members use to locate missing items in the stacks?
  A: This has proved one of the weaker areas of our supplier's product. The battery needs frequent recharging. Again, staff has had their misgivings. But it has proved useful in dramatically speeding up stock checks. (Ward-Marsterson interview, 2006)

Improve Inventory Control

In essence, a library with rows of books on shelves can have rows of RFID tags waiting to send their unique identification to the reader and, in turn, update the database about their location status. If we consider Richard Trueswell's statistical notion, the "80/20 rule," as alive and well in most libraries, then the importance of accurately reshelving materials is paramount for the efficiency of libraries. If 20 percent of the collection accounts for 80 percent of the circulation, the same items are being circulated and reshelved. Long call numbers may cause some confusion if employees are not thoroughly trained on call number shelving and the misshelving of materials.

Therefore, it becomes crucial that items are properly shelved in order to fully understand the logistical and spatial needs of the library. Inventorying a collection is a time-consuming process that requires the buy-in of many stakeholders. Who can afford this?

Staff are removed from normal work assignments and assigned to read the shelves for accuracy and to correct shelving discrepancies. The tedium associated with inventory procedures consists of:

- scanning through shelves for misplaced items
- correcting discrepancies in the OPAC on the fly
- dealing with the sometimes incongruous nature of the shelf list report from the ILS
- acclimating to the repetitive nature of pulling each item off of a shelf to scan using line-of-sight bar code reading technology

Issues such as monotony and boredom affect the accuracy and speed of shelf reading, and thus this activity needs to be broken up into short blocks of time as to prevent errors. Tedium can be a severe liability to the final accuracy of a shelf. This is not to mention the likelihood that a staff member in the stacks will be distracted in some way from the original task at hand. In terms of budgeting, how justifiable is it to assign human capital to shelf reading rows if human error might negate the effort?

For these reasons, inventorying a collection is not at the top of the list for most libraries even though librarians do not want the word "messy" or "disorderly" associated with their branch. Tight library budgets cannot justify paying staff to read shelves for days; rather, the library administration has to assume that there will be some percentage of materials that are at any time misshelved, or (unbeknownst to administration) stolen. The level of confidence in a library's ability to organize data is eroded by repeated "book outs."

A well-inventoried collection is a step in the direction of patron service excellence. Scanning the correct order of something is not a difficult task in and of itself for a set of human eyes, but for anyone that has ever shelf read, the task gets very time-consuming quickly. The focus of the RFID equipment does not get distracted from its task of identifying errors. RFID uses automatic identification and promises an accurate shelf read. Automatic identification of objects applied to this task allows the staff member to become a problem solver rather than just a shelf reader.

Tags and Handheld Readers

Researchers have engineered an application for libraries that uses RFID to inventory a collection. Inventorying takes a fraction of the time with handheld RFID readers. In the time it takes a staff member to walk up an aisle, the aisle is inventoried and shelf-read against a catalog-drawn virtual shelf-list. Vendor software can be loaded onto the reader or used in concert with a laptop on a cart that has a virtual shelf list generated from the ILS. The library's ILS generally needs to be able to produce a list of all items in call number index order. The items have to reflect only the items that are not in active circulation, on reserve, or on hold for a patron as these items should not be expected on the shelf.

The RFID tag's unique identification number actively participates in inventorying the collection for catalog accuracy. As the RFID reader passes, each passive tag "wakes up" and transmits its unique identification number to the reader via radio frequency waves operating at 13.56MHz. This information gets sent to the reader and onto the database. The inventory feature of RFID is like having an invisible, yet potentially ready, army of shelving assistants as each RFID tag tells the librarian's RFID reader if it is in shelf order or out of place. RFID potentially simplifies inventorying and uses staff time more efficiently.

As we learned in Chapter 2, metal can have adverse effects on the way radio waves are transmitted from object to reader. Many libraries may wonder what impact metal shelving might have on the read accuracy of RFID tags while inventorying. From my research, it does not seem to have a negative impact as long as the RFID tags are not placed flush on the bottom edge of the book. Placing a tag midway on the book cover, near the spine, affords an accurate read.

The handheld reader designed for inventory control has an antenna that is for use one foot or less from the item, and is probably best used within three to six inches. Some demonstrations of the inventory function show the staff member physically touching each book on the shelf with the wand, passing it over rapidly. This is so the employee does not read tags from shelves above, below, or behind the shelf being inventoried. This assures that only the shelf in question is read, and that human nature does not creep in and cause one's unguided hand, arm, and a typical three-pound handheld unit to droop below the shelf, or go too high above it. Again, different readers will have different abilities and you will want to check with your vendor on the specifics and technological advancements associated with each.

Customer service is important and inventory control is crucial to ensuring that every book that is available in the catalog is available on the shelf.

- Is assuring that patrons can find every item in the library's physical space justification for the expense of installing an RFID system?
- What is collection omniscience worth to a library?
- How effective is an RFID reader in inventorying a collection?

In a 2005 report, "Floating Bibs and Orphan Bar Codes: Benefits of an Inventory at a Small College," Linda Ernick chronicled the process of inventorying a small collection of 33,000 volumes at Anne Bridge Baddour Library at Daniel Webster College in Nashua, New Hampshire. The collection was scanned in one month "in two-to-three-hour shifts by two people, working about six hours a day, at an average of 307 volumes per hour." (Ernick, 2005) The problem of using the bar code scanners for that length of time was apparent: "one person could not do this alone, if only because one's arm tended to ache too badly after about four hours of the repetitive motion." (Ernick, 2005)

For example: Inventory is something libraries should do on principle. It ensures that everything in the public catalog is indeed on the shelves and in order. However, how many libraries have to forego a comprehensive inventory year after year because of the exorbitant expense of committing precious staff time to the tedious exercise of shelf-reading?

To determine if inventory control is a justifiable reason for introducing RFID at your library, a library should try to estimate the current percentage of books that appear to be lost. Of course, this number is difficult to arrive at since librarians can never tell exactly how many patron trips to shelves end without the successful retrieval of a desired item.

At present, inventory control is in many ways a "killer application" for libraries, but according to the findings of my 2006 survey of librarians, most libraries that have installed RFID are not yet using this function. Only 17 percent of surveyed libraries have used a handheld for this. One library that purchased a handheld was not able to get the handheld to work properly with their ILS to generate a usable report, but noted that the situation was being rectified. Three other libraries stated that they intended to purchase handhelds next to take advantage of this application. A possible explanation of this statistic may be that

- Some libraries had not purchased a handheld yet.
- Other libraries wanted a proof-of-concept with RFID self-check before investing money in handhelds.
- Many libraries had just recently finished converting their materials from bar code to RFID tag and in essence conducted an inventory of materials during the conversion process.
- Some libraries cited current issues with ILS software and report generating as obstacles to using this application, but added that the ILS vendor had committed to fixing the situation.

The key is to see if RFID will change the way libraries view the process of inventory. Will RFID make inventorying such an easy procedure that inventorying a collection becomes a natural part of a library's work routine? Will this become in the next few years a major indicator of RFID ROI?

Trace Missing Materials

In the retail world, a "stock out" occurs when a customer leaves without finding a desired product on the shelf. Repeated experiences of stock outs lessen customer satisfaction and confidence with a store's ability to provide the desired products. A driving benefit of RFID for retail is the proven ability of RFID to reduce stock outs and improve customer satisfaction with finding what they want on the store shelves. RFID could have the same impact on a library. In the library world, patrons cannot benefit from the materials they cannot locate and borrow. Patrons should find what they want on the shelves that we direct them to look at via the OPAC.

If the patron's library experience is viewed in the same way as a retail customer's, then a successful library experience occurs when the patron locates a bibliographic record in the online catalog and then goes to the shelf where the item is listed as being located. An unsuccessful experience (a "book out") occurs when a patron locates the item in the online catalog only to go to the shelf and not find the item where it is supposed to be shelved. Patrons may ask a librarian about the missing item and this will begin a physical search by staff to locate the misshelved item. However, how many patrons simply give up the search at the empty shelf and then settle for data they might locate on the Internet?

Many libraries have circulation staff members that possess otherworldly powers at finding misplaced items in the stacks. We all know those circulation staff members that have great book-sniffing skills mainly because they are aware of typical shelving errors. When a patron ends up leaving a library without the item he/she wanted, it is a failure of the library to satisfy. The RFID handheld reader is a tool that has this power to sniff out items. With future enhancements, this tool should be a catalyst for RFID adoption by libraries.

The earliest adopter of RFID technology was Singapore's National Library Board. It was reported that library staff usually entertained about 150 questions concerning misplaced items each month and that a search for one item could stretch across seven days. With the introduction of RFID, the two-week inventory now took less than a day. (Wong, 2002) Just as a staff member carries a handheld RFID reader in "inventory mode" to inventory a range of books, the staff member can carry a reader that is in "search mode" so it is programmed to read the shelves for a specific item. A library staff member can walk down an aisle of books and pass this wand over the materials. An employee can enter a missing item into the middleware's GUI as the target item to locate. As the wand passes over the spines of the items on the book truck, each tagged item relays its identification information to the reader; when the trigger item is located, a unique sound and/or visual alert is generated.

Again, not every library surveyed had purchased a handheld. It is interesting to note that the two British libraries I surveyed (one public and one academic) both used the handheld for locating missing items in the stacks. My survey indicated that only 12 percent of North American libraries were using a handheld for this purpose.

Track Audiovisual Materials

The motto of this section is "Results may vary among vendors and installations based on a number of factors." Research is being done to improve the read rate accuracy for audiovisual materials. RFID on audiovisual materials provides access and security for media items. There have been serious issues in using traditional 13.56 MHz RFID tags on metal content audiovisual items. RFID tags at the time were configured with books in mind. The same RF waves that make RFID data transfer possible do not interact well with most objects that are composed of water and metal. CDs and DVDs have varying amounts of metal content dependent upon their generation or production. Therefore, the waves bounce off the disc and cause an unacceptable amount of misreads. Some thought putting spacing agents between the tag and disc or using a booster label would rectify this problem.

When we think of the current role of a public library in its community, it is important to think not only in terms of the library as furnishing books for patrons to borrow, but also furnishing audio CDs, computer discs and floppy disks, DVDs, videocassettes, vinyl record albums, audiocassettes, and so on. This category of items is an integral component of the collection and one that is highly susceptible to theft and financially burdensome to the library due to high replacement costs. Having an effective security system is a paramount consideration for administrators. In some libraries, the audiovisual materials are housed apart from their descriptive containers as a security measure, but this translates into additional work for staff members. If a patron wants an item, the material must be retrieved and then discharged by a staff member.

With a properly functioning RFID system for audiovisual, the need for security cases could be obviated. However, audiovisual materials continue to pose problems with irregular reads, due sometimes to varying metal content or the presence of several discs lying against one another that cancel out the data transmission. A reliable RFID system for audiovisuals removes the need for a separate method of security, and also allows the library physically to house a disc with its container and not worry as much about the item being lost or stolen.

Additionally, this releases the circulation staff member whose task it is to retrieve these items to do other work. Combine this with self-check and patrons are empowered and entrusted to select their audiovisual materials for borrowing without having to involve a staff member. This activity lends itself to two important factors for libraries to appreciate: First, the staff member's time is freed up to work on other tasks; second, the patron gains a bit more privacy in selecting and borrowing audiovisual materials, especially if the library has installed RFID self-checkout stations.

All vendors offer some type of solution for audiovisual. In 2004, library RFID vendor Bibliotheca developed a label for use on audiovisual materials during an installation at Mastics-Moriches-Shirley Community Library on Long Island, New York. (Ward, 2004) The company created a "patented booster RFID label" to ensure that the tags on a library's discs will be accurately read 100 percent of the time. The booster label is so named because it boosts the rate of accurate reads from 70 percent for the standard Bibliotheca smart label placed on a CD or DVD . . ." (Ward, 2004) Each CD or DVD has a standard 13.56 MHz copper antenna hub label on the plastic hub. The booster label has an auxiliary aluminum antenna in the form of a ring at the disc's outer edge. It is a clear plastic overlay of the entire disc surface which should not cause any problem during playback. (Ward, 2004) From my follow-up conversations with library staff, there have been very few instances of the labels ever coming off and causing problems for patrons.

Most vendors have a method to assist in multipart audiovisual materials. While converting, a staff member selects the option that he/she wants to create the tags in a "kit" format, which forces the system to remember how many tags are related to one another. For instance, if there is a book with three CDs, each item is labeled. When a staff member initializes the procedure to link the labels to the item records in the database, an option is selected to link them as part of a kit. Therefore, when items are checked out or in, the database expects to read all four of the RFID labels, and alerts the system operator if this number does not match.

RFID-IN-ACTION INTERVIEW: AUDIOVISUAL MATERIALS

I asked Oleg Boyarsky, Chief Executive Officer of LAT:

Q: Has RFID provided any audiovisual solutions?

A: After dealing with the limitation of RFID with CD/DVD collections, probably the highest growing collection of any library, we have introduced an Intelligent Media Manager™ (IMM) system/product line. . . . It is specifically designed for libraries, by librarians (we had a board of consulting libraries assisting us during the design process). The MediaManager allows

- Checkin and checkout, 365/24/7,
- Auto-hold and 100 percent theft prevention without the need for any security measures done to the materials, and
- No tags, strips, marks or anything needed to secure the CD/DVD collection (Ward-Boyarsky interview, 2006).

Kwik Case® is a brand of theft prevention tools designed to house audiovisuals until they are released by a circulation staff member using a keyless magnetic release mechanism. The intent of the product is to allow libraries to house audiovisual materials on the floor with the remainder of the collection. Due to the high rate of theft of audiovisual materials, many libraries display a dummy of the video box or CD/DVD container and ask patrons to come to the circulation desk for item retrieval and loan. The frequent unlocking of audiovisual material containers can be physically intensive for circulation staff in high-volume periods.

The key to making the RFID tag work as both a security and item management tool on audiovisual materials lies in a special adhesive overlay that covers the face of the disc. The antenna is lengthened and the signal is strengthened thus making its read rates much more acceptable. Libraries have to be diligent in making sure that the hub label and booster overlays that are applied to the eye-readable surface of the disc are firmly affixed. Vendors such as Bibliotheca offer tools that allow the staff member to firmly and flawlessly place the hub and overlay tag on the disc. The disc sits on a spoke and the tags are slid onto the spoke and applied.

Libraries have to be diligent in making sure that the hub label and booster overlays that are applied to the eye-readable surface of the disc are firmly affixed.

RFID-IN-ACTION INTERVIEWS: ITEM MANAGEMENT

Q: How do you feel about adopting this new technology?

A: We are very satisfied with RFID for item management, particularly books. However, there are issues with media that impact all RFID users. Many CD and DVD manufacturers use metal in the center of their disks, which is where the RFID labels are affixed. The metal conflicts with the RFID signal, actually preventing it from being effective. As a result, there are some items that require our creativity to figure out how to affix a label to it. For the most part, security for our DVDs and CDs has improved greatly with RFID, and we love not having to use security cases.

Ellen Firer, Director of Merrick Library in New York.

(Ward-Firer interview, 2006)

Q: What is your opinion on audiovisual materials and your Bibliotheca system?

A: We are satisfied and have done away with security cases. As with any security system RFID is not 100 percent; a determined thief is going to find a way around it; and as with regular radio frequency security, metal will block a signal and piling items a certain way will cause tags to block each other, which happened with the RF tags on our security cases with our previous security system as well. Our loss rate has not increased and not having to deal with the security cases at both ends of the process has been a huge plus.

Q: Would you change anything if you could?

A: I am sure RFID will continue to evolve. The changes I would like to see are more in other parts of the process that have been affected by RFID, for example, developing sturdy packaging that permits multiple CDs and DVDs to be offset from each other rather than directly on top of each other (will block signal) and would make it easier for the master tag feature to function (we can program tags for sets with multiple items to account for all parts in both checkout and checkin processes)

Sandra Collins, Executive Director of Northland Public Library, in Pittsburgh, Pennsylvania.

(Ward-Collins interview, 2006)

Edith Sutterlin of Northland Public Library, who presented at the "2005 Computers in Libraries General Conference" on a panel devoted to RFID, demonstrated that if you have difficulty achieving a satisfactory read rate when labeling a multimedia kit, one can always use an amplifying label on the plastic kit container itself.

For more of my interview with Collins and Sutterlin of Northland Public Library, see the video and the demonstration of self-checkout of audiovisual materials.

RFID-IN-ACTION INTERVIEW: CUSTOMER SATISFACTION

Louise Schaper is Executive Director, Fayetteville Public Library, Fayettevile, Arkansas.

Q: Your system was one of the earliest and included components from various sources so it is a unique and customized system. Are you completely satisfied with the way your RFID system handles audiovisual materials?

A: All the vendors I've heard from will either claim their solution works or they will proudly proclaim that there is no perfect solution to-date. I think the latter is the case right now (summer 2006). This is a very difficult problem because CDs and DVDs are made of metal and metal interferes with the signal.

(Ward-Schaper interview, 2006)

Lynne Jacobsen is head of Technical Services, Warren-Newport Public Library, Gurnee, Illinois. The following exchange illustrates how responsive the RFID vendors are to improving any and all aspects of the RFID system that may not be up to optimum efficiency.

Q: Since your library is still using the Kwik Cases® for security, are you satisfied with the way RFID handles media (CDs, DVDs)? Do you know of any plans from vendors about improving the security aspect of RFID for media-related items?

A: Our biggest disappointment with RFID was the way it handles CDs and DVDs. We use the circular RFID hub tags on discs and they don't read well at the security gates because of the metal content of the disc which blocks the signal. They check-out and check-in just fine. As a result, we use Kwik Cases® on parts of the collection for security. These cases are expensive and it takes labor to put them on and take them off. Our vendor, ITG, has provided a solution to accommodate self-service. New self-check stations will have a built-in release so patrons can check them out and take off the cases themselves. We are getting four of these new stations in the very near future.

(Ward-Jacobsen interview, 2006)

In his 2006 ALA/LITA panel presentation, "CDs and DVDs: The Achilles Heel of RFID," Shai Robkin, CEO of ITG, noted that the "approach that [a] library takes regarding the handling of CDs and DVDs should be determined by how two questions are answered:

- How important is security for the CD/DVD collection?
- How important is it to keep the system easy to use for patrons and staff?"

He lists alternative approaches. One could

- tag audiovisual and multimedia materials
- tag a single disc of a multi-part set
- use a tag on the case
- circulate discs.

RFID Patron Cards

Smart cards are a popular way for companies to control access to physical spaces. An RFID-enabled card, similar in look and feel to a credit card, is held near a mounted reader and access is either gained or denied based on the data encoded on the card's chip which ties its user to a file in a networked company database. Smart cards and RFID-enabled key fobs have been used by consumers for years. Many are probably familiar with the Exxon Mobil Oil Corporation's Speedpass™. Since 1997, the small RFID tag operating at 134KHz allows gas customers to purchase gas and products by passing a key fob in front of the company's logo on the gas pump. It has been stated that the Speedpass™ has cut "30 seconds off the average pay-at-the-pump purchase transaction." (Garfinkel, 2006: 181)

However, the standard library patron identification card is not RFID-enabled. In my recent survey of libraries, only 11 percent of the surveyed libraries have installed RF smart cards. It is hard to assess how patrons would feel about an RFID-enabled library card. Will patrons feel that their privacy is threatened by an RFID-enabled card? And will your library provide an opt-out for patrons who are uncomfortable with carrying an RFID-enabled library patron card? These are questions your library needs to address within the framework of your community and what you want to accomplish with an RFID system. Are you looking to future applications, and view an RFID patron card as a way to scale your system to possible fine payment at self-check machines?

RFID-IN-ACTION INTERVIEW: RFID PATRON AND CIVIC CARD COMBINATIONS

Q: Are you interested in obtaining RFID-enabled patron cards that could be used in conjunction with other civic services?

A: We asked about the potential for an RFID-enabled card/civic OneCard in an RFP document, but none of the vendors who responded had a solution that would allow an RFID-tagged card to be used outside of the library (e.g., for transit or recreational facility admissions). The vendor we selected currently does not offer RFID-chipped cards, at any rate, so we will retain our machine-readable bar coded cards and shelve this idea for the moment. I posted a message to RFID_LIB about this issue, asking to hear back from people or organizations that have such a setup; I heard of three.

Adrienne Canty, Manager of the Strathcona Branch of Edmonton Public Library, Edmonton, Alberta, Canada (Ward-Canty interview, 2006).

As with all technology, enhancements are always taking place in the RFID field. RFID technology allows fresh applications to emerge driven by demonstrated need or potential benefits. The utility of a multipurpose RFID user card could provide multiple municipal uses, but would need the buy-in of the community. To secure buy-in, the card needs to be impervious to hacking and carry some type of privacy assurance.

Consider Patron Self-Checkin

The checkin of items is a labor-intensive procedure. Certainly the routine varies among libraries, but certain aspects of the work flow will remain constant regardless of the system.

All returned items need to be:

- resensitized by an electronic article surveillance system to protect from theft
- checked back into the circulation system as being on the shelf and ready to circulate
- updated with a circulation record status in the online catalog
- pre-sorted and then drilled down to more granular levels such as class and class number
- reshelved into the collection

RFID has been integrated into an application of self-check to complement the AMH (automated material handling) and pre-sorting applications available today. Patrons returning materials are invited to place the items into a book drop chute located on an outside wall that transfers the materials gently into the library, or to use a kiosk that is located within the physical space of the library. The patron is immediately presented with a receipt noting all the items that were returned and it is time-stamped. This added feature helps to protect patrons from late fees that might be encountered.

It is a good application of RFID technology but has pros and cons: Pros—it is easy for a patron to use; allows for immediate return to shelf in terms of ILS updates; Cons—it is expensive and cost-prohibitive. The cons have probably impacted its widespread adoption by many libraries. Of the libraries I surveyed, very few had self-checkin stations; however, the application has found more adoption in European and Asian libraries. For maximum efficiency, self-checkin systems should be tied to automatic sorting systems. This option carries a high price tag, but should give a library beehive-like efficiency with conveyor belts and automatic resensitizing and check-in of returned materials in the future.

Automated Material Handling and Sorting

Automated material handling (AMH) is a major benefit of RFID for libraries. The application of using radio frequency to sort materials based on their serialized tags has several aspects that need to be explained. RFID can expedite the check-in of loaned library items. When patrons want to return items to the library, they usually drop the items through slots either inside the library or through an after-hours library slot located on the library's outside wall; however, these slots are often no more than holes that lead to deep bins that do not provide cushioning or protection for items that are dropped off. The same slot used for large coffee-table-style books is also used for DVDs, videocassettes, and paperbacks. Stress upon the physical item is inevitable in this scenario and negatively affects the intended circulation lifecycle of an item. Book-drop systems are constructed to cushion the returned items and can be designed to partner with bin-sorting systems.

Capitalizing upon the automatic identification power of RFID, when an item is returned through the RFID-enabled book drop chute, an RFID coupler wakes up the item's tag, reads its data, and checks it back into circulation. Depending upon your tag, it may also switch the security bit back on to enable security. The items are routed on a conveyor belt to a bin that recognizes their tag as belonging to it as a pre-sort destination. Pre-sort destinations can be housed as data on the tag and can have determining factors such as: branch location, Library of Congress or Dewey Decimal classification number, type (media or book), audience (adult or juvenile), fiction or nonfiction. The sorter routes the items onto specific carts based on parameters that circulation librarians erect in order to make shelving easier. Materials returned after hours in external book drops are transported onto a conveyor belt to be sorted into bins or trucks based on parameters on the tag. For instance, all books destined for a specific section or floor of the library will be identified by the reader in the book drop chute as it is checked back in and resensitized, and then conveyed to the appropriate sort bin and gently dropped in. In the morning, the staff members have a group of presorted materials that are ready for a final call number sort and reshelving. This saves time and reduces much of the repetitive stress activities associated with the return process of circulation.

AMH is the feature that the library works on with the vendor to best suit the needs of the library and its circulation. A library wants to purchase enough bins to make pre-sort and automated material handling an effective investment. A committee should review circulation statistics and determine what are the main categories for returned materials and how best dividing these up would assist in pre-sorting returns. Benchmarking with other libraries using AMH is a good practice.

Several vendors offer automated material handling systems as an optional add-on to an RFID package. In 2006, the cost of an AMH feature varied with the number of bins a library purchased and how the return system and conveyor belts needed to be arranged. Sorting bins ranged from $2,000 to $10,000 depending upon the volume the library contracted for and the type of bin being purchased.

Store and Retrieve Select Materials

Automated Storage and Retrieval Systems (ASRS) are an important solution for the physical space challenges encountered by libraries. Faced with tight budgets, additions to current library space is often not an option, but off-site storage sometimes proves more affordable. However, such off-site storage facilities are not designed for patrons to walk through and pull books themselves; rather, warehouse-like machines are used to assist employees to retrieve requests. In some ASRS implementations, RFID has been used to increase efficiency.

RFID-IN-ACTION INTERVIEW: ASRS USING RFID

Vicki Read, Head of Patron Services, Merrill-Cazier Library
Utah State University, Logan, Utah
One example of a state-of-the-art ASRS system using RFID is Utah State University. Their retrieval system is from Daifuku America Corporation and it services the five-story onsite warehouse.
Q: Will you describe the functionality of tagging RFID books that are going into storage?
A: The monographs we store in the ASRS are RFID tagged. Initially, we were not going to RFID them but realized that we might as well for inventory purposes. We will move RFID-tagged monographs out of our open circulating shelves into the ASRS on a yearly basis so it made sense to have them all RFIDed at the time. We plan on using the tag for inventory only. We do not use the tags to retrieve the items but use the standard bar codes to call materials out of the ASRS and to check the items out to patrons.
(Ward-Read interview, 2006)

Lorraine Lazouskas of Chicago State University described her experience using RFID with ASRS at the 2006 ALA/LITA panel presentation. For the new library building, CSU decided to install RFID and build an ASRS (HK Systems 750 mini-load system) that would provide seven times the storage ability of common shelving. The ASRS features:

- two 134-foot aisles with 48 bays
- thirty-three levels giving rise to a total of 6,336 bins
- housing 350 pounds per bin

CSU uses Endeavor's Voyager which interfaces with the ASRS, and ITG (CSU's RFID vendor) created middleware to interface with the ASRS. This is a challenging environment to install RFID as the metal bins can pose interference problems. For more information on CSU's ASRS, please see Lazouskas' 2006 presentation available at: www.ala.org/ala/lita/litamembership/litaigs/rfidtechnology/ARS-RFID6-2006a.ppt

Government Documents Management

Perhaps nothing is more nightmarish than having to search through boxes housing the myriad of paper government documents that the Government Printing Office (GPO) has published over the years. To provide access to the publications, the GPO has depository libraries that agree to house, archive, and provide access to government documents. In recent years, the GPO has focused on issuing an increasing percentage of documents electronically (around 92 percent in 2006), but there are still thousands of documents issued each year that exist in paper format that libraries cannot weed.

For anyone that has ever had to use government documents on a regular basis, familiarity with the variance in size and shape of issued materials compounded with the complex classification schemes and cramped shelving arrangements makes this research challenging. Many libraries optionally house small, paperbound or stapled documents in boxes with other similar items in an attempt to keep them from getting lost on the shelves. And when one considers the complex construction of government document classification schemes, the importance of properly shelving items is compounded by a need to have the shelving clerk fully understand the flow of the call number.

Documents tagged with RFID provide an immediate way to home in on their whereabouts. A drawback: the paper items are normally very thin and the close proximity of the tags to one another might obviate the optimum functionality of RF transmission during inventory, for example.

Special and Archival Collections

For those that have worked in archival collections, the familiarity with walking down rows filled with non-standardized labeling may bring back unpleasant memories of not being able to successfully locate a specific box for a waiting patron. To the patron it does not matter that the errant box was missing in action due to a staff member misshelving it, a past patron stealing it, or it being in use by another patron somewhere else in the archive collection. The patron walks away with the sense that his/her request for information could not be satisfied by the department whose mission it is to preserve important source documents. For any archive employee, this break in patron satisfaction is unsettling and leaves one with a small sense of failure to serve the public.

Traditionally, when we think of archival boxes, we think of the long, opaque cardboard boxes that have impenetrable sides and cover: the common and affordable type of box to house manuscripts and documents. The difficulty with these boxes comes with the inability to see readily inside the box to ascertain the nature of the contents. Improperly labeled boxes can be an organizational dilemma and an embarrassment for the staff. For any archivist that wished to be able to peer inside the boxes, RFID offers a step toward that goal. Laying an RFID tag inside an archival box, or even affixing it to the box or its contents, benefits the staff member searching the stacks for an item, as well as speeds up the physical act of locating misshelved items. This results in a more efficient experience for the waiting patron, especially if a staff member is adept at using the handheld reader to locate items in the stacks.

The ability for RFID to zero in on a specific serialized item number is a key for archival use. The expense may not be justifiable for all archive collections. The most important point being, is RFID worth its cost of implementation, training, and upkeep for the volume of patrons and activity your archive collection receives on an annual basis?

Historical Artifacts and Rare Books

RFID can offer a unique opportunity to provide collection management of individual items and also provide security for these items. Rare books that are housed in a clamshell box or other type of conservation housing could have the RFID label affixed to the protective housing. Otherwise, a tag could simply be placed in the book without affixing it or peeling it off of its backing.

Historical artifacts pose an interesting opportunity for using RFID. Museums house three-dimensional objects of varying sizes and varying values that might play with the effectiveness of RFID on metal or liquid objects. The key is to tie the RFID functionality to the database and collection metadata for possible future application that may allow for interaction between the tag and portable handheld devices. The associated costs for RFID may pose a problem for smaller, community-based and -supported local historical museums or collections. If they are dependent on public funding for staffing, operations, and collection upkeep, then it is probable that a move to an RFID-based item management and item security system will be seen as an unapproachable budget item.

The first step for a rare books collection or historical objects collection is to assess what true benefit will come from implementing now. A more expensive add-on feature to RFID tags would partner environment sensing sensors with the tag's identification and security bits. There are RFID tags in use in non-library applications which have sensor functionality to monitor temperature and humidity and therefore alert staff members to any sudden changes in the conditions of the materials under their control. Essentially, this will benefit collections physically located in buildings that suffer from roof leaks, basement water seepage, or rapid fluctuations in temperature due to heating/cooling systems problems. RFID is an invisible watchperson.

Review of RFID and Library Applications

RFID technology offers an opportunity for libraries to develop applications to make a library operate more efficiently. Results may vary as no two libraries (like no two snowflakes) are identical. Additionally, continuing work and enhancements on the technology need to happen in order to work through some of the early technological glitches. A caveat: buyers need to ask questions and not just assume that RFID will be a savior to all of their library's problems or challenges.

References

Boss, Richard W. 2006. "RFID Technology for Libraries." ALA Web site. Available: www.ala.org/ala/pla/plapubs/technotes/rfidtechnology.htm

Ernick, Linda. 2005. "Floating Bibs and Orphan Bar Codes: Benefits of an Inventory at a Small College." *Library Resources and Technical Services* 49, no. 3 (July).

Garfinkel, Simson. 2006. "RFID Payments at ExxonMobil." In *RFID: Applications, Security, and Privacy*, edited by Simson Garfinkel and Beth Rosenberg. Upper Saddle River, NJ: Addison-Wesley.

Lazouskas, Lorraine. 2006. "RFID and Automated Storage and Retrieval (ASRS)." ALA/LITA (June 24, 2006 presentation). Available: www.ala.org/ala/lita/litamembership/litaigs/rfidtechnology/ARS-RFID6–2006a.ppt

Robkin, Shai. 2006. "CDs and DVDs: The Achilles Heel of RFID in Libraries." ALA/LITA (June 24, 2006 presentation). Available: www.ala.org/ala/lita/litamembership/litaigs/rfidtechnology/CDs-andDVDs6–2006.pdf

Singh, Jay, Navjit Brar, and Carmen Fong. 2006. "The State of RFID Applications in Libraries." *Information Technology and Libraries* (March): 24–31.

Ward, Diane Marie. 2003. "Radio Frequency Identification Systems for Libraries and Archives: An Introduction." *Library & Archival Security* 18, no. 2: 7–21.

Ward, Diane Marie. 2004. "Tags for CDs Get a Boost." RFID Journal (August 6). Available: www.rfidjournal.com/article/articleprint/1075/–1/1/

Ward, Diane Marie, and Oleg Boyarsky, e-mail interview, July 9, 2006.

Ward, Diane Marie, and Adrienne Canty, e-mail interview, August 16, 2006.

Ward, Diane Marie, and Sandra Collins, e-mail interview, July 5, 2006.

Ward, Diane Marie, and Ellen Firer, e-mail interview, July 5, 2006.

Ward, Diane Marie, and Lynne Jacobsen, e-mail interview, July 11, 2006.

Ward, Diane Marie, and Maureen Karl, e-mail interview, July 12, 2006.

Ward, Diane Marie, and William Marsterson, e-mail interview, July 10, 2006.

Ward, Diane Marie, and Susan O'Neal, e-mail interview, August 3, 2006.

Ward, Diane Marie, and Vicki Read, e-mail interview, August 15, 2006.

Ward, Diane Marie, and Louise Schaper, e-mail interview, July 3, 2006.

Ward, Diane Marie, and Edith Sutterlin, e-mail interview, August 7, 2006.

Wong, Tack Wei. 2002. "Large Scale Application of Radio Frequency Identification (RFID) in Public Libraries: The Experience of National Library Board, Singapore." European Library Automation Group (April).

4

Determining the Return on Investment (ROI) of RFID

Introduction

This chapter will discuss in depth some of the benefits resulting from implementing Chapter 3's applications of RFID through statistics, survey findings, and interviews with librarians that have implemented RFID. The issue for many librarians is how to quantify traditional library activities in terms of return on investment (ROI) since a library is service-driven, rather than purchase-driven: how does one associate a dollar figure with locating a misplaced book for a patron or alleviating the frustration of long lines with RFID self-checkouts?

The reaffirmation of library goals of service excellence and meticulous shelf management is paramount to the longevity and relevancy of libraries in the age of Internet search engines: If we want patrons to patronize a library, we need to ensure that they will find what they want on the shelves we tell them to search. Patrons are customers that "pay" with their time that they spend physically coming into our libraries. RFID is a technological tool that offers us the opportunity to reward their loyalty as never before.

It is a much easier exercise to establish ROI for a business that deals in quantities of product sold, but for libraries that loan materials, and see a good deal of in-house usage, how does one know that the library got its money's worth from RFID? RFID will save time and money, but with any new technology it is difficult to establish hard numbers. In order to build a strong business case for RFID adoption for your library, librarians need real numbers to determine the return on investment. The reality is that most librarians do not record these everyday small personal victories associated with RFID, such as finding lost books or preventing item theft. To determine if RFID will benefit your library, one needs to balance in tandem some of the quantitative and qualitative findings located in this chapter.

Separating Myths from Reality

Applications are developed with the cost of the RFID tag in mind. If RFID tags cost a nickel or a penny, it might be feasible to apply them to disposable objects, but tags still cost about 53 cents (from my survey). Therefore, the library application where an RFID tag is reused and truly serves as a static item identifier is an excellent use of RFID on an item level and a good financial investment for the library.

RFID promises to:

- expedite self-circulation process for your patrons
- provide the opportunity for automated check-in
- offer the opportunity for sorting of returned materials via automatic identification technology
- enhance aspects of security for your materials
- enable easy inventory
- deliver self-charging of audiovisual materials
- make impeccable item management possible
- allow the easy location of misplaced items in an efficient way not possible prior to RFID adoption

Yet, RFID is not a robotic replacement for human library staff. RFID will not transform your library on its own; only library staff members can accomplish that! The application of RFID provides for a level of omniscience that was not available before in libraries. Employees need to know they are stakeholders in the organization and that RFID is a way to make their work life easier—because that is what RFID is: a way to automatically identify objects in an environment focused on providing access to information.

Some of the metrics I will suggest in determining ROI for a library installation are rooted in the qualitative assumptions that

- We strive for service excellence in a library.
- We erect service targets to enable the best possible experience for the user.
- We want accurate, organized shelves that reflect what is in the OPAC.
- We want our staff to interact with patrons in value-added ways.

Therefore, while my metrics may be rooted in the quality of service excellence, it is overshadowed with the desire to offer hard numbers so library committees can have some documented proof. Unfortunately, at this early date, libraries have only been using RFID since 1999, when counting the earliest adopters. The new generation of RFID components promises to alleviate and obviate many of the challenges to implementation that the first generation witnessed.

I surveyed eight vendors and I surveyed 37 libraries in total, 35 of which were North American. The North American responses are the basis for the charts where indicated as survey respondents. These are libraries that have installed RFID systems (majority: 32) or were in the process of installation (three). They are public and private, large and small, rural and urban: a cross section of our North American library culture. As such, they are snowflakes: no two identical. I am offering these statistics (both quantitative and qualitative) as a framework to assist library committees in determining if RFID holds ROI for their unique construction.

> For more detail on Ward's 2006 Survey of RFID Libraries and RFID Vendors, please see RFID Pocket Guide C.

To assess ROI, one needs to balance the qualitative, anecdotal and perhaps subjective responses from interviewed librarians that have installed RFID, with your own service targets for excellence. For instance, you might determine an ROI for inventory control by pairing the positive qualitative statements from the University of Nevada, Las Vegas, and the National Library Board of Singapore with your individual collection size, predictability of fielding patron inquiries, searching for possibly misplaced books, and your typical time to conduct inventory and shelf reading. If RFID poses an obviously less taxing and less financially burdensome path to improved shelf management, and ergo patron satisfaction, there is a return on investment. In the years to come, more time-study research will be available for potential hard numbers, but as with snowflakes, each library is different, so numbers will always have to be adjusted based on the permutations of RFID vendor, ILS vendor, collection size, borrowing volume, FTE (full-time employees) staff size, and commitment to improving library culture and service targets for patrons. Critics have cited that the ROI has not been determined because RFID is so new. A perceived lack of standards and data

Figure 4.1: Benefits of Using RFID			
Locate Misshelved Items	Locate Missing Items	Improves Security System	Item Management
Aids in Weeding	Aids in Sorting	Enables Automated Material Handling	Inventory
Self-Checkout	Self-Checkin	Reduction of Staff Repetitive Motions	Redeployment of Staff

Who is adopting RFID? According to my survey of vendors, around 944 total international libraries and 484 North American libraries have installed RFID systems. The percentage of increase in adoption is growing.

models has only added to existing questions about privacy rights and the projected longevity of the technology.

Comparing Implementation by Public Libraries and Academic Libraries

Opting for an RFID solution means a serious commitment of time and money up-front. The technology's promise is that, in the long run, the benefits will help pay for the system. Libraries need to be realistic about the added value RFID offers. Is RFID worthwhile to install now for your library? According to my survey of vendors, there are at least (in 2006) 944 total international libraries and 484 North American libraries that have installed RFID systems. The percentage of increase in adoption is growing. While administrators hold at the forefront the patron's best interests, however, there are circumstances and scenarios that might assist in selecting RFID. The system might make sense if you:

- recognize that circulation is growing, but no additional funds are being devoted to staffing so self-check is needed
- find that reducing repetitive motions associated with the loan process is appealing

- decrease the number of RSI claims and let RFID pay for itself
- make the library be seen as an early adopter of technology
- make use of self-check usage statistics
- purchase a new ILS and see this as an opportunity to install RFID
- move lesser-used materials into a storage facility and want a new technology for new building
- reduce the handling of materials by staff
- reduce RSI due to less physical manipulation of materials
- provide for streamlined and fast patron self-charging activities
- enable staff to do other less borrowing-centric work
- improve security for materials
- circulate audiovisual materials, possibly without locked cases
- locate missing items
- conduct inventory without a large commitment of staff time
- use the technology with automatic storage and retrieval systems
- improve a security system, or want to install a new one

I surveyed 35 North American libraries to determine why they implemented RFID. The accompanying figures illustrate the type and collection size of the libraries. The breakdown by type was 29 percent academic; 68 percent public; and 3 percent school. The following figure illustrates the size in staff and collection volumes of my survey set. The libraries I surveyed varied in many factors, but especially in collection size, ranging from 8,794 to 13 million volumes. Fifty percent of libraries surveyed were tagging their entire collection, another 22 percent planned on tagging 90–99 percent of their collection.

Figure 4.2: Demographics of Surveyed RFID Users	

Percentage by Type:
     Public
     Academic
     School
	68% (24 libraries)
	 29% (10 libraries)
	 3% (1 library)

Collection Size Range: (Total Volumes)	8,794 to 13 million
Staff Size Range: (Full-Time, Part-Time and Student Employees)	2 to 2,500

Public Libraries

Top questions to consider for Public Libraries in terms of cost and benefits:

- What type of trends in circulation have you noticed in the last year? Five years? Have you had a noticeable increase in circulation?
- What are the numbers related to circulation of media materials?
- How do your patrons access audiovisual materials? Are materials behind the circulation desk with empty cases on the shelves? Or are materials located inside their cases with circulation attendants checking the packaging for the proper contents during the loan process?
- Are the members of your staff willing to learn about RFID, and are they prepared to answer any of the questions that the public might have about privacy issues, etc.? What is their ability to change?
- Have we factored in the importance of stakeholder buy-in to RFID?
- Will you have the municipal funding to purchase the RFID system and also pay for any future maintenance or upgrades?
- Could the cost be justified by the ability to efficiently inventory the collection and produce excellent shelf management?
- Is patron satisfaction in finding requested items an ROI?
- Can we craft a patron survey to gauge service satisfaction before and after RFID installation?

Academic Libraries

Top questions to consider for Academic Libraries in terms of cost and benefits:

- How large is your collection? Would you want to tag all these items or only a portion of your circulating collection?
- Do you have a storage facility for low-use materials that would also have to be tagged—and what will this add to your tag budget? Do you have ASRS there?
- Is the library administration prepared to deal with campus groups or officials that may be hesitant about RFID for libraries due to reports about the technology? How committed are you to championing RFID for your academic community?
- How will RFID positively impact your library? Is your circulation that heavy that RFID self-checkouts will alleviate circulation lines? How many staff do you need to put on during peak times, for instance during exam week?
- Are RSI complaints more frequent at the end of the semester?
- How long in staff hours does it take to presort, sort, and shelve materials?
- Are you intent on using readers to track missing items for patrons? And if so, what will be the parameters of tracking lost items?
- What are the current average complaints relating to lost, misshelved, or improperly organized ranges of books? Will more frequent inventory lead to patron satisfaction?
- How much time do staff spend on shelf reading for missing items?

Questions for All Libraries

- Will purchasing an RFID system truly improve your library's efficiency and its ability to provide service excellence for its patrons?
- What are the benefits that might be realized using RFID tags, that you could not realize using standard bar codes?
- Is the expense and time worth the benefits?
- Will your committee be able to defend that your selection of RFID is not a techno-fad?
- What are the standards and interoperability of the hardware and the tags?
- Will RFID tags become ubiquitous in the next ten years and cost less?
- Is now the right time to partner with a library vendor for advantageous pricing?
- How much will this cost?
- What is our projected system downtime?
- Can you afford the downtime?
- What is our insurance if something goes wrong?
- Will technological improvements be backward-compatible for early adopters?
- How is this going to affect the privacy of users?
- If you are committed to not laying people off if we realize savings, where will they work? And when they retire, will you rehire for that opening? Or will RFID cause a reduction in overall FTE in the near future?

Calculating an Accurate Return on Investment (ROI)

Many questions get to the heart of the decision-making process: What is the ROI? The purchase of an RFID system affects your library for years to come. In some business sectors a return on investment in two years is seen as good; but with libraries, it is difficult to determine cost-savings since libraries are not laying off FTEs when RFID systems are put into place.

> The purchase of an RFID system affects your library for years to come.

An early attempt to establish determinant questions for ROI was Laura Smart's "Making Sense of RFID." Her "ROI Laundry List" includes calculating such things as cost in time and labor for materials processing; time studies on searching for books and inventory; average wait at the circulation desk; how much labor and time is spent on charging activities; and worker compensation costs from RSIs (Smart, 2004). Smart warned libraries to think seriously about tag interoperability and forward compatibility: "If a vendor goes out of business or out of the library market, then it is difficult to recoup the investment if another vendor's tags or equipment won't interoperate. This will also be an issue for sharing materials among libraries. There may be a need to use barcode and RFID" (Smart, 2004) until the market assures compatibility. It is advisable to ask vendors about the interoperability of the equipment you are purchasing.

Berkeley Public Library's Elena Engel completed an examination on ROI for California public and academic libraries as part of a study for the U.S. Institute of Museum and Library Services. The study was conducted by Elena Engel as principal investigator and consultant Karen Coyle. She constructed a thorough document titled "RFID Implementations in California Libraries: Costs and Benefits." I asked Engel about her research. Engel told me: "I just finished a study on RFID implementations in California libraries. It was completed in July of this year [2006]. The study tried specifically to take on the question of ROI, and to look at the benefits and costs of RFID implementation. Berkeley Public was one of the libraries included in the study (we tried to include every public and academic library in California known to have purchased RFID). Overall, there are not yet enough California libraries nor a long enough period from initial implementation to clearly answer questions about ROI/cost-benefits. We did not deal with the privacy issues, except to allude to them because we felt that had been covered elsewhere in detail." (Engel, 2006)

Twenty-four out of 27 libraries returned Engel's survey. The major statistical findings support long-held beliefs about the benefits of RFID: 72 percent wanted to promote patron self-check and 56 percent believed that patron self-check and patron satisfaction were the major benefits. The report also gives insight into the minor and major benefits such as reducing RSI through a reduction in staff handling. Engel also shows that RFID is not that much more costly than installing a traditional EAS system.

Where do the savings come from? Patron satisfaction is the most discussed ROI. Karen Coyle notes in her article, "Management of RFID in Libraries," that ROI statements for libraries fail to account for user satisfaction as an indicator of positive ROI. "In a service business like that of the library, satisfying your users is one of the few measures of success that you have." (Coyle, 2005) Coyle goes on to posit that if a library increases statistics and pursues a user survey before and after installation, then one might have evidence of a positive ROI through documented user satisfaction. (Coyle, 2005)

Surveying Patron Satisfaction, Time Savings, and Cost

I have asked librarians what their patrons think of RFID systems and the response is usually positive. The word "magic" is something that is often repeated. I would have fully expected the self-check systems to be embraced by the techno-centric younger generation, but in my informal survey of patrons in both libraries with and without

RFID, I have discovered that the ease of use of RFID crosses all generational boundaries. The patrons I have asked seem to appreciate the efficiency RFID brings to their library experience. The first response is typically: "It is so fast!" or "I am in and out in no time!" Many are also excited that they can use self-checkout and expedite their library experience, especially when they have young children in tow.

Time Studies

- How many patrons can circulation staff handle per hour? Are there special functions that only staff can provide related to these daily circulation encounters: i.e., new patron card, payment of fines, helping with locating a book, responding to questions?
- How many self-check machines will you need to purchase in order to process the same amount of transactions? Keep in mind you will need staff to troubleshoot, answer questions, and train patrons.
- How much time is spent on presorting returned items? How many steps in the process are involved and how many staff members are devoted to this procedure?
- For the borrowing process of multipart audiovisual and multimedia materials, do you ensure that every component (disc, tape, booklets, etc.) is accounted for?
- What is your policy regarding circulation of audiovisual materials? Do you have a security mechanism on each piece of multivolume items? Or, do you believe that the semblance of security provides enough theft deterrence?
- What happens when a patron wants an item that is listed as circulating in the OPAC, but is not on the shelf? How much time is devoted to finding that item?
- When is your busiest time for returns? How long does it take for a complete check-in to the OPAC and resensitization of one day's load of materials?
- Have you ever had staff members survey patrons about circulation service excellence in regard to long lines?

Estimating Costs of an RFID System

RFID is a new technology and research on average costs for libraries is a movable target. For a quote on what your library needs, it is best to consult a vendor, since these prices will undoubtedly fall in the future, and your library may be able to negotiate more favorable pricing per tag, etc. In my survey, 35 libraries responded with their specifics. And 80 percent (28 libraries) believe it is a success. In my 2006 survey, I asked the eight major vendors to provide an estimated cost for a library with 500,000 items to convert to get up and running on RFID. Five responded and the average cost was $343,923.60. The most common figure was $300,000. Cost varied based on whether self-checks or installation and software were included in the pricing. A self-check system that uses bar codes costs nearly $15,000 and the same model fit for RFID costs around $18,000.

> In my survey, I asked: Do you consider your decision to switch to RFID successful. Respondents answered that 80 percent considered the switch a success/20 percent expressed no opinion at this point.

The expense of a full-scale RFID implementation in a library will vary upon collection size (number of tags to purchase) and if you want automated material sorting, self-charging, and so forth. Cost has been a prohibiting factor for widespread adoption. In 2004, Infopeople and the Information Technology Section of the California Library Association released the results of 113 surveyed libraries regarding their interest in RFID. The report indicated that 55 libraries were not considering RFID, 32 of them because of high cost, five due to privacy concerns, and another 16 because they didn't feel the need for it. (Engel, 2006)

I constructed a survey for the eight major vendors in the United States and Canada: Bibliotheca, Checkpoint Systems, ITG, Libramation, LAT, Tech Logic, VTLS, and 3M. The vendors supplied costs either in ranges or an exact quote. My methodology was to determine an average price for comparable products, but each offering is slightly different. Therefore, products are grouped into categories with an average price. I have left a column for your library committee to formulate a rough approximation of cost for your collection volume.

Other cost targets have been put forward. Richard W. Boss has tried to assemble some cost estimates on his Web page "RFID Technology for Librarians." For a small library of 40,000 items, the budget estimate is $70,000 minimum. A library with 100,000 items, interested in patron self-charging and a book drop unit, should expect a cost of $168,000 minimum. A large library with 250,000 items to tag, and interested in patron self-charging and a book drop unit would see a cost upwards of $333,500. (Boss, 2006)

Gretchen Freeman, the Associate Director of Reference and Technology at Salt Lake County Public Library Services, suggested these figures in her presentation for the Utah Library Association's 2005 Great Issues Forum: RFID, Ready or Not?: A small public library with a collection of 60,000 and circulation of 300,000 wanting a simple self-charging unit would pay around $75,000. A mid-size academic library with a collection of 200,000 and circulation of 150,000 would have a price tag of nearly $217,000, with tagging labor included. (Freeman, 2005)

Figure 4.5 illustrates an average cost of an item based on the five vendors that responded with pricing per item. Please do not hold vendors to these prices. Tags are

Figure 4.3: RFID System Cost Estimate Worksheet		
Item	**Average Cost (2006)***	**Quantity Needed and Estimated Cost**
RFID tags for paper-based items with EAS: Conversion of existing collection	$0.53 Varies by vendor	
RFID tags for paper-based items with EAS: Supply for incoming acquisitions	$0.53 Varies by vendor	
RFID tags for audiovisual items with EAS: Conversion of existing collection	$0.98 Varies by vendor	
RFID tags for audiovisual items with EAS: Supply for incoming acquisitions	$0.98 Varies by vendor	
Handheld RFID reader	$5,886 Varies by vendor	
RFID checkout stations for staffed circulation desk	$2,658 Varies by vendor	
RFID self-checkout stations	$14,300 Varies by vendor	
RFID checkin stations	$15,125 Varies by vendor	
RFID enabled sorter with bins	$111,000 Varies by vendor	
Security gates	$8,636 Varies by vendor	
Conversion station	Varies by vendor—are usually rented	
Middleware (Software)	Varies by vendor	Variable
SIP2 or NCIP fee (if needed)	Varies by vendor	Variable
Server (if needed)	Varies by vendor	Variable
Service contract per annum and installation charge	Varies by vendor	Variable
Miscellaneous items not mentioned but needed	Varies by vendor	Variable

*This cost is an average based on the responses which included price from the eight vendors featured in this book. It should only be used as a guide. Do not expect to attain this price as each vendor sells a unique RFID solution and the prices will vary with determinants such as: product selection, your library's data storage and transmission requirements, your physical layout, number of tags you need, and so forth. The following table gives your committee an idea of what are the start-up costs and what will be continuing costs. Together this will give you a basic estimate of the total cost of ownership. Of course one needs to figure in depreciation on hardware and the cost of software and hardware upgrades but RFID is too new to accurately assess this yet.

Figure 4.4: RFID Installation Costs	
Startup Costs	**Continuing Costs**
Conversion process labor	Service maintenance
Tags for existing collection	Replacement of broken equipment
Readers (handheld and desk-mounted)	Tags for new materials
Self-checkout units	SIP2/NCIP fees
Self-checkin units	Software upgrades
Retrofitting a book drop chute with RFID	Hardware upgrades (new handheld reader models)
Sorting system (AMH)	Additional self-checkout units
Bins	Additional self-checkin units
Conversion station purchase and rentals	Additional bins for sorting system
Training (labor time)	Staff time to monitor advancements in RFID
Committee's time to research RFID issue	Staff time to monitor privacy
Committee's time to draft RFP	Depreciation of hardware when trading up
Committee's time and coverage of expenses for site visits of installations	RFID-enabled patron card

In my survey, I asked the eight major vendors to give me an estimated cost for a library with 500,000 items to convert to get up and running on RFID. Five responded, and the average cost was $343,923.60. The most common figure was $300,000.

priced based on functionality, and often a discount may be offered for buying in bulk quantities. These rolls of tags are not cheap, but the price is dropping from the $1.00 cost from my 2003 survey. As more libraries adopt RFID, these costs will drop as is typically the case with emerging technology products. My 2006 survey shows an average price of 53 cents per tag.

Figure 4.5: System Component Pricing Averages	
Tags for book	$0.53 (US)
Tags for audiovisual	$0.98 (US)
Circulation desk reader	$2,658 (US)
Handheld reader	$5,886 (US)
Self-check station	$14,300 (US)
Checkin station	$15,125 (US)
Sorter	$111,000 (US)
Security gates	$8,636 (US)

Vendor Response to Pricing

The RFID market as a whole is a growth market in the emerging technologies sector of the new millennium. Popular applications are driving researchers and developers to adopt standards and strive for interoperability of all hardware and tags. A hindrance to widespread adoption is the perceived high expense of installing an RFID system. For the industry as a whole, RFID tags are seen as more expensive than standard UPC bar codes, but they add value through the data that they automatically collect. A market driver that most analysts look to is a drop in price per tag which would presumably catalyze the adoption of RFID. RFID tag customers need to buy tags in bulk quantities in order to realize a cost savings. To this end, people predict RFID will take off when tags reach a 5-cent level. However, in an article I wrote for RFID Journal, "5 Cent Tag Unlikely in 4 Years," ARC Research Group believes that a 16-cent price plateau for passive UHF tags and a 30-cent average price for passive HF tags is not likely until at least 2008. Chantal Polsonetti, ARC's vice president of Manufacturing Advisory Services at ARC Advisory Group, commented on the benefits suppliers would enjoy due to RFID: "In order for RFID to be truly successful, the information it holds has to be generated at no cost, so the question becomes how to automate the data collection. . . . The reduced need for manual handling . . . has been attributed to anywhere from a 5 to 35 percent reduction in labor costs . . . ." (Ward, 2004)

A 2003 Allied Business Intelligence (ABI) report "RFID: Emerging Applications Driving R&D Investment and End-User Demand" forecasted global spending on RFID would grow from $1.3 billion in 2003 to $3.1 billion in 2008. (Maselli, 2003) A more recent projection posted on RFID Update was discussed by ABI's Director of RFID and M2M Research, Erik Michielsen in reference to ABI's 2006 report "RFID Annual Market Overview: Vertical Market and Application Market Overviews for Tags, Readers, Software and Services." The report positively characterizes the sus-

Figure 4.6: Conversion Survey Question	
Was the conversion to RFID less expensive, more expensive, or about the same as you budgeted for?	
About the Same as Budget	62% (22 libraries)
More Expensive	29% (10 libraries)
Less Expensive	6% (2 libraries)
No Opinion	3% (1 library)

tainable technical aspects of a market trying to erect standards for the advancement of RFID: "The end result is an industry that is more standardized, multisourced, and solutions-driven. Such virtuous characteristics position the market for sustainable growth." (RFID Update, 2006) In my survey, 62 percent of libraries felt that the final cost came in at about the same as originally budgeted for.

Price Fluctuation

In 2000, Rockefeller University Library became one of the first U.S. libraries to adopt RFID as an item management tool and this made news on the RFID industry's premier Web news resource, RFID Journal. Patricia Mackey worked with Checkpoint Systems to test out their new RFID tag product in a library environment and installed self-checkout stations and tagged 100,000 items (RFID Journal, 2002). As RFID Journal reported, the number of people choosing the self-checkout over a staffed-circulation desk had increased sevenfold. In 2002, the pricing per tag for library usage was estimated to be about 85 cents (U.S.), circulation desk readers ranged from $1,500 to $2,500 per unit; portable readers were about $1,500 each; book drop readers $1,500 to $2,500; long range exit-door reader was about $3,000, and self-checkout stations ranged from $20,000 to $25,000 each according to the RFID Journal report. The report estimated that the Public Library Association estimated "the cost of a complete RFID system for a small library with 40,000 items at least $70,000. A library with 100,000 items would have to spend at least $165,000 for a comprehensive system that includes a patron self-checkout station and a book drop reader." (RFID Journal, 2002). The article concludes that although libraries can realize ROI savings from theft prevention, better use of staff, a reduction in payroll expenses that "The cost of RFID systems has been dropping. The industry, however, faces a chicken-and-egg dilemma. Until libraries are using millions of tags, the price of the tags will remain fairly high. And libraries won't tag millions of items until the price comes down." (RFID Journal, 2002).

Interviewing Early Adopters of RFID

When reading these accounts, think of the extent that they might mirror the potential for helping to steer a committee toward or away from RFID. It may detail various challenges that occurred at a particular library, but those challenges may not be present at your library. For further information on any particular issue, I encourage you to network with your colleagues that work at libraries that have implemented RFID systems. Again, each library will have unique circumstances and it is paramount that library committees work with specialized RFID vendors to accommodate their special situations.

RFID Academic Library Success Story: University of Nevada Las Vegas Libraries

www.library.unlv.edu/index.html

University of Nevada Las Vegas has seen a period of growth that has promoted the importance of the UNLV library to the university community and has made it one of the premier research libraries in the United States. In 1998, 3M's management and the Dean of the UNLV Libraries, Dr. Kenneth Marks, realized that through cooperation they could use 3M's technology to create a state-of-the-art library at the new Lied facility. Opened to the public in January 2001, the $55.3 million Lied Library houses nearly 1,000,000 monographs, 7,950 serial subscriptions, 13,500 media items, and 20,000 maps in a 302,000 square foot new building with over 28 miles of shelving. It has an automated storage and retrieval unit that uses cranes to retrieve any of the 175,000 stored materials in a unit that can store well over 1.2 million volumes at full build capacity. (UNLV Libraries Web site, 2005)

UNLV's redesign and increasing circulation statistics appeared to be a perfect opportunity for administrators to look at integrating new technological advancements in such areas as shelving, weeding, item management, and security systems. This was a tremendous opportunity for both vendor and library to beta test new technology. Jennifer L. Fabbi, the head of curriculum materials at UNLV, confirmed in an interview with Scott Carlson for the *Chronicle of Higher Education* that the library has only a bar code on the tag and that the numbers "are meaningless apart from the library catalog, which is guarded by security software." (Carlson, 2004)

Toni Scire of the RFID installer 3M wrote about the conversion of 600,000 items: "The conversion stations include a touch-sensitive screen, an optical bar code reader and a compact cart that allowed library staff to work directly in the stacks. . . . they converted an average of 170 items per hour and completed the entire conversion project in approximately 3,500 hours." (Scire, 2003)

UNLV uses Innovative Interfaces Incorporated as their ILS vendor. UNLV beta tested the 3M Digital Library Assistant™ (DLA). Staff generated a shelf-order list and loaded these files on a library PC, exported the list to the DLA's memory card in order to check inventory, weed and find missing items. After a shelf was scanned, the staff member could use the DLA's audible tones, lights and screen to address shelf management issues. Using this RFID handheld device, UNLV reportedly found 500 lost items which saved them $40,000 in replacement costs; they frequently do inventories and have not experienced problems with patron privacy infringement. Fabbi has written about this in "Evaluating Academic Library Collections in the Age of Expedience: Weeding with a New Tool." Fabbi wrote about using the handheld RFID reader: "With the ability to pull items in the stacks without a bulky paper list, one is able to look at items in the context of the collection as a whole in that subject area, paying attention to condition and scope of item that may not have made the 'dusty book list.'" (Fabbi, 2003)

RFID-IN-ACTION INTERVIEW: INSTALLING THE SYSTEM

I asked Jennifer L. Fabbi, Head of Curriculum Materials at UNLV, about her experience.

Q: Do you use metal shelving in your stacks, and if so does that play a role in using the handheld reader to locate items in the stacks? Are the read rates affected by the metal?

A: We do use metal shelving. We are able to use certain techniques (for shelf reading and taking inventory), such as pulling the spine of the first book on the shelf out about two inches in order to make sure that we get it. Staff that use the handheld readers on a regular basis learn how to regulate their speed and use other methods to maximize the read rates.

Q: Has the ability to locate misplaced items in the stacks using a handheld RFID reader revolutionized the way you provide service to your patrons?

A: The way we have looked at this is that a misplaced item is a lost item to our patrons. Patrons get frustrated when they go to look for things on the shelf and cannot find them. During the first few years, we were constantly finding items that had call number labels that did not match their call numbers in the library catalog, or items that did not have records in the library catalog. These problems are not atypical for large academic libraries, but ours have all been cleaned up now. We can do inventory on our collection multiple times in a year—this is unheard of for most large libraries. If a patron is looking for an item, it will most likely have a current inventory date, which gives us a clue, or we can just key the barcode into the DLA and do a quick scan of the section where it should be. Also, we can identify items on the shelf that may have been returned to the shelf without being checked in—this is just another way that we can catch mistakes that irritate patrons before they become aware that there is a problem. With a patron base that increasingly expects convenience and self-service, the ability to more easily locate misplaced items has directly and indirectly impacted our patron satisfaction with locating items in the stacks. (Ward-Fabbi interview, 2006)

RFID has had a positive impact upon UNLV's shelf management. John Yorkovich wrote that Dr. Kenneth Marks was proud of the accuracy of his library and quoted him as saying: "staff accurately track and identify every item in the collection so books and other materials can be placed in their correct order on shelves. Students and faculty looking for a specific book or document are able to find it every time." (Yorkovich, 2001: 216)

Circulation increased immediately: Lied Library records visits of "151,423 in October 2001 (an average of 4,885 visits/day and a 123 percent increase over October 2000 visits in the former library." (Eden, 2002) UNLV has been seen as a model library by many. The Parliamentary Library in Australia installed 3M's Digital Materials Flow Management System with their Sirsi Unicorn ILS, and found UNLV's staff to be a resource: "Before installing the 3M RFID system, we wrote to Sidney Watson" of UNLV "to ask how effective the DLA was with thin materials. . . . Watson's response was that at first they were obsessed with counting items by hand to be sure that the DLA did not miss anything." (Khong and White, 2005) Soon it was seen that the DLA did not miss many items and was fine for use with a pamphlet collection. The Parliamentary Library's shelf reading completion time went from six months to six weeks. UNLV is a model to follow because of their dedication to making RFID work for them and for sharing their findings with their colleagues in journals.

RFID Library Success Story: National Library Board of Singapore

www.nlb.gov.sg

In 1998, the National Library Board of Singapore chose to institute in all of its 23 national libraries an RFID system using ST LogiTrack Pts Limited's Electronic Library Management System (ELIMS®). It was the culmination of a long drive to improve Singapore's libraries, which included a study by the Library 2000 Review Committee (1992–1994) that sought to address the needs of Singapore's 4.4 million citizens through library improvements. After a business process re-engineering (1997–1998), goals were established such as to reduce the waiting for borrowing and returning materials from one and one half hours to less than fifteen minutes. Tack Wai Wong writes that RFID: "and an optimized supply chain to ensure the latest materials are on the shelves for customers within the shortest timeframe were 'killer apps'" (Wong, 2002).

Singapore's government agreed to devote $1 billion ($600 million USD) to build an efficient library system (Oder, 2004). The test-site installations started in 1998 and proved to reduce service level targets below the five-minute level during peaks, and provide for instant book checkin for returns. In 2000, 3M Library Systems was selected to install an RFID system to the National University of Singapore's six libraries. They used the 3M Digital Identification System Conversion Station to transition 2 million items from optical bar code to RFID label (Biblio Tech Review, 2000).

Since 1995, NLB saw a "three-fold increase in visitorship and a loan growth rate of approximately 20 percent per years to reached [sic] 27.9 million loans in 2001" (Wong, 2002). More recent estimates confirm these cursory statistics: "They've achieved statistical leaps: annual visits from 5.7 million to 31 million; loans from ten million to 32 million; and inquiries from 50,000 to 1.8 million" (Oder, 2004). Seven million items were tagged. It is estimated they had 84 million transactions in 2002. There was no increase or decrease in staffing as a result of RFID. In a press release from ST LogiTrack, it is proclaimed that RFID saved NLB considerably: "The RFID innovation has enabled NLB to save more that $50 million in manpower cost. In fact, NLB would have needed 2000 staff at its 20 outlets today, just to stamp books for return and loans, to meet the equivalent service standards offered by the RFID system now" (ST LogiTrack, 2002). This extraordinary and remarkably immediate ROI is heralded on the NLB's Web site and most articles written about the library's installation of RFID. While it is beyond my scope to deconstruct the reported quantitative benefit ($50 million saved), the quality metric is solid from all accounts since service quality improved because of reduced queuing time for loans and returns.

In his article, Christopher Chia noted that Singapore libraries attract a young generation because of the do-it-yourself technology and the genius physical locations, including inside shopping malls. The growth of library membership is stellar: In 2001, 50 percent of Singaporeans were members of the library and there were 25 million loans and 21 million visitors. Chia writes: "Just as the creation of shopping mall libraries had a major ripple effect beyond its initial plan, the use of RFID yielded myriad possibilities that NLB aggressively explored. Beyond making borrowing a breeze, the ELiMS® system also addressed another recurrent customer concern that books in libraries are misplaced by other customers" (Chia, 2001: 345). He notes that the inventory procedure has shrunk from two weeks to less than a day. The service target is to reshelve books within fifteen minutes of their return, which was previously a lengthy eight-hour span.

RFID-IN-ACTION INTERVIEW: THE SECOND GENERATION

At the 2006 ALA Convention, Sung Kuan, Senior Manager of NLB's InfoComm Division, told participants about his efforts to roll out a "second generation" of RFID technology in 39 libraries in April 2006. The "first generation" asked users to put an identity card into a slot on the self-charging kiosk. The patron placed an item on a blue pad and watched the screen as each item was identified and a due slip was issued by an integrated printer. The library experienced true 24-hour 7-days-a-week book return services and could rely upon fewer staff for the sorting process associated with returned items.

Q: Will you please describe the difference between the first generation and second generation of RFID systems?

A: Our first-generation RFID system helped us automate our library operation in many ways. It allows for real-time updating of library records, it shortens the time needed to borrow, return and sort the library items. We could also provide round-the-clock returning using our 24-hour Bookdrop, as well as conduct stock check any time of the day. Our second-generation RFID system provides such services with enhanced performance. It also works on an open source system so that we could customize its application to suit our needs. Reporting of statistics can be done centrally via a web browser to provide library managers real-time information. We may also tap on this technology to provide remote bookdrops in order to bring library services closer to our communities.

Q: Did you change vendors or was the technology upgraded?

A: Initially, we used a barcode system for borrowing that requires users to flip open book pages. This system was subsequently replaced with RFID technology at all our branches by April 2002. Our 2nd generation RFID system was rolled out in April 2006 with the introduction of the enhanced features.

Q: Why did you choose to upgrade?

A: We are constantly looking at ways to improve our library operation, thus we have opted to use open source system so that we could continuously tailor solutions to meet our needs.

Q: Do you believe that the return on investment for libraries is substantial enough to warrant RFID adoption?

A: With RFID, we are able to achieve a service level of almost instant book return time as well as the borrowing of four library items within one minute. On a busy day where loan transactions range from 8,000 to 11,000, we would probably need 30 to 40 staff to achieve such service level if RFID had not been deployed. I believe the ROI can be substantial if the current or future business volume is large.

Q: Are you having luck checking in and out your CDs and DVDs or using automatic book sorters?

A: Many DVDs today come with a larger metallic surface that makes detection a challenge. We are in the process of testing a new identification code that will help address this concern.

Q: What is your procedure if a patron cannot find a book on the shelf? Do you use a handheld reader to find it, or do you let them know when it is found after a library inventory?

A: We are currently testing our new "smart shelves" that could help patrons find books more easily. We are also exploring the use of handheld readers to do browse count. Both are still under trial.

Q: You have automatic sorters and bins for returned books?

A: We had previously tried out a conveyor system for sorting of returned books, but it is not cost efficient nor effective for us to continue using it. (Ward-Kuan interview, 2006)

It is therefore not surprising that researchers at the National University of Singapore's Institute of Communication Research have been looking into extending material handling into book retrieval and return applications. The paper "UnManned Library: An Intelligent Robotic Books Retrieval & Return System Utilizing RFID Tags" by Kho Hao Yuan, Ang Chip Hong, Marcelo Ang, and Goi Sio Peng discusses how a system could be created to pull and reshelve books in restricted areas of a library, or to help alleviate the burden of reshelving for circulation librarians. It is natural that Singapore's researchers are trying to build upon those early applications.

Exploring the Administrative and Collection Management Benefits

RFID is an effective way of dealing with a shrinking budget and increased patronage. The one-time outlay of funds for the system may prove more fiscally attractive to financial boards than hiring more full-time employees. An RFID sorter can do a solid pre-sort of returned materials and free staff to actively help patrons rather than pre-sort returns on a cart. Additionally, self-checkout and checkin can expedite the patron's experience and free up circulation staff for other patron outreach activities.

In a 2003 study of self-check machines (non-RFID) in the United Kingdom, Sarah Gollin and Chris Pinder noted that the high cost of self-check equipment was a reason for 75 percent of their survey's responding libraries to not purchase self-check machines; however, 47 percent said they could keep longer hours and 32 percent cited it was cost efficient, and 55 percent said they could make use of self-check if the circulation desk was closed. (Gollin and Pinder, 2003: 47–48)

These findings are in keeping with the findings that I discovered regarding British libraries. I surveyed a large academic library (800,000 volumes and a staff of 85 FTE) and a large public library (370,000 volumes and a staff of 90 FTE). Both had purchased self-checkout RFID equipment as well as checkin RFID equipment and handheld RFID readers for staff to use. Neither library experienced any privacy-related complaints from patrons, nor any job-loss-related worries from the staff. Both libraries used staff to convert the portion of their collection they targeted in two to three months' time, and firmly view the choice to go to RFID as a success for both patrons and staff.

RFID-IN-ACTION INTERVIEW: SUCCESSFUL PUBLIC LIBRARY CONVERSION, SEATTLE PUBLIC LIBRARY

www.spl.org

Seattle Public Library is one of the major libraries that has chosen RFID and to tag all of its collection. Marilyn Sheck, director of information technology at Seattle Public Library, states that her institution is one of the major libraries that has chosen RFID to tag all of its collection. In my survey, she noted, that "We'd be buried if we didn't go this route," which made me think it important to get more details about their experience.

Q: Why do you think RFID has been such a success for Seattle Public?

A: We had capital funding, which would pay for "stuff," but our operating budget was cut four years in a row. People come from operating funds. Our circulation has increased significantly over the past couple of years, but our staff has not increased. We could not keep up with circulation without the sorter, which sorts 1,200 items an hour with two operators per shift. It would not handle anywhere near this volume without RFID. Also, self-service checkout is now so simple that many people just use it, and staff are freed to work with those who need assistance of some kind.

Q: Do you think RFID checkout has allowed your staff to work more efficiently?

A: I think it has. Checkout is much faster, and much of it is done by the patrons themselves. Staff can then concentrate on patrons with fines, registrations, and on other tasks.

Q: Any advice?

A: Win over your customers and staff before you make the final decision. Decide whether it makes sense in your library. We had a definite business need, and RFID was our answer. Don't go with RFID just because it's cool technology or "everyone else has it." It is expensive and should be worth the investment. (Ward-Sheck interview, 2006)

In her article "Meeting New Challenges with New Technology: The Seattle Public Library Experience," Sheck describes the benefits received from automatic materials handling systems (AMHS) combined with RFID. As materials are dropped through exterior book drops, they slide on conveyors to the AMHS where "they pass over an RFID antenna which reads the barcode number from the tag attached to the item. The AMHS then queries our Integrated Library System as to what the item is and where it needs to go." (Sheck, 2004) It goes into a designated smart bin to deliver materials to specific buildings. The throughput of the AMHS is 1,200 items per hour with a plan to reach 2,000 per hour. RFID provided ergonomics, efficiency, processing, and charging benefits to a large, urban public library.

RFID-IN-ACTION INTERVIEW: CUSTOMER REACTION, SALT LAKE COUNTY LIBRARY SERVICES

www.slco.lib.ut.us

Salt Lake County Library Services circulated 12.7 million items in 2005. I interviewed Gretchen L. Freeman, Associate Director of Reference & Technology, about her experience with RFID.

Q: What has been the patron reaction to RFID?

A: Users say it is magical.

Q: Do you believe RFID has helped increase efficiency? Can you detail benefits from automated checkin and sorting systems since the two libraries were using two-thirds the staffing they would normally need?

A: The magical part is the RFID self-checkout where customers place their pile of materials on the antenna and the system "magically" identifies what they have without bar code scanning. Patrons of all ages find that fascinating. RFID self-checkout and sorting have definitely helped us work more efficiently and use staff for other tasks such as pulling holds. I'm pulling together actual data on staffing levels and cost savings that I plan to use to justify additional sorting systems in our system. (Ward-Freeman interview, 2006)

RFID-IN-ACTION INTERVIEW: WARREN-NEWPORT PUBLIC LIBRARY

www.wnpl.alibrary.com

Lynne Jacobsen is the Head of Technical Services at Warren-Newport Public Library in Gurnee, Illinois. I asked her to reflect upon her ITG-installed system.

Q: Are you satisfied with the sortation system? Any problems associated with the sortation system or workflow?

A: Our sorter makes RFID really worthwhile. There are no problems, except that items are checked in so fast that the shelvers have their work cut out for them getting items shelved promptly. I think this piece of equipment has paid for itself after six months of use. It has really helped us handle record-breaking circulation.

Q: You mentioned that you have some statistics related to the time-saving aspects of RFID. For example, checkin that used to take two days is done instantly, and you now need only one staff member at checkin and checkout. Could you expound a little on your feelings about the positive aspects of RFID?

A: We actually now have two people at staff-assisted checkout stations. We used to have three people, so we reduced it from three to two. We no longer have a staff person dedicated to checking in. One circulation person checks in about 10 percent of items manually which are from the "problem" bin, consisting of interlibrary loan items, items without a tag, etc. Two new developments will enable seamless self-check: the new self-check stations with Kwik-Case® release capability and eCommerce (allowing patrons to pay for fines/fees using a credit card during self-check or over the Web). Our staff members don't know how they could get the job done if it weren't for RFID. Patrons welcome self-service—it's available in our community at Home Depot and Jewel Food stores.

Q: How have you been able to use your staff members differently thanks to the time-saving resulting from RFID?

A: Staff members are able to handle the increase in circulation as a result of implementing RFID. We would not be able to keep up without RFID. (Ward-Jacobsen interview, 2006)

For a study on Northland Public Library (www.einetwork.net/ein/northland), see the accompanying DVD, where librarians Sandra Collins and Edith Sutterlin of NPL are interviewed.

RFID-IN-ACTION INTERVIEW: MIDDLETOWN TOWNSHIP PUBLIC LIBRARY

www.mtpl.org

Susan O'Neal is Director of Middletown Township Public Library in Middletown, New Jersey.

Q: How does one determine ROI to assess if RFID is beneficial to the patron and the library?

A: Libraries that can implement business-type decisions and fail to do so will be on the failure end of libraries in the future. Following the models of retailing leaders, such as Wal-Mart, in inventory management is something we as librarians are not used to doing, but our funders now require smarter and smarter management and fiscal accountability. They understand good business models, and our customers do, too. Libraries are places with a lot of inventory that moves out in much the same way as a retailer. If a clerk in a store can complete an inventory with a handheld scanner, why can't a library?

Q: What other questions should libraries ask?

A: How long will libraries be able to deploy an entire staff for a week or two to conduct the same inventory? How long will a customer wait for someone to read seven shelves of books, an action that may also involve sitting on the floor to get to the lowest shelves, to find a misshelved volume, when a scanner could find it in a minute or less? Tomorrow's customer will be out the door, empty-handed with no confidence in the library.

Q: Will self-service be critical?

A: The self-service link with RFID is critically important. RFID systems will give you great inventory management and security, but the combination with self-service is awesome. Taking it to this level goes from the simple, but incredibly important, matter of saving the customer's time to the more complex and subjective contribution staff can make to the library "experience" when they can be deployed for one-on-one time with their customers. The personal touch is what cannot be automated and is what libraries can do really well—when freed from the imprisonment of outdated methods.

True story: I have never hated a store that I shopped in as much as [store name omitted]. It was a discount retailer, lots of variety and very good prices. But every single time I shopped there the checkout lines were atrocious—every time! I couldn't understand why they didn't focus on speedy checkout service since this was the part where they got my money. I valued my time but they didn't respect that. . . . the chain is now out of business. When we were considering the Tech-Logic system, I clearly remembered this story and thought how our library customers might be thinking about us when they stood in line to check out. No lines, no added staff, borrowing up 56 percent—it was practically a no-brainer. How can one NOT consider RFID these days is my question? (Ward-O'Neal interview, 2006)

RFID Library Success Story: Mastics-Moriches-Shirley Community Library

www.communitylibrary.org

Mastics-Moriches-Shirley Community Library in Shirley, New York, was established in 1974 and greatly expanded in 1995 due to growth. It is a very popular library and prides itself on its innovative community programs for patrons of all ages and its ability to embrace new technology. I asked Dennis Fabiszak, Facilities Manager, to tell me a little about his library's experience with time studies. He answered: "In our original cost/benefit analysis we timed multiple staff checking in and checking out items on both the old EAS/barcode system and with the new Bibliotheca RFID system. The results were as follows:

- EAS 8.8 seconds/item checking out
- EAS 7.8 seconds/item checking in
- RFID 1.15 seconds/item checking out
- RFID 0.88 seconds/item checking in

These tests were done before the final integrated version of the III Millennium software to Bibliotheca RFID system had been completed. We are now utilizing the final version of the software. Currently, staff machines are able to checkout or return stacks of up to ten items (including writing to the security bit) in a total of approximately 6 seconds per ten items. The Bibliotheca self-checkout system has by far been the best part of the entire system. The Bibliotheca software allowed me to customize/ change all of the text, buttons, warning messages, and images on the self-check screen. My self-checks are set to allow patrons to checkout stacks of up to five items. From the beginning of a checkout process of five items to the point of receiving a printed receipt takes a patron approximately 4 seconds." (Ward-Fabiszak interview, 2006)

Liberating Patrons from Long Lines

Patrons whom I randomly surveyed indicated frustration with long lines for borrowing materials, particularly on Saturday mornings and afternoons when many families visit the library. When asked about the ability to have an "express" line of sorts for straightforward checkout materials, several were excited at the prospects of having retail-like "self-service" areas to speed up their borrowing process. In this respect, the circulation desk staff can focus their attention on setting up new library patron cards, dealing with overdue fines, advising patrons on materials of a similar topic that might be of interest, and answering patron questions.

The most important lessons that can be learned from installing self-check machines in other libraries are to draw user's attention to them, publicize and encourage patrons to use these new machines, and position staff near the machines to train patrons. It is hard to quantify in dollar figures the ROI of self-checkout in a library, and much harder to quantify RFID self-checkout since many machines have only been in operation for a year or two; however, the qualitative judgment of many surveyed libraries is that RFID is a success and that self-charging machines have helped them to achieve efficiency that would have been impossible prior to their installation.

A British study conducted by Sarah Gollin and Chris Pinder looked at the issues associated with self-checkout in UK libraries. For most libraries, self-checkout is still new and the authors noticed that most surveyed libraries had adopted self-checkout since 1999. In their study, it was noted that self-check "allowed some libraries to cope with increasing demand without increasing staffing levels (noted by 10 percent of libraries). Two other noteworthy points are that 12 percent of libraries felt that they had provided users with a better choice of service and 7 percent of libraries said that self-check had improved the image of their library." (Gollin and Pinder, 2003: 53) Additionally, the authors determined that "The vast majority of libraries reported that their users (93 percent) had some kind of positive reaction to self-check, with a further 24 percent of respondents noting that their users were positive about self-check once they had used the equipment or had been shown how to use it (but had previously found the equipment difficult to use or had been wary of it)." (Gollin and Pinder, 2003: 52) Gollin and Pinder found that 24 percent of respondents indicated that staff had time for other tasks now such as user assistance and training patrons on the machine, and 21 percent felt that their work life improved with the removal of stress of handling less charging activities. (Gollin and Pinder, 2003: 52)

These findings are in line with what I have discovered in relation to RFID self-check installations: staff are liberated to engage in more patron-centric, value-added library work and reduce the stress associated with speeding through the borrowing process in order to move library patrons through as if in a retail line. Patrons that want human interaction and a librarian's book recommendation, offering the option of a staffed-circulation desk is a good option, just as offering a speedy self-checkout is to the busy person who feels competent enough to check out their own materials using RFID.

RFID-IN-ACTION INTERVIEW: KALAMAZOO COLLEGE LIBRARY

---

www.kzoo.edu/is/library

   I asked Mary Griswold why she felt that an RFID system was the right direction to go for her Kalamazoo College Library. Her response: "I am totally convinced that we have done a very positive thing in purchasing an RFID system. The benefits have been enormous and it has been very well accepted by our patrons. They and visitors are amazed to see the self-checkout system at work." (Ward-Griswold interview, 2006)

RFID-IN-ACTION INTERVIEW: MIDDLESEX UNIVERSITY (UNITED KINGDOM)

---

www.mdx.ac.uk

   I asked William Marsterson, Pro Vice Chancellor, Head of Learning Resources and University Librarian at Middlesex University in the United Kingdom, about the adoption percentage for self-charging systems. He responded: "Patrons seem to like the stations and adapt quickly to them (at first the speed of transaction is so fast they don't realize it has happened!). Staff are more critical, because of perceived shortcomings. The supplier has addressed some of these. The stations are certainly easy to use." (Ward-Marsterson interview, 2006)

For patrons that want human interaction and a librarian's book recommendation, offering the option of a staffed-circulation desk is a good option, just as offering a speedy self-checkout is to the busy person who feels competent enough to check out their own materials using RFID.

Freeing Staff from Tedious Tasks

Currently, circulation staff needs to be focused on the dual system of item identification and item security. Staff consumed with tedious tasks related to the checkin and checkout of library materials, are not able to devote quality time to patron interaction. Instead, they need to be focused on lining up a bar code with a reader's laser beam, or double-checking that they deactivated the security bit. The irony is that these staff members are the public face of the library for most of your patrons, and there is little opportunity for them to interact with patrons apart from discussing deactivation of security mechanism and locating bar codes. RFID changes this process completely. If a library committee does not choose to implement self-checkout kiosks, RFID terminals will be used by trained circulation staff members. An RFID tag with item identification and security on one tag cuts down considerably the time spent on checkout for the patron. The average time it takes a patron to self-check four items is under a minute.

An RFID tag with item identification and security on one tag cuts down considerably the time spent on checkout for the patron. The average time it takes a patron to self-check four items is under a minute.

Circulation staff members are the public face of the library, and RFID offers an opportunity for them to interact with the patron on a more meaningful level, and apart from discussing deactivation of security mechanism and locating bar codes.

RFID Library Success Story: Mooresville Public Library

I asked John Pritchard, Director of Mooresville Public Library in Mooresville, North Carolina: http://mooresville.nc.us/library/ "What do your patrons and staff think about the RFID-enabled self-checkout stations?" Pritchard replied: "The patrons like it. It is more popular with the children users of the library, but adult users like it as well. It is not an operation that eliminates staff from the circulation functions. If a patron owes fines or fees, the self-check refers the patron to the Circulation staff. Moreover, there are always patrons who prefer to speak with a staff member. It functions very well as an alternative to the staff-assisted checkout and with staff supervision could function as the primary circulation point. Using it as a primary circulation point, however, would require design decisions and changes in the layout of the traditional circulation services desk. The staff is divided on the issue. Some see the self-check system as requiring too much staff supervision to be of great benefit. I believe that as our library users become more adept in using the self-check stations the staff will see it as a greater benefit. It is, after all, the ATM of the library." (Ward-Pritchard interview, 2006)

Reducing Repetitive Stress Injuries

One of the greatest benefits of RFID is the apparent reduction of Repetitive Stress Injuries (RSIs) and Cumulative Trauma Disorders (CTDs) that are often associated with circulation activities. For some, soreness may be caused by the frequent and repetitive action of aligning a bar code with a line-of-sight reader, and then maneuvering the item through the EAS desensitization process. These twist and turn actions to maneuver an item for an optical read can affect nerves, joints, tendons, and produce associated pain such as carpal tunnel syndrome in some people. A high volume of patrons increases the frequency that a staff member has to manipulate books, and also increases the frequency of moving an item back and forth over a sensitization bed.

Repetitive stress injuries associated with circulation procedures of item charging and desensitization are a serious issue facing many libraries and are a growing cost. The time in dollar amounts for payout to workers that are on worker's compensation or undergoing physical therapy or surgery is growing and is a real concern for many large libraries. Also, the loss of valuable staff members due to these injuries may not necessarily mean that their specific workloads will be picked up by a new hire—often a shrinking staff is called on to do even more work in the name of service excellence for the public. The costs associated with health insurance and time off for rest and recuperation are high. It is a lose-lose situation.

RFID appears to help to alleviate RSI's associated with circulation routines, but the information up to this point is anecdotal: RFID is too new to prove conclusively that it causes a reduction in RSI and work-related injuries. The handheld readers are designed to be ergonomic and the mounted circulation RFID readers do not require repetitive motion for borrowing or security deactivation.

The process of charging an item has several necessary steps. The current system design for most library circulation operations requires staff to check the item out in the catalog and also to desensitize the item's security component. Additionally, the checkout process is also subject to cause successive events of repetitive movement since with a bar code system the operator has to have dexterity to maneuver the item for an optical read.

What I am presenting is anecdotal, qualitative information from my survey and interviews with librarians that work with people who have mentioned issues with RSIs. I asked Marilyn Sheck of Seattle Public Library's Technology and Collection Services unit about RFID's impact upon RSI. Her opinion: "We used to have a lot of incidences of carpal tunnel syndrome. We have not had any lately. Also, we had lots of back injuries and strained muscles from lifting bins full of books. We now have a sorter, thanks to RFID, that eliminates almost all lifting. It also eliminates the repetitive motion of scanning a bar code on every item and there are fewer cases of muscle fatigue." (Ward-Sheck interview, 2006)

In my recent survey of librarians using RFID, I polled libraries that had implemented RFID or were in the process of completing their installation. Of these libraries that have noticed a decrease in RSI complaints, about half of them purchased handheld RFID readers in addition to the stationary RFID that readers found at the circulation desk or in self-check machines. When asked "Did your library circulation staff notice any decrease in repetitive stress-related complaints after the implementation of the RFID system?" almost half of respondents said yes.

Susan O'Neal of Middletown Township Public Library informed me in terms of the clunky audiovisual cases and their relation to RSI's: "The system we have has dual screens, a receipt printer, card slot, and the antenna. All library materials are self-selected and can be checked out. There are no materials with security cases and, of course, with RFID, the security is deactivated without repetitive swiping of the material against another piece of equipment. So, we have reduced to zero the two labor-intensive repetitive motions, the swiping and the twisting/turning of cases. One employee, young 40s I guess, had started to wear a wrist brace; others were talking a lot about discomfort and pain. One told me, 'I figured if I was going to continue to work at the library, this is the way it's going to be. This is what we have to do.' Well, she no longer wears the brace." (Ward-O'Neal interview, 2006)

I asked Jean Foster, Director of Public Services at Windsor Public Library, if the RFID system and its readers are more ergonomic and better for them in terms of avoiding RSI, and she replied: "This was the first positive response from staff . . . it was much more comfortable to pass the items over the reader than use a hand scanner." (Ward-Foster interview, 2006)

In an e-mail to Camille Cleland of Skokie Public Library, I asked: "Why do you think that RFID has helped to decrease RSI? Was this a problem for your library with your previous system?" She responded: "RFID has decreased repetitive stress injuries. We now 'slide' the books, rather than pick up each one individually for bar code reading. Our circulation is over one and a half million, so we did indeed have a repetitive stress injury problem pre-RFID." (Ward-Cleland interview, 2006)

RFID-IN-ACTION INTERVIEW: RSI

I asked Adrienne Canty, Manager of the Strathcona Branch of Edmonton Public Library in Edmonton, Alberta, Canada, about her experiences.

Q: Do you think your newly purchased RFID system will help with RSI?

A: Staff members at the Edmonton Public Library literally move tons of material every year, and particularly in our branches with high volumes of materials returned/placed on hold, repetitive strain injuries have been a recurring problem. Most of our processes for handling holds, route-outs/route-ins, returns, checkouts, etc., are manual, and while we have begun to make the changes we can to improve the ergonomics of our physical set-up and reduce the need to lift/move/manipulate items, our gains are small to date. While statistics are not kept on the nature of Workers' Compensation claims either locally or at our provincial WCB, our HR department reports that the vast majority of the claims EPL submits are for injuries associated with repetitive motions. Our hopes are high that automating the back-room processes that can be automated (checkin, sorting) and having the majority of our customers themselves checkout their materials will lessen the incidence of work-related injuries. . . . Self-check stations will off-load the majority of check-out transactions to our customers—we plan for a minimum 60 percent of checkout transactions to be performed by customers themselves once we install self-check stations. (Anecdotal reports from other libraries implementing self-check indicate adoption rates for the self-check units by customers of 60 to 90 percent, some as high as 100 percent.) We intend to purchase automated checkin units for all service points, with automated sorting in the branches that can physically house such equipment—fortunately, these are our branches with the highest volume of library material throughput.

Q: What's in your plan?

A: Our Business Plan for the project states: "The self-check stations will allow customers to check out their own materials, removing a significant number of daily transactions from staff members' responsibility. In those cases where customer-assisted check-out is required, RFID will allow staff to check out multiple items simultaneously, thus reducing the time spent by staff on each customer transaction. Automated return and sorting will reduce the number of times that staff members must manipulate items upon their return. With reduced numbers of transactions and reduced physical handling of items, it is expected that staff members will experience fewer repetitive strain injuries, and those that are experienced will be less severe. The RFP asked proponents to comment on the ergonomics of their equipment in various areas; across the board we received responses from vendors commenting that their equipment was designed with ergonomics in mind and complied to ADA standards, but very few specific details were provided." (Ward-Conty interview, 2006)

Cutting Down on Work-Related Injuries

As many circulation clerks and librarians will attest, the checkin process of handling and reshelving returned materials is physically exertive and tedious at times. Checkin is heavier at predictable intervals: for instance, academic libraries will see an influx of returned items at the end of the semester and public libraries may notice a plethora of returned audiovisual material on a Monday morning. Sorting room injuries from repetitive stooping, loading, and shuffling heavy books have been identified by some as a concern for libraries in compensation claims. Awkward postures and repeated motions requiring a tight grip associated with retrieving books from book drops and the circulation process are being researched. Many vendors reference the problems of human stoop-load-sort injuries in their Web pages detailing and promoting their automated material handling system (AMHS). A fully integrated AMHS which relies upon RFID should have a positive effect upon work-related injuries associated with the back and legs that are a result of grabbing the books out of the return bins and then sorting them onto carts.

San Francisco Public Library lists on their Web site information about "RFID Technology and Reducing Factors for RSI Injuries." The library experienced from January 2001 through January 2004, 36 public service employees filing Worker's Compensation claims. The impact on SFPL was "260 loss work days; 500 modified/restricted work days; $265,000 paid costs." (San Francisco Public Library, 2006) Couple this with risk factors from a March 2004 report from an ergonomic consultant: "Workload: 12 events per minute/768 per hour (highly repetitive when events exceed 3 per minute). Awkward and forceful hand/arm motions to desensitize material. Check-in Desk: Excessive grasping and handling to process returns. Each piece of media must be handled individually and 70% must be opened. 70% of books are being lifted, turned and flipped over in order to scan. Workload: 10 events per minute/575 per hour (highly repetitive when events exceed 3 per minute). Sorting Room: Excessive grasping and handling to sort/process returns. Workload: 16 events per minute/940 per hour (Highly repetitive when events exceed 3 per minute)." (San Francisco Public Library, 2006)

For more details, please see the report on San Francisco Public Library Web site available at http://sfpl.lib.ca.us/news/releases/rsi.htm

Lynne Jacobsen of Warren-Newport Public Library in Gurnee, Illinois, noted: "We experienced a reduction in wrist stress-related injuries, but some of the shelvers were bending over to retrieve items from the bins at the sorter which caused some back problems. They have since changed their work process to sitting down as they load carts and fine-sort materials." (Ward-Jacobsen interview, 2006)

Many do not realize the serious issue of workers compensation claims for library administrators. In Anne M. Turner's *Library Journal* column "Your Money's Worth," she talks about the growing budgetary problem for libraries dealing with musculoskeletal disorders or repetitive stress injuries. Turner writes that although automated systems brought us accuracy and speed, and unforeseen problems when "we use technology to enable our staffs to do more and more work. Demand for service is on the rise, putting pressure on not just the people working the public desks but the behind-the-scenes folks as well. The result of this 'self-speedup' can be a plague of worker injuries." (Turner, 2004) RFID systems may eliminate some of the repetitive motions associated with the process of checkin and checkout that may eventually lead to repetitive stress injuries since data is transfered and uploaded automatically through the use of RF waves.

References

Biblio Tech Review. "3M to Install RFID in Singapore." April 2000.

Boss, Richard W. 2006. "RFID Technology for Libraries." ALA Web site. Available: www.ala.org/ala/pla/plapubs/technotes/rfidtechnology.htm

Carlson, Scott. 2004. "Talking Tags: New High-Tech Labels Help Libraries Track Books, But Worry Privacy Advocates." *Chronicle of Higher Education* 50, no. 48 (August 6): A29.

Chia, Christopher. 2001."Transformation of Libraries in Singapore." *Library Review* 50, no. 7/8: 343–348.

Coyle, Karen. 2005. "Management of RFID in Libraries." *Journal of Academic Librarianship* 31, no. 5 (September): 486–489.

Eden, Brad. 2002. "The New Lied library at the University of Nevada, Las Vegas: Introduction." *Library Hi Tech* 20, no.1 (2002): 8–11.

Engel, Elena. 2006. "RFID Implementations in California Libraries: Costs and Benefits." U.S. Institute of Museum and Library Services (July).

Fabbi, Jennifer. "Evaluating Academic Library Collections in the Age of Expedience: Weeding with a New Tool." Mountain Plains Library Association 2003 Conference. Available: www.mpla.us/documents/handouts/2003/fabbi.doc

Freeman, Gretchen. 2005 "RFID: Ready or Not?" Utah Library Association, 2005 Great Issues Forum. Accessed July 21, 2006. Available: www.ula.org/organization/attachments/greatissuesforum/RFID—Great%20Issues%202005.ppt

Gollin, Sarah, and Chris Pinder. 2003. "The Adoption of Self-Check Technology in UK Academic Libraries." *New Review of Academic Librarianship* 9, no. 1 (December): 42–58.

Khong, Gaik, and Shirley White. "Moving Right Along: Using RFID for Collection Management at the Parliamentary Library." Information Online Conference 2005. Available: http://conferences.alia.org.au/online2005/papers/a11.pdf

Kuan, Sung. 2006. "What Went Right & What Went Wrong with RFID: The National Library of Singapore." ALA/LITA: RFID in Libraries: An International Perspective presentation (June). Available: www.ala.org/ala/lita/litamembership/litaigs/rfidtechnology/What-Went-Right6–18–06.ppt

Maselli, Jennifer. 2003. "ABI: RFID Market Poised for Growth." *RFID Journal* (July 18). Available: www.rfidjournal.com/article/articleview/506/1/1

Oder, Norman. 2004. "A Day in the Life of International Libraries: Ambitious Meets Audacious." *Library Journal* (February 1). Available: www.libraryjournal.com/article/CA374952.html

RFID Journal. 2002. "Libraries Adopt RFID by the Book." *RFID Journal* (September 2). Available: www.rfidjournal.com/article/articleview/191

RFID Update. 2006. "Strong RFID Optimism from ABI Research." *RFID Update* (April 10). Available: www.rfidupdate.com/articles/index.php?id=1092&from=rss

San Francisco Public Library. "RFID Technology and Reducing Risk Factors for RSI Injuries." April 28, 2006. Available: http://sfpl.lib.ca.us/news/releases/rsi.htm

Scire, Toni. 2003. "What's Next for the Radio Frequency Library?" *Library & Archival Security* 18, no. 2: 51–58.

Sheck, Marilyn. 2004. "Meeting New Challenges with New Technology: The Seattle Public Library Experience." *Library Hi Tech News* 10: 22–27.

Smart, Laura. 2004. "Making Sense of RFID." *Library Journal* (October 15). Available: www.libraryjournal.com/article/CA456770.html

ST LogiTrack. 2002. "All Public Libraries in Singapore Is [sic] Now RFID." (August 18, 2002). www.stlogitrack.com/pr_publiclibraries.htm

Turner, Anne M. 2004. "Your Money's Worth." *Library Journal* 129, no. 1 (January): 64.

University of Nevada, Las Vegas Libraries Web site. 2005. "University Libraries Fact Sheet." (Updated September 7) Available: www.library.unlv.edu/about/facts.html

Ward, Diane Marie. 2004. "5 Cent Tag Unlikely in 4 Years." *RFID Journal* (August 26). Available: www.rfidjournal.com/article/articlereview/1098/1/1/

Ward, Diane Marie and Adrienne Canty, e-mail interview, August 16, 2006.

Ward, Diane Marie and Camille Cleland, e-mail interview, July 3, 2006.

Ward, Diane Marie and Sandra Collins, e-mail interview, January 24, 2006.

Ward, Diane Marie and Sandra Collins, e-mail interview, August 7, 2006.

Ward, Diane Marie and Elena Engel, e-mail interview, August 31, 2006.

Ward, Diane Marie and Jennifer Fabbi, e-mail interview, July 11, 2006.

Ward, Diane Marie and Dennis Fabiszak, e-mail interview, August 24, 2006.

Ward, Diane Marie and Jean Foster, e-mail interview, July 4, 2006.

Ward, Diane Marie and Gretchen Freeman, e-mail interview, July 4, 2006.

Ward, Diane Marie and Mary Griswold, e-mail interview, July 5, 2006.

Ward, Diane Marie and Lynne Jacobsen, e-mail interview, July 11, 2006.

Ward, Diane Marie and Sung Kuan, e-mail interview, August 19, 2006.

Ward, Diane Marie and William Marsterson, e-mail interview, July 10, 2006.

Ward, Diane Marie and Susan O'Neal, e-mail interview, August 3, 2006.

Ward, Diane Marie and John Pritchard, e-mail interview, July 3, 2006.

Ward, Diane Marie and Louise Schaper, e-mail interview, July 3, 2006.

Ward, Diane Marie and Marilyn Sheck, e-mail interview, July 6, 2006.

Ward, Diane Marie and Edith Sutterlin, e-mail interview, August 7, 2006.

Wong, Tack Wai. "Large Scale Application of Radio Frequency Identification (RFID) in Public Libraries: The Experience of National Library Board, Singapore." European Library Automation Group (April 2002). Available: www.ifnet.it/elag2002/papers/pap14.html

Yorkovich, John. 2001. "Lied Library: At the Forefront of Technology with 3M Digital ID Collection Management." *New Library World* 102, no. 6: 216–221.

Yuan, Kho Hao, Ang Chip Hong, M. Ang, and Goi Sio Pen. "UnManned Library: An Intelligent Robotic Books Retrieval & Return System Utilizing RFID Tags." IEEE SMC, 2002.

5

Deciding to Put RFID
into Operation

Introduction

In Chapter 4, the process of deciding whether or not to select an RFID solution was discussed in terms of quantitative and qualitative benefits and upfront and ongoing costs for the institution. Securing budgetary funding for an RFID system is an overarching consideration for many committees. For those in my survey who were successful at bringing RFID to their library, all were nearly unanimous in justifying the cost based on the benefits of RFID: saves time, staff can accomplish more using RFID, reduction of RSI complaints, patrons are satisfied, and so forth. For a qualitative analysis, this was a positive finding, but it does not necessarily make it easier for committees to construct a business case for selecting RFID. Most RFID installations are in their nascent stage and therefore it is difficult to quantify with certainty the ability of a library to recognize ROI. Do we in the library field have granite ROI figures for the realization of short-terms goals? How do librarians determine if RFID is right for their library? Each library must make this determination for itself. This chapter is designed to assist you in that process of discovery.

Striving for Service Excellence

While librarians wonder what experiences the retail industry might offer to them, it is important to consider how large multinationals make similar decisions to migrate their operations to a new technology and not put off their customers or employees in the process. Librarians are apt to shudder when "patrons" are referred to as "customers" since they are not transacting business with them: librarians as a profession do not "charge" patrons for reference information, nor for the privilege of borrowing items or using them in-house. Therefore, the comparison to business models is often eschewed as the profession is focused on servicing the intellectual needs of its community.

A patron cannot get intellectual feedback from a search engine in the same way one would receive it from a person who has devoted his/her career to sharing information with the public. To this high mission of providing excellent service to a patron, in many ways, the library is a business with customers who pay with their time. If library staff members can free up their time from performing routine tasks, which RFID is able to effectively automate, then why would any library committee not choose RFID as a natural way to increase patron service excellence and reallocate precious staffing to where it is most needed: interaction with the public?

Gathering Feedback from Library Associations and Interest Groups

American Library Association (ALA)

www.ala.org

The American Library Association has been attuned to the use of RFID in libraries for years. ALA's Library and Information Technology Association sponsors annual conferences where RFID is highlighted as a top trend.

- ALA's Web page on RFID has links to external data resources, privacy rights advocacy organizations, and news stories. Available: www.ala.org/ Template.cfm?Section=ifissues& Template=/ContentManagement/ ContentDisplay.cfm& ContentID=77689
- Additionally, at the 2006 Annual ALA Conference, The Council of the American Library Association adopted: "RFID in Libraries: Privacy and Confidentiality Guidelines." Available: www.ala.org/ala/oif/statementspols/ otherpolicies/ rfidguidelines.htm

Additional library association documents dealing with privacy aspects of RFID can be found in Chapter 9.

Library and Information Technology Association (LITA)

www.lita.org

www.ala.org/ala/lita/litamembership/litaigs/rfidtechnology/index.htm

LITA is the American Library Association's Library and Information Technology Association. Each year, LITA sponsors a conference where RFID is discussed as one of the many new technological innovations. Panel speakers include librarians who have steered their libraries through an RFID installation, RFID company executives, and privacy rights advocates. In 2005, LITA created an RFID Technology Interest Group. The Group is currently chaired by Chicago State University System Librarian Connie Haley and vice-chaired by Head of Technical Services at Warren-Newport Public Library Lynne Jacobsen. The Group discusses issues and seeks to educate the library community about RFID usage and constructs a panel for the ALA annual conference.

> LITA publishes the presentations of speakers of its RFID Interest Group Conference at www.ala.org/ala/lita/litamembership/litaigs/rfidtechnology/programs.htm

International Federation of Library Associations (IFLA)

www.ifla.org

International libraries are also reaping the benefits of RFID in libraries. IFLA's Information Technology Section (ITS) has sponsored informational programs on RFID for years for their members. In 2003, their session on "Wireless Technologies for Library Services: RFID in Use" featured a presentation by ITS chair, Mats G. Lindquist of Göteborg University Library, Göteborg, Sweden (now Senior Executive Officer at the Royal Library's Department for National Co-ordination and Development). The presentation, "RFID in Libraries: Introduction to the Issues," was valuable because Lindquist had gone through an installation and was aware of the technology pitfalls with integration and unreliable functionality. He predicted "general growth in the industry should also benefit library applications"; cautioned that developers needed to examine "the means to bypass an RFID station unnoticed" just as they had discovered that paper printout of bar codes could fool a bar code reader; cited a "lack of standards" as a "major reason why RFID technology has not reached its potential adoption level"; and asked colleagues to think seriously about the trap of technology: "What 'permanent' bindings are there to the chosen system solution (or supplier)? . . . How many of the choices made in choosing a particular RFID system are irreversible?" (Lindquist, 2003)

Book Industry Studies Group

www.bisg.org

Jonathan Collins reported in "Publisher Tags All Library Books" that NBD Biblion, a Dutch publisher with annual sales of 2.7 million books to Dutch libraries, is going to place the tag on the inside of the book's back cover at the spine. With 80 percent market share among libraries in the Netherlands, NBD Biblion saw RFID as a method to meet the needs of libraries and gain a strategic advantage. It is reportedly using Philips Semiconductors 13.56 MHz I Code SLI chip which is ISO 15693 compliant, with labels provided by UPM Rafsec and Smartag and is going to adhere to the data model set forth by the Dutch Library Association. (Collins, 2004)

But some postulate that the book industry will go with the EPC tag to please retailers. As it stands currently, the RFID tag found in a library book is at 13.56 MHz and is not on the same frequency as a retail EPC tag. Therefore, a different reader would be needed to read the tag's data. The worry comes in that perhaps the library industry will not have as much muscle as retailers, and thus the 13.56 MHz tag will be cast aside for the more common EPC tags.

RFID-IN-ACTION INTERVIEW: THE BOOK INDUSTRY STUDY GROUP

I asked BISG's James Lichtenberg about RFID and the book industry.

Q: What is the BISG's opinion on RFID?

A: BISG enjoys a very diverse membership including libraries, distributors, publishers, retailers, and wholesalers, each of whom has a different perspective on RFID.

Libraries are, of course, very interested, and RFID is being adopted exponentially by libraries across the country. A very few publishers are mildly curious, most are wait and see to completely disinterested, and some are strongly against recommending it at all. After an initial flurry of interest in 2003, booksellers are definitely in a wait and see mode, discouraged by the privacy issues and some of the more "radical" and vocal opponents of RFID (as well as cost, I would imagine). Distributors/wholesalers find themselves caught between libraries who are using it and want their support, and publishers/retailers who aren't.

Q: Have there been privacy issues raised regarding RFID tagged books for retail sale or sale to libraries by BISG, or by those in the book publishing, printing, and marketing industries?

A: Privacy was our first focus, with the thought being that it is really important to get out in front of the privacy questions and reassure the customer/patron that the book publishing value chain respects and will protect their personal information. To this end, the RFID Working Group created a Privacy Policy (available on the ALA Web site) now officially adopted by BISG and ALA, that emphasizes that no personal information will be encoded on the tag, and that patron privacy will be strictly protected. Most libraries simply put a "dumb" barcode number on the tags, which only the internal library system can de-code.

Q: If an RFID tag becomes standard fare on a book (regardless whether it is going to a library or a bookstore or a big box retailer), do you think BISG will lean toward a 13.56 MHz tag, the type used by libraries?

A: We aren't there yet. The RFID working group has asked NISO (National Information Standards Organization) to begin work on the standards for the data structure of the tag. I am also on that committee.

Q: I am curious if you see RFID as an opportunity for libraries and the book trade to work cooperatively to benefit both parties, rather than having one group dictate to the other?

A: Right now I feel like one of those Roman charioteers trying to drive a team of two horses. . . . Of course, working together cooperatively is the best possible outcome. (Ward-Lichtenberg interview, 2006)

Balancing the Tangible and Intangible Benefits

For this book, I surveyed libraries that had installed RFID systems and also separately surveyed vendors of RFID products. Many of them expressed what they believed were the major benefits realized by their transition to RFID. I distilled and organized results into categories of tangible and intangible benefits. Figure 5.1 lists some of the tangible benefits that can be measured in some way by cost savings, visibly shorter lines, time savings, decrease in RSI complaints, and ability to locate items misplaced or thought missing. Intangible benefits represent things that are measured qualitatively such as user satisfaction, less frustrated patrons, service excellence, reputation for exemplary shelf management, staff and user confidence in the system.

Any large-scale technology-related implementation may elicit strong reactions from the affected parties. Prior to opening up a discussion about RFID to the whole library community, it is beneficial to form a core group of people from cross-representational departments to assess if RFID might be feasible for your library, your staff, and your community. It may be perceived as risky for administrators to choose RFID. Deloitte's Consulting and Retail Systems Alert Groups issued a paper entitled "RFID: How Far, How Fast: A View from the Rest of the World" in 2004 where they allude to this: "Fear of change reflects that many companies have one or two internal RFID champions who are not C-level. Most C-level executives do not want to risk their positions by getting involved in RFID or any other new technologies that will significantly change the way their companies do business." (Deloitte, 2004: 8) Deloitte's survey of retail RFID adopters indicates the main benefit from RFID is a decrease in human error during the first five years of implementation. (Deloitte, 2004: 6)

Administrators contemplating a move to RFID routinely charge planning committees with the task of investigating the need, the benefits, and the potential impact on service and budget. The results of my survey point to a trend toward instituting planning committees to wrestle with the issue of RFID. The committee's work should

Figure 5.1: Patron and Staff Benefits of RFID	
Tangible Results	

Patrons	Self-check increases efficiency
	Self-check reduces long lines for charging
	Can adjust number of staff at circulation desk
	Staff time spent on patrons can increase
	Ease of use: Circulation process can be measured
	   in seconds, not minutes as it takes well under a
	   minute to check out a stack of books with RFID

Staff	Do not have to open up AV cases to charge Perhaps will not have to use AV cases at all No alignment needed to charge items like with bar codes Multiple items can be charged simultaneously Ability to deal with increase in circulation Staff reassignment to other work duties Staff become problem-solvers Do not have to open up item for optical read Can have a security system component No separate step for security deactivation Tags do not degrade Decrease in RSI complaints Saves money in terms of items not stolen Locating items thought to be missing or stolen Saves replacement costs of books Staff time saved locating missing items Improved shelf management Enables frequent inventorying of collection Saves labor cost for inventorying a collection
Intangible Results	

Patrons	Patrons empowered
	Service excellence
	Patron's bags will not have to be searched
	   physically if security alarm sounds as staff will see
	   item on screen
	Privacy in borrowing for patrons with self-check
	Confidence that items in OPAC are on shelf
	Loyal patrons want to interface with staff
	Cool factor of new technology

(continued)

Figure 5.1: Patron and Staff Benefits of RFID (*Continued*)	
Intangible Results	
Patrons	Fun for patrons to use new technology Patrons do not feel rushed by long lines Less frustrated patrons
Staff	Staff feel challenged to do value-added work Job satisfaction increases due to less stress Better work environment Technology offers accuracy Ability to gather usage statistics via reports Reputation for accurate shelves Less pain from repetitive movements

culminate in RFP, vendor demonstrations, and solid recommendations either to adopt a system or to uncover alternative means to fix whatever problem RFID was thought to fix. The committee will challenge one another and in turn challenge the vendor to provide the best package for the most reasonable price and time commitment.

Of the libraries surveyed in 2006 by this author, 53 percent chose to form a formal committee to investigate RFID's impact upon their libraries.

RFID-IN-ACTION INTERVIEW: MAKING THE DECISION

Mooresville Public Library
www.ci.mooresville.nc.us/library

Mooresville Public Library in Mooresville, North Carolina, did not form a committee to determine if RFID was right for it. Mooresville Public Library has a collection size of 85,000 volumes and made the decision to tag all their collection. With a staff of 25 FTE, it took about six months to tag their collection using employees reallocated to the conversion process. The tag has both item management and security. I inquired of John Pritchard, Director of Mooresville Public Library:

Q: Tell me about your decision to introduce RFID to your staff and patrons and how you chose an RFID system in only two months.

A: I had seen the 3M PAMS (Public Access Management System) card in operation at the High Point Public Library and realized that the RFID card was an excellent method for controlling usage of the public access computers. In researching the public access control cards, I learned that RFID tagging could be a solution to our security issues with the audiovisual material in the library. Two companies, ITG and 3M had RFID products. Both companies used similar technology and both promised high-level security on the audiovisual materials. Security tags on book-type material is a flat tag (2 1/8" x 2") that glues to the inside cover of the book. The security tag that is used with DVD/CD material is a circular tag that attaches around the hub of the DVD/CD. In addition to the security system, both companies offered self-check capabilities and partnership with Sirsi/Dynix, our existing library automation vendor. The decision on which vendor to use was made by the IT director, the library director, and the assistant town manager. In the end, we decided to use 3M as the public access control vendor and ITG as the RFID solution for self-check, security, and circulation control. The 3M PAMS card had proven itself over time in other libraries for public access computer control. ITG used, at that time, a nonproprietary tag for security and circulation control functions. Knowing what functions are essential to the project and having the right people in the decision-making process is the key to correct decision making. This was the case in our project and, as a result, the project moved very quickly. (Ward-Pritchard interview, 2006)

RFID-IN-ACTION INTERVIEW: EUGENE PUBLIC LIBRARY

www.ci.eugene.or.ub/library

In Chapter 1, I mentioned Margaret Hazel, who manages the RFID_LIB blog. She works at Eugene Public Library in Eugene, Oregon, which has installed RFID. I interviewed her via email for her thoughts on the state of RFID today and about the details of their installation since Eugene Public Library is such a large library and provides a good model for other public libraries.

Q: Could you describe in detail what the scope of RFID implementation is at Eugene Public Library? (What is the scope of your collection: circulation figure, number of volumes, what percentage of the collection you chose to RFID tag, which vendor installed your system, how long it took to tag everything, etc., did you install self-charging machines, RFID-sorters, etc.)

A: We chose to RFID our entire collection, other than non-circulating materials. We use Tagsys equipment and tags, sold through Tech Logic. We have five self- or assist-stations at the large Downtown Library, one more coming at one branch, and three other assisted-only checkouts, at our two small branches. We used volunteers to begin tagging the collection, and it took about a year to complete. We tag only circulating materials, as there is not a security-only tag that could be used on reference materials and non-circulating items such as newspapers. We circulate about 2.1 million items a year—a figure that is about double what it was in the old building. We own about 500,000 items. We also have a sorting system, and three book drops that connect to the sorter with conveyors. Two are exterior, and accept materials 24/7, including a drive-thru.

Q: What are the top three benefits you feel that the staff have realized from RFID? And what are the top three benefits that patrons seem to like about the RFID system?

A: The staff spend less time checking out materials, and much less time wanding materials, both in and out, so the ergonomic benefits are great, as well as our being able to reallocate staff to other needed duties. Staff also do less troubleshooting of on-the-fly records related to mis-typing or wanding barcodes. For patrons, I believe they like that there is a techno-cool factor of placing things on a pad, touching a screen, and checking things out all by themselves. Most transactions are faster, which they like, and it's actually a bit more private, since there isn't someone right there handling your items as you check them out.

Q: Do you have any advice for libraries that are looking for an RFID solution? Any pitfalls to avoid? Any lessons learned you could share?

A: I have a lot of advice for libraries looking for an RFID solution, and share it freely. I've done six conference presentations and panels on the topic in the last few years, around the country, and do participate on a number of library e-mail lists where the topic has arisen. My most recent advice is to not consider RFID if you are looking solely for a security solution—even the vendors aren't trying to sell it as such these days. Choose it if you are willing to be part of a new technology, and willing to help shape the future of RFID. Choose it if you want good self-check and inventory, and ergonomic improvements for staff, and even for the possibility of being able to reallocate staff to other tasks. Do not choose it as a means of reducing staff—but I say that more as a philosophical issue, as I believe that most libraries already have too much work for the staff they employ. Make sure, when you implement it, to be thorough and constant in your communication with staff. Not only will the project change as you go, and you need to keep everyone's expectations for functionality and policy on the same page, but it is a fundamental change in how you provide your front-line service, if you go to entirely self-check, and it will be hard for many staff to let go of that cherished contact with the public—for some patrons the only human contact they have is at a library. (Ward-Hazel interview, 2006)

Commissioning a Library Planning Committee

The first step a library should take when considering an RFID system is to call a committee to order to investigate what strategic benefits RFID affords your:

- patrons
- budget
- staff:
  - circulation
  - technical services
  - reference
  - administration
  - collection development
  - preservation

It is perhaps the most honest path to formulating answers to the questions raised at this chapter's beginning. A cross-departmental library committee should survey the near- and long-term goals to assess if an RFID solution fits into the plan and the budget. The committee needs to assess the work processes that occur on an hourly and a daily basis related to circulation checkin and checkout and shelving. These are costly, but absolutely necessary functions of a circulating library collection. Fifty-three percent of my surveyed libraries did form a committee. It is a step that I would suggest should be a best practice.

Committee Duration

The amount of time that a committee is active will vary. For example, if you are on schedule to move into a new library and RFID has been budgeted into your plan, your committee may have two or three years to weigh the option of RFID. However, if you are experiencing increased circulation of items with no increase in staffing, then RFID may be an attractive option to lobby for in the near term. In that scenario, the window for a committee is more urgent and financially restrictive and might range from three to six months to create a request for vendor proposals, conduct site visits, and craft a plan for implementation with a vendor. In my survey, the most popular time frame from the charging of a committee to the point of system purchase was six months.

Figure 5.2: Ward's Survey Results: Inception to System Purchase Averages	
2 months	1 library
5 months	1 library
6 months	7 libraries
12 months	4 libraries
18 months	1 library
20 months	2 libraries
22 months	1 library
24 months	1 library
30 months	1 library
48 months	2 libraries

RFID-IN-ACTION INTERVIEW: MERRICK LIBRARY

Ellen Firer, Director of Merrick Library in Merrick, New York.
Q: Was it an easy choice for your library to select RFID?
A: We did not form a committee to investigate RFID because we were building a brand new $10 million library, and did not have a previous security system at all. Without a security system, we did not feel going to old technology made sense, and we knew we wanted to be cutting edge with an RFID security system. (Ward-Firer interview, 2006)

Work of Committee

- gather interested parties
- research RFID
- assess library's needs
- decide if RFID is right for your library
- draft an RFP
- assess vendor proposals
- bring in vendors for demonstrations
- site visit other installations
- decide on vendor
- establish installation timeline

Determining the Rate of Implementation

When one embarks on a new technology adventure, one may begin with preconceived notions as to the successful effects this new technology will deliver. But after some time elapses from the implementation, staff begin to sort out what was a myth and what benefits were truly delivered by the technology.

Process Reengineering

One of the paramount issues which a committee needs to grapple with is what impact RFID will have on the existing work processes of staff. Will the introduction of an RFID system entail a reengineering of work procedures? If the answer is an immediate yes, then the committee has to start weighing the psychological impact RFID might have upon their staff, and the financial impact upon the budget. The library staff should understand that an RFID system is not a threat to their livelihood and be promised that they will not lose their livelihood to a wireless technology.

The library committee needs to look carefully at how things are currently accomplished by staff in the circulation and technical service departments. Some library staff view automated sorters and checkin and checkout stations as threats. In my survey, some respondents echoed this issue of job security. So far, it appears that library jobs have not been lost to the installation of RFID, but 51 percent of survey respondents encountered staff that had concerns about the RFID system. Some expressed doubt that the system would deliver all the bells and whistles that marketing promised and shuddered at the thought that it might not work, and maybe there was a better way to spend the money.

A major question for the library planning committee to assess is "How will RFID impact the daily work routine of technical services and circulation staff?" If implementing RFID translates into having to reengineer every process from technical services to circulation, then perhaps the cost of implementation is beyond what your library may be able to afford.

The technical services department (where books are ordered, received, and cataloged) is the genesis for all books on library shelves. The traditional practice of technical service staff members affixing a bar code to a book and then linking it with a handheld bar code reader to an item record in the online catalog is employed by many libraries. The additional step of including an electronic article surveillance mechanism is usually also accomplished by technical services staff.

RFID vendors offer conversion stations for rental or purchase. They are straightforward in operation and take a few minutes to learn. Libraries can rent these stations per month from a range of $250 to $500. A standard conversion station for purchase can run from $2,200 to $4,000 and can make the process of linking items to their records no different from the processing of bar coded items.

But, the question remains how easy it is for the technical services staff members to map their bar code related tasks to the environment of an RFID system? Is it an easy transition or a challenging one? Of course, this is a very qualitative assessment of the ability of technical services staff to adapt to change. RFID tagging impacts the workflow, but in no different manner than affixing a bar code and a security mechanism. It can be assumed that eliminating a two-step process in favor of a one-step process is a benefit in terms of time and the reduction of RSI.

Therefore, my 2006 survey of libraries that installed RFID systems, either a total system or only component parts, contained a question concerning the ability of technical services to adapt to using an RFID conversion station during collection conversion, and also how they adapted to a new process of affixing the RFID tag to an item. One hundred percent responded that their technical services staff felt the change to a system using RFID tags was easy.

Some book vendors are selling books that have RFID tags in the book. These items need only to be linked to a library's bibliographic record and they are ready to shelve. For libraries that lack a technical services department and rely upon ready-to-shelve items, the increased availability of already tagged books will be a time-saver.

RFID-IN-ACTION INTERVIEW: STAFF REACTION

Middletown Township Public Library
www.mtpl.org
Susan O'Neal, Director of Middletown Township Public Library in Middletown, New Jersey.
  Q: What was your staff's reaction to RFID?
  A: First, I have a great staff to begin with. They have the normal mix of aversion to change and go-for-it types in the department. The primary reservation, shared by many, was fear of losing jobs due to the technology. But we brought them in on the planning in the early stages, and administrative assurances did help assuage these fears. We did not have a hidden agenda to reduce staff, but did think there might be some staff re-assignments over time, and we were honest about that. The staff knew how to do their tasks very well and could quickly see the time-saving benefits of the new system. If it worked. There was a little apprehension on this matter, but since it works very well, and we trained slowly and carefully, staff were on board, vigorously promoting the system with the public from day one. It didn't hurt that we had a beautiful new building to showcase new technology. Isn't there some degree of expectation of new systems in a new building? So keeping the old methods in a new building didn't seem to come up. In terms of security, well, we had no confidence in the old system at all. It was ready for replacement, so the prospect of a new system was enthusiastically welcomed. (Ward-O'Neal interview, 2006)

RFID In Action

In many ways, Australian libraries are at the cutting edge of RFID technology as they are trying to formulate a data model and have been some of the earliest adopters. The third largest city in Australia, Brisbane, has a very progressive library system: Brisbane City Council Library Services (http://elibcat.library.brisbane.qld.gov.au) is an example of reengineering process to deliver amazing and positive results for patrons and staff.

Christine Mackenzie and Michael Aulich wrote a breakthrough paper, "Self-Service—The Revolution's Here!" In it, they described how RFID brought positive change and real benefits to the Brisbane City Council Library Services in terms of patron satisfaction, better use of employee time, and increased efficiency to handle growth. They wrote that they hoped to redefine the library as a "community hub" and "increase customer-contact programs" through the use of RFID self-check. There is a sense of urgency in their writing about reengineering their library to accommodate twenty-first-century needs and that they "adopted retail merchandising techniques to make our libraries more attractive." (Mackenzie and Aulich, 2002) They strove to increase the 30 percent of staff time spent on work associated with customers and did a time study to analyze where the most time was spent. They determined that the routine of borrowing books required so much time that self-check would be a logical option to free up time to reallocate staff for service excellence-type of work.

They wrote: "We need to shift from being lower-valued circulation-centric. . . . We can use technology as an enabler to achieve this vision by introducing technology that frees library staff from the more routine tasks so they can concentrate on value-added services for customers." (Mackenzie and Aulich, 2002)

Mackenzie was Manager of Brisbane City Council Library Services and is now the CEO of Yarra Plenty Regional Library in Bundoora, Victoria, Australia. She told me that she has crafted a business case for bringing RFID to her new library based on the success in her previous post. Yarra Plenty Regional Library is experiencing high circulation and therefore a great deal of material handling which puts stress on the staff. Knowing the success Brisbane had, she has built a business case that includes a matrix or the total cost of ownership over the next ten fiscal years.

The cost and benefit analysis is not easy to create since RFID is new, but her attempt is inspiration to all libraries that it can be done, perhaps not just with the traditional amount of statistics that libraries are used to. In regard to RFID, Mackenzie and Aulich, cite that 40–80 percent of libraries using RFID have found improvements in the loans and handling processes. In 2001, Brisbane City Council Library Services worked with 3M to bring RFID to Wynnum Library (40,000 volumes, circulation of 425,000 per year, 10 FTE). The library experienced a positive acceptance of the self-check RFID equipment from patrons and from staff, and a reduction in RSIs.

Solving Problems with Circulation and Security

I noticed in my survey responses that there was a trend toward accepting a theft prevention system that was around 85–90 percent effective, because self-check benefited the staff (less RSI) and patrons (short lines). Many survey respondents felt this risk was acceptable for the benefits brought to the library by RFID.

RFID-IN-ACTION INTERVIEW: SALT LAKE COUNTY LIBRARY SERVICES

Gretchen Freeman, Associate Director for Reference and Technology Services at Salt Lake County Library Services.

Q: How would you convince other libraries that RFID is an effective business case, but that you have to be willing to accept some tradeoffs to achieve other benefits, such as a reduction in repetitive stress injuries?

A: I don't know that I would try to convince any libraries that an 85–90 percent theft prevention rate is acceptable for them. It's acceptable for us and we accepted that risk of loss when we started the RFID project. RFID for us was about patron convenience, reduced handling and repetitive stress, and easier inventories, not about theft prevention as our first priority. Each library needs to start the project with a clear understanding of goals and realistic expectations of what RFID can deliver. (Ward-Freeman interview, 2006)

This sentiment mirrors that of many librarians I talked with: RFID is not perfect, but the benefits it offers currently, and promises to deliver in the future to libraries, are worth the creative workarounds that need to be developed to allay its short-term shortcomings.

In order to make a case to a library board of trustees or other library advisory council, a library needs to fully delineate how the implementation of an RFID system will benefit it. The main benefit should be an increase in good services to patrons and a more efficient work process circulating and securing the library's materials. Many libraries chose to table the RFID decision for a year or two, monitor the market, its prices and new applications, and then revisit it in a year or two. Or, some libraries may choose to implement incrementally. For example, this is what a three-year plan might resemble:

- Year 1: Convert existing collection and design workflow so that all new materials are tagged.
- Year 2: Install self-checkouts.
- Year 3: Install automated material handling and sorting system.

But when does RFID not make good fiscal sense? If your library has millions of books and other media materials, the cost of retagging each item will be exorbitant at the current market for RFID tags. Additionally, many might see a move to an RFID system as frivolous, especially if all the items presently housed and circulated are bar coded and have some type of electro-magnetic security device. When administrators compare the near 100 percent accurate read rate of the inexpensive (a few cents each) bar code as compared with the RFID tag (53 cents average), it is difficult to make the case to transfer your circulation system to RFID.

If RFID is such an improvement over bar code technology, one might rightly question what is causing the slow adoption of RFID tags as their natural technological replacement? The main hindrance to the ubiquity is pricing of RFID tags and system components. Secondly, RFID tags have to achieve the types of sustained accuracy rates on media that traditional bar codes have achieved. Until RFID tags reach a 100 percent read accuracy rate, many library committees and circulation administrators will be hesitant to switch over to a system with an accuracy rate that is less than what they currently have in place. This is a very logical reaction and one that RFID research and development professionals are working to remedy.

RFID-IN-ACTION INTERVIEW: SUNY BUFFALO UNIVERSITY LIBRARIES

Karen Senglaup, Director of Access Services at the State University of New York at Buffalo University Libraries.

Q: Why might or might not RFID fit into the plans for a proposed new-build 16,000 square foot, off-site storage facility?

A: The facility will house 1.5 million of the total 3.3 million volumes the library holds. SUNY Buffalo is a unique library with multiple physical special branches spread between two separate city locations.

Q: Was RFID considered for item management in the new storage facility, or is it too cost prohibitive given the sheer size of the collection?

A: The bar code is a 100 percent error-free transaction and for circulation that is a perfect technology. RFID is not 100 percent accurate and from a circulation standpoint, if you have 100 percent error free and a million volumes to move to storage in a short amount of time, why go to RFID? It would be a better opportunity for an un-bar coded collection that lacks security.

Q: What were the major factors weighing against selecting an RFID solution?

A: Well, size is a concern. The existing bar code system is complete: every piece is bar coded. And this is going to be a low-use storage facility with retrieval accomplished by staff. For the storage facility, RFID is not compelling enough to do it. The recovery cost for implementation has to be there and in our scenario, it is not. Academic libraries may not have the same types of circulation numbers as public libraries. Auto sorting is the second piece. For a public library with many branches, you want that benefit. Inventorying, too, is a back-end benefit. You can create what no other libraries can without RFID: a pristine library collection with nothing out of shelf order. (Ward-Senglaup, 2006)

Likewise, Santa Clara County Library District Joint Power Authority RFID Analysis Committee decided in October 2005 to table selecting an RFID system until prices come down to under 50 cents a tag, interoperability of tags and vendor hardware is widespread, and cost benefit analysis indicates RFID is a prudent investment. Their detailed final report is available at: www.santaclaracountylib.org/about/jpa/Report_SCCL_RFID_10.27.05.pdf. Their library has a collection of 1.6 million items and annual circulation of 10 million. Even though their staffing has declined 2 percent since 1999, their circulation increased 27 percent even though they were open 16.8 percent fewer hours in 2004–2005. The Committee wrote that the two main reasons for considering RFID "as a solution to the large volume of materials handled by library staff. First, RFID may allow staff to be more productive. Second, it may be possible for the library to sustain quality service with the same level of staff . . . " (Santa Clara County Library District, 2005)

Brainstorming Seven Key Areas of Consideration

I asked in my RFID library survey, "What are the top 3 questions you would encourage other libraries that are considering RFID to ask of themselves (their library staff and committees) before they make the change to RFID?" As evidenced from the volume of questions listed in Figures 5.3 through 5.7, respondents contributed plenty of them.

> Brainstorming Worksheet 1: Motivation
> Brainstorming Worksheet 2: Technology
> Brainstorming Worksheet 3: Finance
> Brainstorming Worksheet 4: Staff
> Brainstorming Worksheet 5: Service Excellence
> Brainstorming Worksheet 6: Ability to Change
> Brainstorming Worksheet 7: Vendor

Figure 5.3:   Brainstorming Worksheet 1: Motivation

Are we clear about our library's needs?

_____

_____

What issues are we trying to resolve with RFID?

_____

_____

Is RFID the only way to resolve them, and is RFID proven as a solution?

_____

_____

What are we attempting to achieve for our staff, our patrons, and our budget?

_____

_____

Do we have a problem with inventory?

_____

_____

Do we have realistic expectations that match documented reports by other users? What are the current circulation statistics?

_____

_____

If circulation statistics are increasing, are we hiring additional staff to meet the needs? If not, will RFID be the best way to go?

_____

_____

How many staff could we hire for the cost of the system?

_____

_____

Will we implement a sort system?

_____

_____

How many bins do we need to start with? Will it be more economical to buy extra up front?

_____

_____

Will staff support RFID and understand its implications to library services?

_____

_____

What can RFID do for us in the coming years?

_____

_____

Figure 5.4:   Brainstorming Worksheet 2: Technology

Are we willing to accept that not everything works seamlessly at first?

_____

Does RFID satisfy the needs of our multimedia?

_____

What is the importance of media security?

_____

As there are conflicts with metals in CDs and DVDs? Do we know for sure if tagging our multimedia will work effectively?

_____

Do we want our circulation system and security system to be one system?

_____

What if we cannot reach our target read rate accuracy with RFID?

_____

Should we continue with our current way to provide security?

_____

Will the new system work with bar codes as well as RFID?

_____

How much in-house IT support do we have/need?

_____

Do we have a well-thought-out time line for installation?

_____

If we are a multi-branch library system, how do we envision the plan for implementation for all the branches?

_____

_____

(continued)

Figure 5.4:   Brainstorming Worksheet 2: Technology (*Continued*)

If we are a part of a consortium, how do we envision the plan for implementation for other members? Do we have reciprocal borrowing privileges?

_____

_____

What future applications might we be interested in?

_____

_____

Do we want to be able to inventory our collection without having to handle the actual materials?

_____

_____

Figure 5.5:   Brainstorming Worksheet 3: Finance

What is the business case for implementing RFID?

_____

_____

Will the ROI justify the cost of the project? What is the payback period?

_____

_____

Will we recoup our investment within three years? Will it save the library in the long run?

_____

_____

Is this project really necessary? Are there other ways of realizing efficiencies or employing technology?

_____

_____

Have we budgeted for the system's cost exceeding what we planned?

_____

_____

Will the benefits we hope to achieve outweigh the costs?

_____

_____

Maybe we don't need to buy the whole system at once. What would be the consequences of phasing the system in over a year or two?

_____

_____

Do we have the ongoing commitment of financial resources to purchase additional tags, etc.? Do we have financial resources to support the service contract?

_____

_____

What are our benchmarks for satisfaction? How will we know if we got our money's worth? How do we quantify patron satisfaction and increased efficiency?

_____

_____

(continued)

Figure 5.5:   Brainstorming Worksheet 3: Finance (*Continued*)

Are we committed to no layoffs? What about five years from now? Will we replace retirees, or do we just assume RFID will make certain paraprofessional positions obsolete?

_____

_____

Should we tag magazines?

_____

_____

What are our success metrics? How will we know if we succeeded?

_____

_____

Are we clear about the processing costs for technical services?

_____

_____

Is the installation affordable and good value?

_____

_____

How big is the collection we want to tag?

_____

_____

Do we want to tag all of it? Can we afford that? Do we need to tag our low-use items?

_____

_____

What is the budget-related gain from RFID products that benefits staff in terms of time/money saved, easier processing, quicker handling of materials, etc.?

_____

_____

Figure 5.6:   Brainstorming Worksheet 4: Staff

Can processing and circulation routines be changed to accommodate new tasks?

Do we have the staff and resources to convert existing collections?

Are the handheld readers ergonomic?

Can the staff handle the extra tasks without additional employees?

What redesign of the circulation stations needs to occur? Will the vendor do this?

Are we shutting down during our installation and conversion?

How do we plan to tag items that are circulating during installation?

How best should we involve circulation staff in resolving issues of transition?

Who will convert the collection? Existing staff or volunteers?

How much staff time will RFID save?

Do we have staff capable of maintaining the system if something goes wrong on the self-check-out units?

(continued)

Figure 5.6: Brainstorming Worksheet 4: Staff (*Continued*)

After we looked at potential staff savings, are we committed to retraining and reallocating some staff because of workflow changes associated with RFID?

_____

_____

What existing procedures will change with the installation and use of RFID?

_____

_____

Figure 5.7: Brainstorming Worksheet 5: Service Excellence

Will this allow us to offer better service to our customers?

_____

_____

What are the advantages/disadvantages for our institution and its population? What do our users gain from RFID?

_____

_____

Have we made sure all the equipment we are purchasing is ADA compliant?

_____

_____

Have we walked through the checkin/checkout process to determine if the process will work?

_____

_____

Is it easy for people to use?

_____

_____

Do we want self-service checkin and checkout? Or, do we have self-check stations already, and if so, what happens to them?

_____

_____

Are there better self-checkout units? Are there better self-checkin units? Are there better sorting systems?

_____

_____

What are the present and future possibilities of RFID in the library? Do we want an RFID-enabled patron card?

_____

_____

Do we have a patron privacy policy in place?

_____

_____

How do the vendors ensure privacy? How best should we publicize and explain RFID to patrons?

_____

_____

Figure 5.8:   Brainstorming Worksheet 6: Ability to Change

RFID will change the way we do business. Are we prepared?

_____

_____

Have we allowed enough planning time? Are we good planners and motivators?

_____

_____

We need to develop a plan for conversion. Then, question ourselves: Can we realistically complete this plan?

_____

_____

What result does our organization really want to accomplish with RFID technology?

_____

_____

If we convert, what will improve? What will be worse?

_____

_____

If we convert, what will we be able to do differently?

_____

_____

Do we realize how much this will all really cost?

_____

_____

Have we sufficiently addressed our physical space design?

_____

_____

How compatible is it with other systems such as PAMS?

_____

What is our logic for change? Are we renovating the building and redesigning workflows?

_____

_____

Figure 5.9:   Brainstorming Worksheet 7: Vendor

Who will oversee installation?

_____

_____

What is the response time of the company we will be calling when problems arise?

_____

_____

Will the service come from our vendor, or is it outsourced to local technicians?

_____

_____

Is the company we will be dealing with primarily library-oriented or are their RFID resources spread thin?

_____

_____

Who on the committee will check references and research the track record of a company before we commit to a purchase?

_____

_____

Do we have the release time and financial support of the administration to visit libraries currently using RFID?

_____

_____

What are the main points of their customer support contract?

_____

_____

Do we get an item-by-item guarantee?

_____

_____

What is the service contract for each of our new system components?

_____

_____

Do they offer an extended guarantee?

_____

_____

(continued)

Figure 5.9:　Brainstorming Worksheet 7: Vendor (*Continued*)

Do we understand the limitations of RFID? What happens if we are not satisfied with the system once it is installed?

_____

_____

Do they sell non-proprietary tags?

_____

_____

Has our vendor worked with our ILS before? Did that library experience any bumps in the road after implementation?

_____

_____

References

Collins, Jonathan. 2004. "Publisher Tags All Library Books." RFID Journal (September 22) Available: www.rfidjournal.com/article/articleprint/1128/–1/1/

Deloitte. Consulting and Retail Systems Alert Groups. 2004. "RFID: How Far, How Fast: A View from the Rest of the World." Deloitte and Touche.

Lindquist, Mats G. "RFID in Libraries." Presentation at the World Library and Information Congress, 698th IFLA General Conference and Council, August 1–9, 2003, Berlin.

Mackenzie, Christine, and Michael Aulich. 2002. "Self Service—The Revolution's Here!" VALA 2002 Conference. Available: www.vala.org.au/vala2002/2002pdf/44MacAul.pdf

Santa Clara County Library District. Joint Powers Authority RFID Analysis Committee. "Final Report." October 27, 2006. Available: Santa Clara County Library Joint Power Authority RFID Analysis Committee www.santaclaracountylib.org/about/jpa/Report_SCCL_RFID_10.27.05.pdf

Ward, Diane Marie and Ellen Firer, e-mail interview, July 5, 2006.

Ward, Diane Marie and Gretchen Freeman, e-mail interview, July 4, 2006.

Ward, Diane Marie and Margaret Hazel, e-mail interview, August 30, 2006.

Ward, Diane Marie and James Lichtenberg, e-mail interview, August 17, 2006.

Ward, Diane Marie and William Marsterson, e-mail interview, July 10, 2006.

Ward, Diane Marie and Susan O'Neal, e-mail interview, August 3, 2006.

Ward, Diane Marie and John Pritchard, e-mail interview, July 3, 2006.

Ward, Diane Marie and Karen Senglaup, e-mail interview, February 3, 2006.

6

Designing Your RFID Solution: RFP

Introduction

As discussed in Chapter 5, the decision-making process is very important for a library in order to be clear about its reasons for going with RFID. With any large technology implementation, libraries will issue a "Request for Proposal" or RFP. The RFP clearly expresses what the library wants. It forms the framework for contractual discussions about system implementation. This chapter is written to counsel RFID investigative committees or library administrators during the RFP process. It should be used as a framework only, as each library has its own methodology and format for drafting an RFP, receiving proposals, and evaluating best and final offers of a vendor.

Drafting a Request for Proposal

When an RFP is issued, vendors are invited to send detailed bids in response to the questions. This is the formal beginning of the vendor-library communication. Vendors demonstrate RFID systems onsite at the library, and then submit a best and final offer (BAFO). If your library chooses not to discuss specifications with the vendor and simply wants prices, you might want to issue a Request for Quotation (RFQ). If you are at an information gathering stage, you might want to issue a Request for

Information (RFI). Your committee will want to be clear about the date by which proposals have to be received in order for consideration. This chapter can help with all three requests, but was designed with a comprehensive RFP in mind.

> An excellent resource for writing a library-related RFP is Cynthia Hodgson's The RFP Writer's Guide to Standards for Library Systems" published by *NISO Press* in 2002. It is available at: www.niso.org/standards/resources/RFP_Writers_Guide.pdf

The keyword to associate with RFP is "specificity." Your committee should be firm that you want detailed responses from the vendor. One of the most important things a library committee should do is to familiarize itself with radio frequency identification technology. Libraries should use their RFID knowledge to craft a solid RFP.

Remember, what you might take for granted about your library is probably unknown to the vendors who will respond to your RFP. Describe everything in detail. When you describe your physical space, give dimensions to the best of your ability so that the vendor has a visual image of what your library is trying to accomplish with RFID. The committee should also consider the future scalability of RFID. How many tags might be needed in the future, and how will they be used? Is your library considering remote storage? Is there a new physical space in your budgetary horizon?

We are still early in the technology lifecycle of RFID since our innovating RFID libraries started their installations in the period 1998–2001. We are now at the end of what I see as the "early adopter phase" of 2002–2006, and fast approaching what I feel will be an oncoming "early majority phase" once standards are ubiquitous and privacy rights are addressed (2007 and beyond). It will be apparent when reading through an RFID RFP that the potential library customer is very interested in the experience level of the vendor with installations on similar integrated library systems.

> For more on adoption phases and product lifecycles of emerging technologies, see Geoffrey A. Moore's *Crossing the Chasm* (2002 Revised Edition, New York: HarperCollins)

I e-mailed privacy rights expert Lee Tien of the Electronic Frontier Foundation about what steps he thinks a library committee should take in preparation for sending out a RFP for a RFID system? Should the committee publicize its interest in RFID plans to a local paper, a library town forum, a paper-based or online patron survey? Tien replied: "I don't think libraries should do this yet. I think that right now they are going to get very imperfect systems. Libraries should move very slowly and do a lot of homework before sending out a RFP. One thing they absolutely need to do is find and listen to informed, tech-savvy RFID critics. . . . IMHO [In my humble opinion] the library community as a whole needs to evaluate RFID and pressure the industry to build a truly privacy-sensitive architecture. Individual libraries cannot do this well." (Ward-Tien interview, 2006)

Finding the Right Price

There is an old expression in the business world that "no one gets fired for choosing IBM." The expression reinforces that information technology managers like to purchase systems from tried and true vendors; however, with RFID technology there are no companies that are analogous to IBM's; since RFID has only been an option for libraries since the new millennium, it is not readily apparent which vendor is the "IBM" in the industry. While one RFID vendor has the most installations of RFID systems in libraries to date, other companies have pioneered in the market in product development and customer service. Therefore, all vendors should be looked at objectively for their individual strengths and for what they can offer your library in terms of personalizing the RFID installation to suit your needs.

Always strive for the lowest price. If budgetary concerns seem to prohibit doing everything you want to with RFID at one time, you might want to investigate options with your vendor about installing the system in phases. Perhaps starting out with the conversion of your collection to RFID tags and installing self-check readers, and then the next stage would be installing book drop chutes and automatic sorters. Staging your installation might prove to be fiscally attractive.

> For a thoughtful guide to potential questions for RFID and RFP, please see San Francisco Public Library's "Radio Frequency Identification and the San Francisco Public Library," which features a section on RFPs. It is available at http://sfpl.lib.ca.us/librarylocations/libtechcomm/RFID-and-SFPL-summary-report-oct2005.pdf

If you are fortunate enough to have a pool of money for technology, you still might want to architect your system in stages and spread your library purchase of over 1 million over three years. I asked Salt Lake County Public Library's Associate Director of Reference & Technology Gretchen L. Freeman if she would suggest to other large public library systems that spreading out installation and payment over a couple of years is a good idea. Freeman answered: "We have spread it over two years for the first phase of the project. Additional phases depend on building and remodeling projects, so I can't say for sure how the funding will spread. We are unique in having a reserve fund available to us to fund part of our technology initiatives like RFID." (Ward-Freeman interview, 2006)

RFID-IN-ACTION INTERVIEW: THE RFP PROCESS

Waterloo Public Library
www.wpl.ca

The city of Waterloo, Ontario, Canada, has seen rapid population growth in recent years. Known in the Province, as Ontario's Silicon Valley area, the region is known for being a technology incubator and having a very high literacy rate. Set in the heart of a bustling main street area that is home to scores of boutiques and "mom and pop" stores, Waterloo Public Library's high volume business is reflective of its growing population. In response to the increase in circulation, the government marked over $2 million (CD) to the library board to purchase new materials. In order to make room for all the new materials, some materials had to be weeded. Eventually, it was determined that a new physical space was needed for all the new books and audiovisual items. With a new building on the horizon, the librarians at Waterloo Public Library decided to look into the possibility of integrating an RFID solution into their library system.

I asked RFID Project Manager and Manager of Systems at Waterloo Public Library Ellen Jones and Manager of Technical Services Sheila Mehes about their RFP process and their hopes for RFID.

Q: Tell me about your experience.

A: Jones: I hoped that an RFID system with self-checkout would help to alleviate the strain on the circulation staff since WPL had experienced a sharp increase in the circulation. An additional factor is the reciprocal borrowing agreement with its neighboring city of Kitchener.

A: Mehes: RFID self-check will allow patrons that know what they want to borrow to do so in an express manner, thus freeing up staff to do other work that requires analytical skills. (Ward-Jones and Mehes interviews, 2006)

For more on Waterloo Public Library, see the accompanying DVD which features interviews of Ellen Jones and Sheila Mehes.

Crafting Sample Questions for the RFP

An RFP could be divided into the following broad areas:

- Introduction: describe the library and its motivation; give essential facts about circulation, ILS, physical space, collection size; provide a time frame and contact information.
- Questions about RFID: information about the proof-of-concept tests for RFID applications; data regarding the vendor's experience installing the type of system you are interested in purchasing.

- Request for cost of each component of the RFID system, and a grand total for hardware, software, tags, installation and maintenance.
- Your requirements for proposal documents from the vendor: timetable; the form in which you want their bid; how your library will determine and notify a vendor for a possible demonstration; and how you will make your decision and contact the successful vendor.

For the more detailed suggestions on crafting your RFP, see the following brainstorming worksheets (Figures 6.1 through 6.3).

Figure 6.1:　Brainstorming Worksheet: Questions to Ask the RFP Vendor

Sample Structure and Questions

Introduction

Essentials

- Identification area (is this an RFP, RFI, or RFQ)
- Library name
- Date

Introduction: About Your Library

- Write a little about the library (public or academic) and the size of the community it serves. Include how many volumes your library houses and daily/monthly/annual circulation statistics.
- What is the physical size of the library in square feet or meters. Also, do you have more than one branch? If yes, how many branches are to be converted to RFID?
- Briefly list your objectives and expectations.
- Is the library part of a consortium? If so, give details about reciprocal borrowing or any special ILS restrictions.

Scope of RFP

- What are you looking for in this RFP? Give details on the type of RFID system envisioned.
- What do you want the vendor to supply in equipment, maintenance, and tags?
- List the items you would like to install, but reserve the right to increase or decrease the quantity of each, if found necessary. Give the quantity and type of RFID products you want. For example, the following is a list of what a library *might* like to purchase or rent:
  - New RFID hardware and software installed by the vendor
  - Staff workstations (quantity: four)
  - Handheld RFID readers (quantity: two)
  - Self-checkout station (quantity: eight)
  - Self-checkin station with book drop (quantity: two: one internal, one external)
  - Sorting system with four bins
  - Purchase a conversion station (quantity: one) and rent additional conversion stations (quantity: two) for three months
  - A service contract for at least one year and renewable thereafter

Timetable

- Date of proposal issuance.
- State when you want proposals returned to you (include day/hour).
- Expressly state your policy regarding late submissions.
- What is your time frame? Do you have a schedule for onsite vendor demonstrations? When do you want to install the system?

Contacts

- Provide the address for vendors to send the RFP.
- Provide a contact for vendors in case they have questions for you.

Figure 6.2:   Brainstorming Worksheet: Common RFID Questions

ILS-related
- State your ILS provider and the version/release you use.
- Is the vendor a certified partner with the ILS?
- If you change the ILS in the future, what happens with the RFID system?
- Has the vendor installed on this ILS before (where and when)?
- Does the vendor's staff have technical competence working with your ILS to bring the installation to fruition?
- Is there a need to contact the ILS vendor to make them aware of the potential RFID installation? If so, will the ILS vendor need to supply information?
- Ask if SIP2 or NCIP is used? (Determine if you have SIP, SIP2, or NCIP). Do you have the money budgeted for this protocol?
- Will you need a server for the vendor's RFID application, or will an existing server need to be partitioned for RFID event activity? Or, will SIP2/NCIP be sufficient? If you have multiple branches, will you need a server at each site?
- Will you be able to use your current circulation staff GUI during staffed charging activities, or do you need to have an RFID GUI screen up also?
- Ask vendors to explain the middleware in detail.
- If the ILS or the server goes down, will you still be able to charge materials? If so, how? Will the RFID events be saved somewhere? Is there a way to bulk load the tag information into the ILS when the system comes back up?

Technical Specifics
- Does the vendor test equipment and have third-party test results as verification?
- Will metal in your shelves, desks, walls, cabinets, or furniture affect the read rate? Can they provide exact specifications regarding metal or water in the area near readers and how they might affect read rates?
- What typically causes a read failure? What does the vendor consider an acceptable rate of read failure through the gates?
- How will the vendor complete the site survey? How far in advance of installation does the site survey occur?
- Are standards stable enough that the system will not change dramatically in the near future? Will their products work with another vendor's products? Interoperability commitment?
- Is the vendor's software compatible with your Windows-based system? What are the requirements for each computer that hardware and software will be tied to?
- Will a bar code scanner work on the same computer as the RFID reader?
- How would we remove or deactivate an RFID tag from an item if we want to withdraw it, or offer it in a book sale?
- Will the RFID system cause any interference with (or receive interference from) wireless hotspots

(continued)

Figure 6.2:   Brainstorming Worksheet: Common RFID Questions (*Continued*)

using 802.11 (abg), cellular phones, 2.4GHz phones, laptop computers with wireless cards, RFID tags that might be in patron credit cards?

- Do you want prospective vendors to commit to a proof of concept test at your library?

Security

- Detail for the vendor what type of security system you currently have (if you have one) and if you intend on using it, or if you're looking for a chip with both item management and security. Discuss if you want the security bit on the tag or if you are open to another type of security mechanism, such as querying the database or a legacy security system.
- What is the vertical/horizontal read area of gates? Are there any dead spots in the security gates? If someone walks through the security gates with an item in a bag held close to the ground, or an item held above their heads, will the RFID gates detect it and set off an alarm? How wide is the RF field? (18 inches for each gate equaling 36 inches?)
- Will gates alarm when tags from other libraries or vendors pass through the gates?
- What is the recognition rate for detecting materials exiting security gates?
- Are the alarms audible and visible?
- What type of information is generated on the screen when the alarm sounds?
- What happens to your existing EAS materials that are either embedded in or affixed to the book? You probably don't want to remove them as it would damage materials, but will they negatively impact the RFID read accuracy?
- Any questions about ADA compliance?
- How might a patron circumvent the RFID system? (Foil, metal, lead, etc.)

Tags

- Are the vendor's tags proprietary? Will this company be the only supplier of tags? Will other tags work with your RFID system?
- Do your tags meet all current industry standards for interoperability?
- What ISO standard is followed: ISO 18000–3, ISO 15693?
- Do the tags come preprogrammed or can you program them with item bar codes? Is there a preprogrammed number on each tag which is burned onto the tag at the point of manufacture?
- What data do you want on the tag?
- Will the bar code (unique identifier) be in a locked field?
- How many areas or fields of data are on the tag?
- Can tags be rewritten to easily? Can you reuse tags? Can the label be easily pulled off? How strong is the adhesive?
- How are fields locked? Can you lock and unlock the tags? Ask if their tags could be subverted or killed by subversive or non-library readers?
- What are the dimensions of the tag?
- Is data transfer encrypted? Does the reader talk first and authenicate itself to the tag?

(continued)

Figure 6.2:   Brainstorming Worksheet: Common RFID Questions (*Continued*)

- Do you want other data stored on the tag: title, location?
- How many bits of memory are available from the vendor? What is the average?
- Who manufactures the RFID tag? Ask the vendor for a history of the development of their tag. Was it designed specifically for library applications?
- Indicate if you want Read/Write tags (that allow one to rewrite data in unlocked fields) or Write Once Read Many (which allows the tag to be written once).
- Will a security bit be on the tag also?
- What is the average RF transmission distance between tag and reader?
- How long will it take to deliver the tags for conversion? Ask if the vendor will be able to supply tags in this volume. (Remember to buy more tags than you think you might need, in case you realize your numbers were off.)
- Ask if the tags will last for the life of the item to which they are attached.
- Are they environmentally hardy? Do they sustain functionality during a disaster such as a fire, flood, etc.? How long will it last before it can no longer be read and how will you know when it no longer works?
- Can they be killed?
- In general, what is vendor's response to supplying an order for tags? How long will a shipment take to arrive? Is there a specific bulk quantity you have to order for the lowest possible cost?
- What kind of information can you print on the label? Are tags preprinted by vendor or can your library print the tags on a vendor-supplied printer?
- What is the reputation of the chips used? What is the failure rate? Do you have third-party testing results supporting this?
- Ask for lowest price per tag.

Circulation

Ask for details about how their system handles:

- Books: thick; thin; pamphlets; books with accompanying audiovisual items; books with metal or reflective foil in the cover
- Magazines: unbound; bound (What happens if you bind several tagged issues?)
- Sound recordings: CD, sound cassette, vinyl record
- Video recordings: DVD, VHS, BETA, laser disc
- Computer discs (CD-ROM) and computer disks (floppy)
- Multimedia kits with a combination of some of the above

Additionally:

- What about data associated with each RFID event? Where is it stored and what is required in terms of storage space for information?
- Can the vendor provide you with a percentage or statistic on read rate accuracy?
- Will the circulation RFID stations be able to read your bar code system also? This is important if your patron card has a bar code and not an RFID tag.

(continued)

Figure 6.2: Brainstorming Worksheet: Common RFID Questions (*Continued*)

Self-Checkout Station
- What kind of self-charging stations do you want? Do you want free-standing furniture, or desktop models so you can use existing furniture?
- Should you rearrange where your self-checks are located and should you do so in conjunction with the vendor to guarantee the best read rates?
- Can you use existing self-check equipment and just add RFID readers on flat beds, or do you need to buy the stations as a complete package?
- Will your self-checkout machines be near the main desk so staff can help patrons?
- Bleed-over occurs when the RF travels a bit further than expected or planned. Ask about bleed-over of RF emitted from self-checks or circulation desk stations.
- How many items can be charged-out at one time? What is the recommended number of items to place on an RFID bed at once?
- How flexible are the self-checkout screens?
- Will your library be able to customize the wording on the screen? What languages are available for the touchscreen: English, French, Spanish, Chinese, etc.?
- Are users alerted if an item is unrecognized?
- If the patron experiences a problem with self-checkout, how will the software prompt staff intervention?
- Are there diagnostics that can be set to run automatically?
- Can audiovisuals be charged at self-check, or do they need a separate process?
- Are receipts issued from the vendor's self-checkout machine?
- Can overdue payments be made at this station? Can patrons check their borrowing record from the GUI? Will entering a PIN number be allowed?
- Are the stations or kiosks ADA compliant? What are the physical dimensions? Will the patron use a touchscreen or will a keyboard and mouse be needed?

Self-Checkin Station
- Is this a separate station, or just an additional feature of the self-checkout unit?
- Do you want a station located inside the library that would issue a receipt?
- Do customers need the item in hand to request a renewal or will patrons be able to enter a PIN number to check their account?
- Will your library be able to customize the wording on the screen?
- Will a receipt be printed showing their return?
- Will items be immediately checked back in with security components turned on?

External Book Return Chutes
- Can the chute's coupler check in and resensitize multiple items simultaneously?
- How will the chutes be linked to the sorter?
- Will you be able to identify material marked as holds?

(continued)

Figure 6.2: Brainstorming Worksheet: Common RFID Questions (*Continued*)

- Is it possible to retrofit existing chutes for RFID?
- Give dimensions of the chutes.

Sorting and Automated Material Handling

- Have the vendor describe in detail the self-checkin and sorting system.
- Will the sorter work with bins and/or book carts?
- How expandable or modular is the system? Can you add bins/carts in the future?
- Will the library need to remodel to accommodate sorting?
- Will it be possible to separate incoming holds? How are these items identified?
- Will the sorting system separate materials which lack an RFID tag?
- Will you need to buy additional software?
- What is the average hourly/daily throughput for the sorting equipment?
- What is the expected lifespan of the sorter? What is the cost of ownership?
- How does the sorter handle book jams? Will staff be alerted about jams?
- If a conveyor belt system is required, who supplies that?
- What are the specifications in terms of speed, capacity, and size of a conveyor system? A drawing of the area for the book return, conveyor belt, and automated material sorting area might be helpful.
- How many sorting bins will be needed?

Audiovisual Materials

- Ask vendors to explain in detail the way they handle audiovisual materials.
- Ask the vendor if they can substantiate their read rate accuracy.
- Will you need to buy hub and booster labels and apply them directly to the CD or DVD, or does the vendor encourage tagging the security cases? What is the cost?
- Will you still need to buy and use lockable security cases?
- Will each disc in a kit have to be tagged? What are the options?
- Is there a way that the RFID tag can be programmed to indicate the item is a kit and then can check to read all the expected tags associated with that record?

Conversion

- Can you rent conversion stations, or do you have to buy them?
- Can the vendor help suggest a plan for your conversion based on their experience with other libraries similar in collection size and amount of conversion staffers?
- Is there a way to verify that the tag has been successfully converted?
- What is the estimated time to convert a book or audiovisual?
- Do the tags come in rolls or some type of dispenser?
- How long in staff hours does it take a library of our size to convert its collection?
- Ask about the vendor's third-party option to tag items.

(continued)

Figure 6.2:   Brainstorming Worksheet: Common RFID Questions (*Continued*)

Training
- What type of training do you offer? In-house or train the trainer?
- Is there a limit as to how many staff can attend?
- What happens if you need more training?

Handheld Portable Readers
- Explain the portable handheld reader. You will need details on if it is wireless or if you need to connect it with wires to an accompanying laptop?
- What is the weight and ergonomics of the reader? What else is carried with it?
- How resilient is it when dropped? What is the guarantee on this product?
- What is the power source? Does the battery have a long life? What type of battery is it? How long does it take to recharge? What is the cost of batteries?
- For shelf reading, how far away can you stand with the handheld reader?
- Does the portable handheld reader transmit data in real time or do you have to download/upload data to the ILS during inventory?
- Ask vendor to describe the processes of inventory, weeding, locating items, and shelf reading.
- What is the handheld reader's data storage capacity?

Equipment
- Will you be able to trade-up to newer models and get some credit for residual value? Or will this equipment be upgradeable through new loaded software?
- How does the equipment connect to your circulation computers or laptops?
- Is transmission of data wireless or through hardwires?
- Does the vendor offer credit for trade-in of non-RFID equipment?
- What exactly is needed for installation? Will the vendor's crew require anything from your library facilities or staff on installation day?
- How long will installation take?
- What is the life expectancy of the equipment?
- What is the RF exposure from the vendor's products? Are they within acceptable OSHA, ICNIRP, WHO and IEEE levels?

Privacy
- What format is data in when transferred between the RFID system and the ILS?
- How is data encrypted?
- Are readers authenticated or passwords used prior to data transmittal?
- Do vendor's systems comply with organizational guidelines for privacy?
- Will the vendor continue to research ways to prevent the RFID tag from being defeated or hacked by third parties?

(continued)

Figure 6.2:   Brainstorming Worksheet: Common RFID Questions (*Continued*)

- If improvements in authentication or encryption become available, how will it be communicated to your library? Will the system become forward-compatible?
- What is the vendor's position on privacy and RFID? How will this affect your library's patron privacy statement?

RFID Patron Cards

- Are you interested in upgrading your patron card to an RFID-enabled card?
- Describe your present patron card and ask vendor to describe card options.
- Are you interested in having a card that has the ability to carry money in order to pay fines? If so, how does that affect privacy?

Data Management and Reports

- What kind of reports does the vendor's system offer that you can use to improve your library efficiency and service excellence?
- Will data be gathered about holds or items that did not properly deactivate when going through the security gates?
- What kind of reports can be generated?

Guarantee and Maintenance

- What are the main points of the guarantee for the equipment's functionality?
- What read rate should you expect to get on a consistent basis?
- Can you get an item-by-item guarantee for the equipment?
- What type of service contract is offered? What happens when the initial service contract runs out? Can you purchase additional years of service?
- What happens if something breaks? What is the turnaround for replacements?
- What is the policy for onsite maintenance calls? Where is the service center located?
- Will the vendor stand by its work and assure that it has secured the proper copyright and patent rights for the technological applications and the equipment?
- Do you expect the vendor to carry insurance for workman's compensation in case their installers are injured?
- Do you have a 24/7 technical service number? Is there centralized tech support only, or do they partner with local technicians to provide onsite support?
- Are there software and hardware upgrades? What is the cost, process, and time frame for repairs and upgrades?
- Will the vendor certify equipment is FCC compliant and the level of non-ionizing radiation is at safe levels?
- What happens if your real read rates do not match your expectations? Will vendor commit to onsite troubleshooting?

Figure 6.3:   Brainstorming Worksheet: Costs and Vendor Requirements

---

Creating a Cost Chart
- Create a chart for vendors to input prices of components.
- Ask for the total cost of ownership to bring up the RFID system.
- Ask for the total cost of ownership for the system over a three- or five-year period.
- How long does it take to recover the initial investment through savings generated throughout the system? Do you have any framework for a payback period?
- Are there any hard figures for similar-sized libraries, in terms of customer adoption rates, time savings, etc.?

RFP Proposal Document Requirements
Suggestions for vendor returned proposal and bid:
- Set a page limit. Explain if you want a few pages of prose at the beginning of the RFP with information about the vendor, their history, corporate structure, experience with RFID installations, etc.
- Ask vendor to provide specifics such as year of founding, ownership, etc.
- Ask vendor to list their experience in delivering the desired RFID products.
- Ask for references that you can contact of similar-sized libraries using your ILS.
- Ask for references which can be contacted of successful installations.
- Ask the vendor to submit the proposal in multiple copies.
- Do you have a metric to determine depreciation value of equipment?
- Detail what the vendor must agree to deliver and within what period of time.
- Explain the bid process and how the successful winner will be determined.
- Is the vendor committed to ongoing R&D for future applications?
- Is the company viable? Are they financially solvent?
- Describe how vendor will be engaged in BAFO.

Vendor Demonstration
- Do you want the vendor to site visit your library and its branches?

Your Library's Rights
- Detail any rights your library reserves in the RFP process such as the right to change quantities from time of RFP to system purchase if necessary after vendor-client consultation, or for other reasons.
- State that it is within your library's prerogative to withdraw the RFP.
- State that bribery is not allowable.
- Describe how you will determine the winning bid. Will it be a points system?
- Spell out what would disqualify a vendor from the RFP.
- Will you grade or weigh certain aspects over other aspects, and if so what will your scale be? It is courteous to make the vendor aware of these procedures so they can address the issues

(continued)

Figure 6.3:   Brainstorming Worksheet: Costs and Vendor Requirements (*Continued*)

which are most important to your library without guessing. Will cost be more important than references? Will the inability to supply a single product in the quantity or exact specifications, immediately disqualify the vendor, or is your library open to flexibility?

- If you are a publicly funded library, you may need to look at asking vendors for disclosure of political contributions or connections to public officials, if you are so regulated by state or local ordinance.

References

Ward, Diane Marie and Gretchen Freeman, e-mail interview, July 4, 2006.

Ward, Diane Marie and Ellen Jones, e-mail interview, April 25 2006.

Ward, Diane Marie and Sheila Mehes, e-mail interview, April 25, 2006.

Ward, Diane Marie and Lee Tien, e-mail interview, July 10, 2006.

7

Selecting Vendors

Introduction

As a whole, the RFID vendor market has elasticity due to retail and governmental implementations. Despite the presence of large RFID vendors such as Alien Technologies and Symbol that satisfy major RFID mandates, they have not gained a noticeable share of the library RFID market. The focus of this chapter is to familiarize readers with the main North American RFID vendors that focus on the library market.

As with most technologies, market forces reward specialized vendors that tailor applications for specific customers. Application development is done in concert with customers and mindful of the need to integrate with an ILS. A core group of eight vendors has emerged that is devoted to forwarding RFID systems for libraries:

- Bibliotheca RFID Library Systems, Inc.
- Checkpoint Systems, Inc.
- Integrated Technology Group
- Libramation, Inc.
- Library Automation Technologies, Inc.
- Tech Logic Corporation

- VTLS, Inc.
- 3M Library Systems

Finding Reputable Vendors for Libraries

Librarians are best served by working with RFID vendors focused on the library market as they have proven experience integrating an RFID system with a variety of ILS platforms. While libraries are not bound to use library-specific RFID vendors, it does make the conversion process more efficient since library-specific vendors understand the needs of their clientele and how best RFID might be applied to patron-driven operations. Library-focused RFID vendors hire librarians and often some have librarians on their board of directors. The presence of a librarian on staff creates a handshake of trust and empathy between vendor and client. Of the vendors I surveyed, four (Bibliotheca, LAT, Tech Logic, and VTLS) have librarians on their board of directors; two (3M and Checkpoint) did not have a librarian on the board of directors; and two companies (ITG and Libramation) do not have a board of directors.

Vendors proficient at installing the common retail/supply chain RFID applications are not familiar with the specifics and possible pitfalls of a library installation. A library choosing such a vendor risks having to allocate time upfront to explain workflows and associated patron privacy concerns to a vendor that has never implemented an RFID system in a library, and may never do so again. What type of service guarantee will a one-time purchasing library receive when in competition with repeat customers (like Wal-Mart suppliers) for onsite technical support? It is not in the best interest of a library to buy readers, tags, and middleware from vendors that cater to retail and logistics implementations, unless the library is certain about the interoperability of the equipment and the viability of the company. In the future, the true and tested interoperability of hardware will mean that librarians can be vendor-agnostic, but that is not where the market is currently. As Lori Bowen Ayre notes in "Wireless Tracking in the Library: Benefits, Threats, and Responsibilities": "Once a library purchases tags, it is committed to the tags and the vendor." (Ayre, 2006: 236)

RFID Journal provides a searchable database of all RFID vendors, including some of the library-specific vendors we will look at in depth: www.rfidjournal.com/article/findvendor

RFID Tag Manufacturers

A library RFID vendor may choose to partner with a third-party RFID manufacturer to supply tags and readers that comply with ISO standards to cut costs associated with in-house research and development and component manufacture. The most frequently identifiable tag manufacturers for library applications are: Phillips, TAGSYS, Texas Instruments, and UPM Rafsec/UPM Raflatac. The tags are usually square or rectangle about 2" x 2" or 2" x 3" in size.

Texas Instruments developed their Tag-It™ Smart Labels for a variety of applications. Rather than Texas Instruments offering a complete RFID solution for libraries and competing in this market, it chooses to partner with a company that does offer an entire package and already has a library clientele. Texas Instruments tags have been used by 3M, LAT, Tech Logic, and VTLS, which benefits each partner and keeps the cost down for customers. For more information, see: www.ti.com/rfid/default.htm

TAGSYS is often associated with RFID installations in North America as they have manufactured the Folio™ Smart Label for many years for a variety of applications including libraries. At 2005's ALA Conference, TAGSYS, Inc. debuted their Folio™ 320 tag that had 256 bit memory which was specifically designed for library applications. Early on, in 2003, TAGSYS partnered with VTLS, Tech Logic, and Vernon RFID (now ITG) and participated in 30 North American, European, and Asian library projects. TAGSYS also manufactures readers used for inventory procedures and circulation desk charging. For more information, see: www.TAGSYSrfid.com/html/rfid–52.html

Philips Semiconductors is the manufacturer of the ICODE SLI-S Smart Label that will be used to tag four million items in the Shenzhen Library in China. Philips tags have been used by Bibliotheca, Libramation, and LAT. The smart labels are compliant with ISO 18000, ISO 15693, and EPC protocol standards. The chips have enhanced security measures such as the ability to password protecting portions of the data on a tag. For more information, see www.semiconductors.philips.com/applications/smart_cards/index.html

UPM Rafsec was founded in 1997 and creates passive RFID smart labels, but merged with UPM Raflatec in 2006. Bibliotheca RFID has used their tags in several European and North American installations. For more information, see www.rafsec.com or www.raflatac.com

Growth

It is probably safe to estimate that the majority of libraries do not have RFID in their immediate budget. In 2004, Infopeople and the Information Technology Section of the California Library Association released the results of 113 surveyed libraries about their interest in RFID. Only seven of these surveyed libraries had an RFID system in place, and they were either clients of Checkpoint Systems or Tech Logic. They found 54 libraries were considering RFID during the survey (August–September 2004) and

Figure 7.1: Ward's Vendors Survey Results: Top Vendor Selections		
Vendor	**Percent of Libraries**	**Number of Libraries**
Tech Logic (formerly Library Corporation)	32%	11
Checkpoint	29%	10
Bibliotheca	17%	6
ITG (formerly part of Vernon)	11%	4
3M	11%	4

31 libraries indicated a plan to consider and implement such a system within two years. (Infopeople and CLAITS, 2004)

In my survey of RFID libraries (conducted between January and March 2006) the responding libraries illustrated a variety of vendors. I contacted 50 libraries and was happy that 35 North American librarians responded and took time to fill out my extensive survey considering how much work we are all asked to do. While my respondents are not representative of every vendor discussed in this chapter, their responses to individual questions give an overall view of the effectiveness of RFID as a new technology for library applications.

Market Share

At the turn of 2003–2004, I conducted a survey of RFID library vendors that appeared in the March 2004 issue of Computers in Libraries. (Ward, 2004) The results were presented in a matrix and featured the number of library innovators that had installed RFID from 1998 to 2003. I surveyed Bibliotheca, Checkpoint Systems, Vernon (now ITG), VTLS, 3M, and ST LogiTrack and asked for the number of installations completed.

Since then the number of vendors has increased, while the vendors I surveyed remained in business which indicates the market is expanding to allow for new competition and is strong enough to sustain the original companies. To support this fact, the number of companies listed as ALA exhibitors that sell RFID solutions and products has doubled from 2003 to 2006.

For the survey, I contacted the major North American RFID vendors to libraries:

Figure 7.2: Ward's Vendors Survey Results: Libraries with RFID		
Region	**2003**	**2006**
Global		944
North America	168	484
U.S.		463
Canada		21
Europe	24	360
Australia	21	30

Bibliotheca, Checkpoint, ITG, Libramation, LAT, Tech Logic, VTLS, and 3M. It is often estimated that there are about three hundred libraries with RFID systems in the United States, but my estimate using numbers supplied by vendors indicate 463. Figure 7.2 illustrates the growth of RFID adoption from a field of a few innovators to swelling early adopters.

The RFID vendor market is healthy and this is due to librarians challenging vendors to competitively price products and installations. In my survey of vendors, I asked companies a variety of questions regarding pricing, product offerings, guarantees, and technical aspects. The numbers in Figures 7.3 and 7.4 were supplied by vendors in response to my June–July 2006 vendor survey question regarding the "Total number of RFID implementations completed by your company since company inception—breakdown of that number by geographic region."

This breakdown is typical of emerging technologies: one company in the lead; two companies nearly tied for second place; and a few companies that have a smaller market share but are known for innovation or customer service which keeps them as attractive vendors.

For example, Bibliotheca RFID has a high number of RFID implementations in libraries due to a strong presence in the European RFID market. 3M has a high number as they were the first vendor piloting RFID in U.S. libraries. Companies that may have fewer installations should not be discounted; rather, these emerging vendors may be able to uniquely address your library's needs because of their ability to focus more time on your installation. Numbers should not be construed in any way as a promotion of one vendor over another: it is wise to issue an RFP and carefully look over as many different vendor proposals as possible to address your library's needs. The value of not overextending company resources is sometimes not considered, but can turn out to be a very important consideration. I found that the emerging vendors were among the most eager to complete my survey and answer any and all of my questions.

Figure 7.3:   Ward's Vendors Survey Results: Vendor Market Share (Based on vendor-supplied numbers to 2006 survey)

Vendor	Percentage of Total U.S. Installations
3M	43%
Checkpoint	33%
Bibliotheca	8%
Tech Logic	7%
ITG	3%
VTLS	3%
Library Automation Technologies	2%
Libramation	1%

Figure 7.4:   Ward's Vendors Survey Results: Total Global Installations (Based on vendor-supplied numbers to 2006 survey)

Vendor	Percentage of Total Global Installations
3M	51%
Bibliotheca	19%
Checkpoint	17%
Libramation	4%
Tech Logic	4%
VTLS	3%
ITG	1%
Library Automation Technologies	1%

This chapter is not internationally exhaustive. For instance, a major European RFID vendor is Intellident, but as it has not penetrated the North American marketplace, it was not included in this survey. For more information, visit: www.intellident.co.uk/ or take a look at the RFID library case study: "Intellident RFID Library Installation: A Colchester Library Case Study" Version 1.4: www.intellident.co.uk/downloads/ColchesterCaseStudy.pdf

As discussed in Chapter 5, the most important building blocks to creating a RFID solution are:

- assess what issues your library has, and how you think RFID might fix those issues
- ask your committee to determine if RFID is the only way to fix this issue.
- determine if you have buy-in from stakeholders—staff and patrons
- review (or create) a privacy statement in order to address any questions that might arise
- consider the financial impact and be ready to accept that ROI may be immediately qualifiable, but not immediately quantifiable

Another good way to assess potential systems and associated costs is to talk with colleagues about their experiences with vendors, but be cautious of comparing "apples and oranges." Look at libraries that have:

- similar collection sizes
- similar circulation statistics
- same ILS, and
- have the vendors made significant improvements in the RFID systems since that library was installed? Were they among the early adopters and perhaps may have experienced problems that you will not because of technological advances? Be careful what type of information peer libraries give you: weigh the negative and the positive.

When you determine that RFID is for your library, and your committee formulates an RFP, you will want to become familiar with the vendors of RFID solutions. When the RFPs are returned, you will be ready to meet with vendors and have them demonstrate their system to you in person to show what RFID can do for you to address the issues you feel are paramount.

Comparing the Eight Top Vendors

The following vendors are the major vendors of RFID solutions with installations in North America. I contacted each of the major vendors of RFID equipment for libraries. Most were overjoyed that a book was being devoted to this topic and they were eager to give me requested interviews and fill out my survey. The presence or absence of materials under a vendor heading should in no way be inferred as a promotion or demotion of one over another, as I have no vested personal interest in any of these companies and only wish the best for all of them as they are all very devoted to RFID and libraries. All companies were given the same opportunity for interviews and I have included material that I received. It should also be known that I cannot verify any claims on the RFID systems that are described by the various companies.

Bibliotheca RFID Library Systems

Bibliotheca RFID Library Systems	
1566 Silo Road, PO Box 595, Yardley, PA 19067	Address
1–877-BIBLIO	Telephone
1–215–369–0841	Fax
www.bibliotheca-rfid.com	Web site
USA@bibliotheca-RFID.com	Contact

Bibliotheca RFID Library Systems designs and implements RFID solutions for libraries worldwide. It is an international company with a management structure that has representatives in Europe and North America. Bibliotheca's "BiblioChip™" was introduced in 2002. Its tags are nonproprietary and follow ISO standard ISO 15693 and ISO 18000–3. Bibliotheca offers products for many applications for the library including self-check stations, automatic book drops, and sorting systems. Bibliotheca sits on the ISO board in Europe.

Bibliotheca RFID has a board of directors that includes librarians. The U.S. company is a subsidiary of Bibliotheca RFID Library Systems AG of Zug., Switzerland. Emmett F. Erwin is President and Chief Executive Officer in the United States. The installation of RFID systems in libraries is the company's sole focus. It conducts in-house research and design of hardware, but its 1024 bit tags are made by Rafsec and Philips. They offer tags with and without a security bit, which is beneficial for libraries that do not want to give up their current security system. Bibliotheca RFID offers onsite training for library staff members and onsite support for libraries post-installation. Currently, its guarantee offers one year on all hardware and software, which includes all labor. Bibliotheca has installed RFID systems at libraries that have the following ILS: Innovative Interfaces, Sirsi/Dynix, Polaris, Endeavor, ExLibris, Surpass, and assorted European ILS vendors. Bibliotheca RFID offers a per-item fee-based option for customers where it will convert the collection to RFID for the library. On average, it estimates 180 items per hour can be converted to RFID using its conversion stations. Bibliotheca RFID highlights its great software as something that differentiates the company from the competition.

RFID-IN-ACTION INTERVIEW: BIBLIOTHECA

Emmett Erwin is President and CEO of Bibliotheca in North America.

Q: Which ISO standard does Bibliotheca use and how many lockable and unlockable fields are on your chips?

A: 15693 and 18000-3. We sit on the ISO board in Europe. We use encrypted software, so all of the fields are locked. That is why West Point just chose us for their RFID system.

Q: Could you tell me a little about how you came to work with RFID applications for libraries?

A: While I was heading up the library program at Checkpoint; libraries were not happy with the security systems we and 3M had at the time. I came up with the idea of using an RFID tag to automatically turn the security off on a book when the library's ILS system checked it out. Before that time it was a manual process. RFID applications basically evolved from there.

Q: What are your thoughts on the standards work being done for library applications of RFID to provide for better interoperability of equipment?

A: I believe standards are necessary and should be adopted.

Q: Where do you think the RFID market for libraries will be in five years?

A: I believe it will be a standard in all new libraries and every library will be budgeting for RFID systems.

Q: Can you provide the readers any statistics on the success of your booster labels for CDs and DVDs to achieve successful read rates?

A: We can booster the signal up to a 95 percent detection rate between the security gates, the highest of anyone in the industry. (Ward-Erwin interview, 2006)

Checkpoint Systems, Inc.

Checkpoint Systems, Inc.	
101 Wolf Drive, Thorofare, New Jersey 08086	Address
1–800–257–5540	Telephone
1–856–848–0937	Fax
www.checkpointlibrary.com	Web site
Pamela.Rollo@checkpt.com	Contact

Checkpoint began selling its RFID solution in 1999. The company's Chief Executive Officer is George Off and it has a board of directors, but does not have a librarian on the board. It has a large staff of 3,500 and RFID is not the sole focus of its business. Checkpoint has been long associated with electronic article surveillance in retail settings and in libraries. Predominantly, Checkpoint conducts in-house research and design of hardware, but is always looking for the best technical solution. Checkpoint manufactures its own tags with 1,024 bits. It offers tags with EAS, but its own system does not activate or use the security bit segment. Checkpoint offers onsite training for library staff members and onsite support for libraries post-installation. In 2006, its guarantee offered one year for hardware and software. It has installed RFID systems at libraries that have the following ILS: Sirsi/Dynix, GEAC, VTLS, Innovative Interfaces, and Polaris. Checkpoint offers a per-item fee-based option for customers where it will convert the collection to RFID for the library; only a few libraries have used this option. On average, Checkpoint estimates at least 300 items per hour can be converted to RFID using their conversion stations.

Checkpoint highlights its security architecture as something that differentiates it from the competition. Its security system is protected within its server structure and formatting. Customers of Checkpoint's EAS can continue to use their EAS with an RFID system due to Checkpoint's unique usage of servers to query the status of the items. Circulation transactions do not require writing to the tag directly which Checkpoint says results in a faster processing of an item and fewer false alarms. Security information is stored in a cache on the installed application controller and locally collects data. When an item physically leaves the library, each item is checked against this security cache. If the item is not recognized as in the cache already, the security alarm sounds and the title and item identifier (bar code) displays on the screen. In the survey, Checkpoint indicated that privacy was an important issue for the company. It uses DiscMate™ to enable self-checkout of audiovisuals. Administration tools monitor the health of the system and generate reports.

RFID-IN-ACTION INTERVIEW: CHECKPOINT

Michael Jermyn and Pamela Rollo are representatives of Checkpoint Systems.

Q: What do you foresee for the RFID library market in the next five years? Do you feel the development of standards will help to increase the adoption rate?

A: Most of us have seen that technology is adopted once a problem and solution is communicated well. Historically, RFID was imagined as a security technology, but increasingly it will only enjoy greater success when it is appreciated as a technology that helps libraries interact with their patrons/customers more effectively. Most businesses know that inventory control, while very important, shouldn't be the thing to which most of the team should devote most of their time, and I think that librarians and other information professionals would agree. RFID provides patrons/customers a convenient way to checkout materials, quickly and easily, enabling the evolution of the traditional paraprofessional role, creating opportunities for more quality interaction among library team and patrons/customers. We are looking forward to working with libraries to enable them to develop that model in a way that suits their community and their staff.

Q: What advice would you give librarians thinking about adopting an RFID system?

A: There is the obvious advice that one hears when entering into any technical project, making sure that all the right players are spoken with at the right time to ensure success. If you have a circulation manager, enable her/him to work closely with your team in acquisitions and cataloging and if the system is being entertained during a renovation or a building program ensure that the architect and the right contractors interact effectively. Embed what you know about patron flow/behavior in your library in your plans to bring patrons into contact with the right members of your library team. Use RFID and self-check to ensure that staff time is devoted to those activities that make the library a stimulating, inspirational, fun, and safe place for everyone in the community. Our staff is available to help in that process. I would suggest that this is a great time to involve your marketing specialists and your programming specialists to brainstorm what could be done if they had more time, staff, and opportunities to interact with patrons. Think as to why the library is entertaining the decision. Make the adoption of RFID part of a grander plan, because it can be a great tool.

Q: What makes Checkpoint's history of providing item security management for libraries uniquely suited for RFID installations?

A: Checkpoint has been working in the library space for about 40 years, and it is our desire to learn from, work with, and support libraries that makes us a good match for libraries. We anticipated the initial need for library security when libraries were predominantly book oriented and now we are anticipating the need for libraries evolutionary relationship with their patrons/customers. We know and celebrate that libraries are community destinations and that people go to libraries to pursue their interests and investigate solutions to their problems. We know that patrons/customers go to libraries to learn from each other and to have a place where regardless of how young or old they are, they can learn about new things—things new to them personally and things new to society. Working within RFID and installing those systems is just one stage in the evolution of how we work with libraries and how we concentrate on the patron experience. When we designed our RFID system, we knew that patron privacy was just as important as patron convenience and our unique technical design ensures patron privacy by never storing unique patron data on the tag on or in the material. Our new self-check works with a variety of systems in this same method as we want to concentrate on providing the patron a convenient way to check out. Our future projects take advantage of what we have learned during the RFID stage and concentrate on providing patrons with a great experience and providing libraries with the tools to do so. (Ward-Jermyn/Rollo interview, 2006)

Integrated Technology Group (ITG)

Integrated Technology Group (ITG)	
2851 Cole Court, Norcross, GA 30071	Address
1–877–207–3127	Telephone
1–877–207–3129	Fax
www.integratedtek.com	Web site
information@integratedtek.com	Contact

Integrated Technology Group (ITG) was founded in 2003 as a subsidiary of Vernon Library Supplies, Inc. ITG does not have a board of directors, but does have a growing staff of 25 professionals. Shai Robkin is Chief Executive Officer and has a long history of working with the book industry and libraries. Although ITG is focused on installing its APEX RFID™ systems in libraries, it also provides other library-related services. ITG conducts in-house R&D and also outsources some development. TAGSYS manufactures ITG's tags: the 320, which is 256 bits, and the 370 tag, which is one kilobit. All their tags contain an EAS component. ITG offers onsite training for library staff members and onsite support for libraries post-installation. In 2006, its guarantee offered one year parts and labor on hardware, and one-year software support and upgrades. The tags are guaranteed for the life of the items to which they are affixed. Additionally, ITG guarantees backward and forward functionality as long as support and maintenance contract are maintained. It has installed RFID systems at libraries that have the following ILS: Sirsi/Dynix, Innovative Interfaces, ResourceMate, Carl, TLC, Endeavor, Follett, and Polaris. ITG offers an option for customers that they will convert the collection to RFID for the library. The price of this is dependent upon the size of the collection and the time frame. On average, ITG estimates 200 items per hour can be converted to RFID using their conversion stations. ITG highlights its great software as something that differentiates it from the competition.

RFID-IN-ACTION INTERVIEW: ITG

Shai Robkin is Chief Executive Officer of ITG.

Q: What do you believe makes ITG suited to deliver RFID solutions for the future, and what differentiates your company?

A: ITG provides a full-service solution from the sale through the implementation and beyond. Our ability to work with other vendors' products makes our solution flexible, while providing great functionality. And because we are privately held and have been focused specifically on the library market for the last 33 years, we can be more responsive to customer needs and provide more personal service to librarians than the large corporations we compete against. ITG's solutions are real-world solutions that take into account not only the power of the technology but also its pitfalls. We also take into account the fact that real, not ideal, patrons and staff will be working with the system and provide safeguards to make sure that the pitfalls do not lead to dissatisfaction. (Ward-Robkin interview, 2006)

Recently, ITG and TAGSYS teamed up to donate and deploy an RFID system in a New Orleans library that had been destroyed by Hurricane Katrina in 2005. The library reopened in July 2006 with 13,000 books. (O'Connor, 2006) Robkin is featured on this book's accompanying DVD.

Libramation, Inc.

Libramation, Inc.	
12527 129 Street NW Edmonton, Alberta, Canada T5L 1H7	Address
1–780–443–5998 or 1–888–809–0099	Telephone
1–780–443–5998	Fax
www.Libramation.com	Web site
info@libramation.com	Contact

Libramation began selling its RFID solution in 2001. Franklin H. Mussche is President and oversees a growing staff of twelve RFID professionals with a sister company in the Netherlands. The sole focus of Libramation's operation is to provide quality RFID solutions to libraries, and to that end it has an in-house research and design department for hardware. Its tag, the Lib-Chip™, offers read/write tags with an EAS security bit. Libramation offers Phillips tags in both 1,024 and 2,048 bits on a 5 x 8 cm. label and follows ISO 15693. It offers onsite training for library staff members and onsite support for libraries post-installation. In 2006, its guarantee offered one year on parts and labor on hardware with additional extended warranties available. It can install on any ILS that supports the SIP Protocol. It offers a service to outsource conversion of the collection priced per tag. On average, it estimates a two-person team could tag between 250 and 300 items per hour and can be converted to RFID using their conversion stations. Libramation highlights that it is not a proprietary system as a quality that differentiates it from the competition. It notes that their software has a staff and patron friendly interface, and that its chip is password protected which helps to eliminate privacy concerns. Libramation also offers special monitoring features on materials that do not leave the library, providing statistical data on periodicals for circulation management reports. Its corporate Web site features dozens of color photographs of the Princeton Public Library installation in Princeton, New Jersey, which highlight its sleek self-check stations. Libramation also vends a Media Bank CD/DVD self-charging unit. President Frank Mussche said, "The Media Bank can be purchased to use RFID tags, barcodes or both. The use of RFID tags is a much more economical choice when deciding whether to use barcodes or RFID, as barcodes are limited to an eight-digit number in order to fit on the label. The amount of information that can be stored on an RFID tag is considerably larger." (Ward-Mussche interview, 2006)

RFID-IN-ACTION INTERVIEW: LIBRAMATION

Franklin H. Mussche is President of Libramation, Inc.

Q: Where do you see the market going in the next few years? Do you see indicators for sustained growth and a healthy adoption rate for libraries choosing RFID?

A: Libramation has been involved in the development of RFID solutions for over four years. RFID is a very powerful technology which is revolutionizing library workflows; easing the ergonomic challenges librarians face, and increasing patron self-sufficiency. Not unlike the migration of libraries to an automated system, RFID is slowly gaining acceptance as librarians watch the early pioneers in the technology benefit from the changes. We believe that over the next five to ten years many libraries will embrace the benefits which are realized with the implementation of RFID. Public libraries will be the first wave to move to this technology, followed by the academic libraries that often have larger collections to be converted. The migration to RFID is quickly gaining momentum as indicated by the amount of libraries that are implementing this technology as they are being renovated or new branches being built.

Q: Tell me a little about the software (middleware) your system uses? Is it easy for library staff to get used to?

A: Libramation's Lib~Digit Staff Workstation software is designed to act as an overlay to the library automation's circulation workflow, providing the communication between the library automation system and the RFID antenna via SIP protocol and changing the security status for each item. Library staff can complete almost all circulation procedures using the Staff Workstation software without having to revert back to the integrated library system, wait for the ILS to catch up to the data being read via the RFID antenna, or change the security status of an item using another piece of equipment. The only time library staff may be required to go into the circulation workflow of the ILS is to provide an override of a circulation function, or to make changes to a patron record.

The Lib~Digit software is extremely user friendly, and all circulation functions take place in the same window. Items that are placed on the RFID antenna are immediately visible on the screen along with their circulation status and other pertinent information. Staff can simply choose to sign out or return items by pressing a command ("F") key, using the mouse to click on a button on the screen, or, if using a touchscreen, simply touch the function on the screen. Patron information is also visible on the screen including a list of the items they currently have signed out and the amount of fines they have outstanding. Materials that are currently signed out to a patron can also be renewed by selecting the items by selecting a box in front of the item to be renewed and selecting the renew button. Items that are being returned can also have hold or routing slips printed using the Lib~Digit Software. The use of the EAS bit for security adds to the functionality of the system as the security bit is turned on and off automatically during the circulation process. The system can also change the circulation status of an item by using one of the function buttons on the screen. Library staff have little difficulty switching to the Lib~Digit software for circulation, as one of the many benefits of our RFID solution is that there are fewer steps required for the circulation process. The switch to the Lib~Digit software makes circulation faster, easier, and more ergonomic.

Q: Your products have a very state-of-the-art appearance. Do you get many comments on their sleekness from patrons?

A: Yes, patrons and library staff appreciate the contemporary style and feel of our products. Both our tabletop self-check and our SCOT units have been featured in the Library by Design Issue of the *Library Journal*. Libramation builds each workstation specific to the library's requests. Library staff can choose the style of counter as well as the wood, laminate, and countertop that is used for each station. This allows our equipment to look like its part of the library décor, not an add-on. Libramation even offers an assembly package that allows our equipment to be built into new or existing cabinetry that is in the library ensuring that it is an integral part of the library. (Ward-Mussche interview, 2006)

Library Automation Technologies, Inc. (LAT)

Library Automation Technologies, Inc. (LAT)	
2 East Atlantic Avenue, Somerdale, NJ 08083	Address
1–856–566–4121	Telephone
1–856–346–9099	Fax
www.LatCorp.com	Web site
olegb@latcorp.com	Contact

Library Automation Technologies (LAT) began selling an RFID solution in 2003, but its management team has ten years of R&D with patron self-checkout systems. Since then, it has grown to a size of fifteen RFID professionals. This privately held company has a board of directors with librarian presence on the board. The Chief Executive Officer is Oleg Boyarsky. The company provides other services to libraries in addition to offering RFID solutions. LAT has an in-house research and design operation for hardware. It offers tags manufactured by Philips, Texas Instruments, Omron, and Alien Technologies, with bit ranges from 64 to 2048, with 2048 bit being its standard tag. It offers tags both with and without EAS. LAT offers onsite training for library staff members and onsite support for libraries post-installation. In 2006, LAT's guarantee was a one-year unconditional guarantee, with complete support for both hardware and software, including free software updates. Additionally, there is 100 percent tag verification and a full guarantee that its RFID-enabled components will work with any tag manufactured by any vendor as long as the tags are ISO standard compliant. LAT has installed on Sirsi/Dynix, Innovative Interfaces, and TLC. They can offer to outsource to a third party the process of converting the collection to RFID for a library. Using teams, about 500 tags per hour can be converted.

RFID IN-ACTION INTERVIEW: LIBRARY AUTOMATION TECHNOLOGY, INC. (LAT)

Oleg Boyarsky is Chief Executive Officer of Library Automation Technology.

Q: What is the distinction between your company and the competition?

A: The value that we bring to our customers. For instance, all of our RFID-enabled products contain a staff-conversion station, built in, at no cost. Or, that we offer alternatives to highly expensive and unreliable "donut" tags via our Intelligent Media Manager (IMM) system. In addition, all of our products are self-updating, thereby ensuring that the software is always the latest, that faults are automatically reported and acted on. But, for RFID in particular, we are the only company that is RFID-vendor agnostic. We guarantee, unconditionally, that our equipment will work with any tag, bought from any vendor, as long as the tags are standard. This provides the libraries tremendous leverage in having the ability to go out and "bid-out" the tags to get the best possible price.

Q: Could you tell me a little about how the company came to be?

A: LAT is a unique company in that we grew out of the needs of the librarians themselves. With our roots firmly established in designing the very first patron self-checkout systems for libraries nearly a decade ago (under OEM contract for someone else), we have emerged as a stand-alone company with our flagship product line of patron self-checkout solutions titled "FlashScan®" a few years ago. Within a few short years, we have achieved hundreds of successful installations across the country, and have been named #1 Fastest Growing Company in N.J., 2005. . . . We offer at no cost, wireless options, remote enterprise tools, remote assistance tools, RFID conversion station, multiple form-factors, multiple animations, multiple languages. . . . For RFID implementation, in particular, we . . . don't force the customers to have us as a sole source vendor. This unprecedented flexibility allows the library the ability to take advantage of price and function changes that occur in the marketplace daily, without being locked into some custom or proprietary RFID solutions.

Q: In terms of adoption rates for libraries, where do you think RFID will be in five years?

A: Certainly, five years is a long time, and even at the snail's rate that the RFID adoption is taking place now, many more libraries will be on board. Nevertheless, there will be a number of key changes though. For one, there will be a basic definition of the ROI specific to libraries. It will be much more detailed and measurable, compared to the standard "excuse" of "patron satisfaction." It is unfortunate, but to date there is still not even a glimmer of hope for ROI for RFID in libraries. Also, the notion of the "conversion process" will disappear—something that I have been speaking about at length at all the RFID gatherings to date. As a company, here at LAT, we have made every effort with our products to make this a reality now. Unfortunately, this is largely dependent on ILS vendors, who at this stage, have done virtually nothing to enable RFID—to them, RFID is still a glorified bar code. Thirdly, I don't think the cost of the tags (at least the ones that will be used in libraries) will substantially go down, but the cost of RFID implementation as a whole will, because most of these tags will be already embedded into materials/books. This will virtually eliminate any manual labor required to implement RFID, which accounts for a substantial portion of the overall cost. (Ward-Boyarsky interview, 2006)

LAT's self-checkout FlashScan-RFID™ and IMM-RFID™ supports all RFID vendor tags ISO/IEC 15693 and 18000–3 compliant. Their LAT-Direct™ customer service program features "preventative care" such as onsite training, promotional signs, and ongoing Web-based training for enhancements. LAT offers one-hour response time to support calls, and promises "24 hour escalation for any unresolved service problem." LAT-Total™ Coverage features renewable annual contracts. Libraries interested in encryption and Application Program Interface (API) might want to explore DataShield™, a privacy-related software available with their FlashScanRFID™ product.

Tech Logic Corporation

Tech Logic Corporation	
1818 Buerkle Road, White Bear Lake, MN 55110	Address
1–800–494–9330 or 1–651–747–0492	Telephone
1–651–747–0493	Fax
www.Tech-Logic.com	Web site
info@tech-logic.com	Contact

Tech Logic Corporation began selling its RFID solution in 2000. Its parent company is The Library Corporation and its Chief Executive Officer is Annette Murphy. The company has librarians on its board of directors and has a growing staff of 35 professionals. Tech Logic outsources its research and design of hardware. It uses tags of 1024 bits from TAGSYS, Smartag, and Texas Instruments. It offers tags with EAS, and also tags without the EAS bit that have an AFI byte that can be used for security. Tech Logic offers onsite training for library staff members and onsite support for libraries post-installation. In 2006, its guarantee offered one year for all hardware and software. A full-service agreement is available for following years. Tech Logic has installed RFID systems at libraries that have the following ILS: Sirsi/Dynix (Unicorn, DRA, Horizon, Dynix ILS), TLC (Library Solution & Carl Solution), Innovative Interfaces (Millennium), and Polaris. Tech Logic offers a per-item fee-based option for customers that it will convert the collection to RFID for the library. On average, it estimates 60 items per hour can be converted to RFID using its conversion stations. Tech Logic highlights the fact that the ability for customers to buy just the self-check software and source all self-check hardware differentiates it from the competition. Tech Logic prides itself on its custom, flexible American-manufactured sorting systems.

RFID-IN-ACTION INTERVIEW: TECH LOGIC CORPORATION

Gary Kirk is executive director of Tech Logic.

Q: As Executive Director of a library-focused RFID solutions vendor, where do you see the market going in the next few years? Do you see indicators for sustained growth and a healthy adoption rate for libraries choosing RFID?

A: There are many indicators pointing toward sustained growth of RFID in the library market. Among those is the need for patron self-services dictated by the constraints placed on library staffing budgets in an environment of ever-increasing demand for public services. Libraries must find new ways to serve the public while keeping staffing levels down. Self-service is a perfect solution and RFID lends itself to better self-service models than do barcode systems. RFID holds promise for more efficient and accurate inventory counts and enables efficient Automated Material Handling systems in high volume libraries. All of these by-products of RFID will help libraries run more efficiently while maintaining current staffing levels. As well, these by-products of RFID will reduce staff injuries related to repetitive stress and handling of library materials. I see an increased deployment of RFID over the next ten years and I see more standardization of the technology that will protect libraries from investing in "proprietary" technologies.

Q: Please tell me a little about the software (middleware) your system uses. Is it easy for library staff to get used to? Do libraries need to buy a server for your system?

A: Tech Logic's currently deployed software (ACS) is an easy-to-use distributed package. Library staff generally need only a couple hours' training to be fully comfortable with all features of the software. The skins or interface are completely customizable by the library. Any language can be deployed. Tech Logic is in beta testing of its new software called "CircIT". We expect a general release of CircIT in the fall of 2006. CircIT will be just as easy to use as ACS and will have all the features of ACS including customizable skins. CircIT will be a web-server-based system allowing libraries to manage all clients from a central command center. All statistics and reporting can be done centrally.

Q: What is the best advice you could give a librarian or a library committee that is considering RFID for their library?

A: My first suggestion is to talk to libraries that have deployed RFID. Find out all the good and bad for each vendor solution. Understand that this is not a perfect science and be ready to grow with the technology. My second suggestion is to make sure that you purchase a system that has been proven in many libraries of different size and circulation. If a vendor can handle the volume of a large urban library, chances are they can handle anything. My third suggestion is to be sure that you buy an ISO standard system. ISO standards are RFID tag related only at this point in time. ISO standard does not mean interoperable today but buying an ISO 15693 standard product will give you the best chance at survivability over the long run. Purchasing a proprietary system is very risky and could end up costing the library a lot more than just the original cost of the system. (Ward-Kirk interview, 2006)

VTLS, Inc.

VTLS, Inc.	
1701 Kraft Drive, Blacksburg, VA 24060	Address
540–557–1200	Telephone
540–557–1210	Fax
www.vtls.com	Web site
pillowr@vtls.com	Contact

VTLS began selling its RFID solution in 2000. The company has librarians on its board of directors and has a growing staff of 85 professionals. VTLS outsources its research and design of hardware and sells other library products such as an ILS. It uses tags between 256 and 2K bits from TAGSYS, Texas Instruments, and others. It offers tags with EAS, and also tags without the EAS bit. VTLS offers onsite training for library staff members and onsite support for libraries post-installation. In 2006, its guarantee offered one year for products, but can vary by component supplier. It has installed RFID systems at libraries that have the following ILS: Sirsi/Dynix, Virtua, Innovative Interfaces, Endeavor and CARL. VTLS' Fastrac is peer-to-peer, so no server is required. VTLS offers a per-item fee-based option for customers that it will convert the collection to RFID for the library. On average, it estimates 100–120 items per hour can be converted to RFID using its conversion stations. VTLS highlights its devotion to standards and peer-to-peer (not requiring a server) designed solutions as what differentiates it from the competition. On the survey, they indicated the security of the system and explained in detail how a potential hacker would need to have access to a library reader and the ILS in order to rewrite data on a tag. The company wrote a good deal about how the technology will not affect privacy rights since the only information stored on a tag is the item's identity and perhaps shelf location for sorting. VTLS highlights the ability of RFID to enable library staff to give the "personal touch" to patrons since much of the routine work can be automated.

RFID-IN-ACTION INTERVIEW: VTLS, INC.

Vinod Chachra is Chief Executive Officer of VTLS.

Q: You were one of the earliest proponents of RFID for libraries. Where do you see the RFID market in five years?

A: VTLS was the first library automation vendor to embrace the RFID technology. Our first contract for RFID installation is dated March 2000. Today, there are two major deterrents to the widespread deployment of RFID technology. The first is cost and the second is concern about personal privacy. In five years, the cost of the technology will probably be less than a third of what it is now. In addition, there will be widespread international adoption of RFID standards. The two together will further encourage the adoption of the RFID technology. The second concern, one of personal privacy, is trickier to predict. It does not depend on technology, but on emotions. Whereas, some privacy concerns are well founded, most are based on a misunderstanding of the capabilities and limitations of this technology. One of the goals of the NISO RFID Committee is to provide reliable information that will help put the privacy concerns in perspective. It is possible, though not likely, that the adoption of RFID technology will be completely derailed by exaggerated privacy concerns. The more likely scenario is that privacy concerns will be better understood and accounted for. The economic case for the technology will become so compelling that RFID adoption decisions will shift from whether this technology is appropriate for the library to whether this supplier is appropriate for the library. It is not unreasonable to expect that RFID tags will be as common in five years as barcodes are today. The savings in processing time, the increase in employee productivity, the improvement in workflow management, and the benefits of better inventory control are already making many converts.

Q: VTLS is very progressive in that it tries to incorporate new technology early (i.e., FRBR, RFID). Do you believe more ILS vendors will try to integrate an RFID solution into their offerings in the near future as hardware becomes more interoperable, and RFID standards become more publicized?

A: I believe that all major ILS vendors will offer an RFID option to their customers. Whether they develop their own solution or integrate somebody else's solution in their offerings, will depend on their financial and technical strengths, but I feel confident that there will be such an offering available from all major vendors.

Q: Is the process of installing an RFID system made easier when it is combined with an ILS installation?

A: Yes. A combined decision makes for smoother workflows and allows faster return on investment. However, RFID standards will allow libraries to separate or postpone the decision with little loss of efficiency. It is always easier to work with a single vendor than it is to work with two or three. VTLS has already achieved the role of a "system integrator" providing solutions to libraries with "foreign" ILS systems. (Ward-Chachra interview, 2006)

3M Library Systems

3M Library Systems	
3M Center, Building 0225–04–N–14 St. Paul, MN 55144	Address
1–800–328–0067	Telephone
1–800–223–5563	Fax
www.3M.com/library	Web site
jhaas@mmm.com	Contact

3M is a well-known, global company. It is publicly traded and has a diversified offering of solutions. Chief Executive Officer George Buckley oversees a total 3M staff of 70,000. 3M has a board of directors, but there are no librarians on that board. In 2000, it began to offer RFID solutions for libraries with well-publicized pilots at UNLV and in Singapore. It conducts in-house R&D and its own tags have 256 or 2,048 bits, based on need. As 3M is known for the library security device Tattle-Tape™ strip, it provides an RFID chip with the EAS bit as requested by clients, but can design a system to work with their traditional EAS. 3M offers onsite training for library staff members and onsite support for libraries post-installation. In 2006, its guarantee offered one-year product performance when purchased with a one-year service agreement, and its tags and strips are guaranteed to be free from defects in materials and manufacture for the lifetime of the materials they are adhered to. 3M has installed RFID systems at libraries that have all the major ILSs and some others at the client's request, but it cannot implement self-check in or out if the vendor does not support SIP Protocol. 3M offers a per-item fee-based option for customers that it will convert the collection to RFID for the library and is discounted based on quantity. Thus far, four libraries have chosen this option. On average, 3M estimates 400 items per hour can be converted to RFID using its conversion stations.

3M provides detailed descriptions of all its products on its Web page, including the Digital Library Assistant™. The DLA has four hours of battery life and requires six to eight hours of charging. It weights 25 ounces, which is less than the first bulkier models. The uses of this tool were discussed in detail in the case study on the University of Nevada, Las Vegas.

3M offers a solution that allows a library to maintain its legacy EAS such as 3M's Tattle-Tape™ Security Strips. It also responded to customers that were interested in a tag that would have both security and item management on one tag, and introduced the 3M™ One Tag RFID System. Its Web page features case studies and information on its library installations. It has installed the most of any other vendor using both approaches. 3M has enjoyed holding a significant share of the library RFID installation market and has promoted the use of the technology on its Web site as well as at library conferences around the world.

RFID-IN-ACTION INTERVIEW: 3M LIBRARY SYSTEMS

Jacob Haas is a representative of 3M Library Systems Marketing.

Q: Where do you see the RFID for libraries market in the next five years?

A: I believe there will be a large shift of libraries moving to RFID in the next five years. I also envision that the competitive landscape you see today will change, because of the high cost of developing RFID technology and the speed with which the industry is moving. You will see some competitors exiting the industry and new competitors entering the industry. I also believe that RFID standard will be implemented in North America which will increase the adoption rate of RFID.

Q: What advice can you offer for librarians investigating an RFID solution?

A: Investigate each company thoroughly and understand its financial position as well as the quality of management. If you believe in the management of the company and the financial outlook is acceptable, you can feel confident that they will take care of your library now and in the future. Make sure that the RFID company complies with all regulatory approvals such as UL, CE, RoHS, Weee, and FCC. This will minimize the safety risk of the equipment you purchase and guarantee that you will comply in the future. Weee/RoHS positively impacts the environment by reducing the amount of lead and other hazardous materials entering the environment when electrical/electronic devices are disposed. Also make sure that the company has the service infrastructure to support the technology purchase that will drive your library operations in the future and on which you will rely.

Q: Will 3M continue to offer libraries an option to use their 3M Tattle-Tape™ security strips with their RFID system?

A: 3M will continue to offer RFID with enhanced security. RFID security has its limitations and until there are breakthroughs in RFID security, there will still be a need to provide our customers with this high security solution. Therefore, we will continue to provide this world-class solution to customers who truly need the best security available today. (Ward-Haas interview, 2006)

Working with Vendors, RFID Success Story: Fayetteville Public Library

Winner of the 2005 Library of the Year Award from Library Journal, Fayetteville Public Library in Fayetteville, Arkansas (www.faylib.org), is a model for progressive libraries. Steered by Executive Director Louise Schaper, Fayetteville has risen to be a library to emulate. Schaper negotiated excellent prices for each component of the RFID system, and worked closely with vendors to provide a solution that suited her library's needs, including a SIP-less check out: "FPL had a single computer when Schaper arrived and was just installing its first integrated library systems. Now it has some 200 computers . . . a RFID-based self-checkout system and through shrewd negotiations managed to pull off the whole transition for $50,000—plus the cost of the tags." (Berry, 2005) The new $23.3 million FPL library has 88,000 square feet, three times the size of the previous library. Schaper and Assistant Director Steven Thomas "targeted several repetitive work processes for radical rethinking prior to the 2004 opening of the new library. We felt that if we could streamline our most-labor-intensive processes, we'd be able to handle the anticipated jump in service levels that would come with opening a new building." (Schaper, 2005)

Some libraries may choose to purchase tags or products from a variety of library-RFID vendors or even vendors that are not in the library world. FPL was fortunate to have great technical expertise to get the system working. FPL saw SIP as an obstacle both in price and functionality for its system. In a special arrangement, Bibliotheca's RFID software was imbedded into GIS Information Systems, Inc.'s Polaris library automation system so that Polaris' ExpressCheck self-check could be accomplished without an intervening SIP protocol. Thomas, Schaper, and Robert Ford wrote "in Europe SIP-less systems are common. RFID vendors provide their system "code" or API (application protocol interchange) to the library catalog vendor, which builds the RFID application into its system—just as we had envisioned." (Thomas, Schaper, and Ford, 2004) GIS' president Bill Schickling was interested and worked with Bibliotheca's American President Emmett Erwin to deliver the type of self-check system FPL envisioned. FPL also installed Tech Logic's 9-bin conveyor sorting and check-in system, and Bibliotheca's RFID tags, BiblioGates, BiblioWand, and station readers.

RFID-IN-ACTION INTERVIEW: FAYETTEVILLE PUBLIC LIBRARY

Louise Schaper is the executive director of Fayetteville Public Library.

Q: I am wondering if you could offer other librarians advice about creating an off-grid implementation RFID system like you did (tags, readers, gates from Bibliotheca; check stations and software from Polaris). Do you suggest this route for other libraries?

A: For us, this was the way to go. Our tight budget made us scrutinize the various vendor offerings. We were able to do far more by going off-grid than buying a turnkey system. As a librarian, I think that our vendor/partners too often think of proprietary turnkey solutions instead of thinking how they can offer an interoperable solution at the lowest possible price. Most libraries have limited budgets. I'd rather put my library's money into providing content and other direct services to our customers than into operational solutions. As an industry we will eventually end up with interoperable RFID systems. The quest for interoperability is an issue for all industries, not just libraries. It's not uncommon that new technologies emerge as proprietary and then move toward non-proprietary and interoperable. How can we as librarians who struggle with tight budgets every single day justify paying $15,000 or $20,000 for a self-check station that should really cost about $5000 to $8000? Now, I'm not saying that a $20,000 self check kiosk isn't warranted. There may be aesthetic reasons or even functional reasons why that amount of money is justified. But I am sure that the airlines are not paying $20,000 per kiosk. For 99 percent of the self-check kiosks I've seen, the cost isn't warranted. If you buy five self-check kiosks at $20,000, you've spent $100,000 versus the $40,000 we spent. I think what we did in Fayetteville did make some vendors uncomfortable and perhaps even some librarians. But, we think our effort had an impact on the development of this technology and we're glad. After our system was built (June 2004) we began to see other vendors dramatically drop the price of their self-check stations. Also, we began to see library automation system vendors offer self-check modules. This may have been a coincidence, but I don't think so. I remember people's expressions when they saw our system on exhibit at the 2004 ALA annual meeting in Orlando. Some said we'd regret it. Some said it would never work. Well, it's worked great with the exception of media. And, that's a problem that every-one is having. I will say that if RFID technologies for libraries were offered in an interoperable manner at an affordable price for us, we would not have done what we did. There simply would not have been a need. FPL derived other benefits from going off-grid—we understand the tech-nology better, we can communicate with vendors more intelligently, and we can more directly shape the direction of the technology. (Ward-Schaper interview, 2006)

The net results were a success: circulation has increased 2.5 times since 1997 and more than 48,000 of the 58,000 citizens have library cards making 576,000 library visits in 2004/2005. (Berry, 2005) The impact of instituting RFID in the library has been extraordinarily beneficial for patrons and staff and it is this proactive manage-ment style which has brought the Fayetteville Public Library installation of RFID so much attention.

Constantly trying to assess their level of service excellence, Fayetteville issues calls for input such as their 2006 "Strategic Plan: An Assessment of Library Goals for the Fayetteville Public Library" to measure how their services meet public expectations. Hopefully, this report will lend some patron-based assessments of the success and ROI of RFID. Schaper sits on the recently created NISO board charged with estab-lishing standards for RFID in libraries.

Figure 7.5: Asking Vendors the Right Questions

Please use the following list of "questions to ask vendors" to help you understand RFID as it applies to the vendor's solution. Many of these are a result of my survey that asked librarians to offer the top three questions to ask vendors before you buy.

Tags
- Do your tags meet all current industry standards for interoperability?
- Are they open architecture or proprietary?
- Can our library buy tags from other vendors? Will they work with your readers?
- Does your system read all industry standard tags, regardless of vendor/source?
- Can your tags be reprogrammed with additional/different information as industry standards and capabilities progress?
- What is the delivery time for the tags?
- What is your lowest price per tag?

Audiovisual Materials
- What are the performance ratings for your tags on audiovisual materials?
- How does your product handle multiple-item kits—such as books housed with multiple CDs?
- Do we still need to use audiovisual security cases?

Read Rates
- What read rate do you guarantee for your tags on books and on audiovisual materials?
- What happens if our real read rates do not match our expectations? Will you commit to onsite troubleshooting?
- Can you provide exact specifications regarding metal or water in the area near readers and how they might affect read rates?
- Will the type of shelving or storage units we have impact read rates or affect our ability to use RFID as an inventory tool?
- Are there any dead spots in the security gates? If someone walks through the security gates with an item in a bag held close to the ground or an item held above their heads will the RFID gates detect it and set off an alarm?

Interoperability and Standards
- Are standards stable enough that the system will not change dramatically in the near future?
- What is your position on proprietary versus open architecture in regard to tags and reader antennae?
- Will your products work with another vendor's self-check systems?

Circulation-related
- How far apart should our checkout stations be to ensure good reads?
- Are the self-checkout screens touchscreen, or are a mouse and keyboard required?
- How flexible are the self-checkout screens? Are they ADA compliant?

(continued)

Figure 7.5: Asking Vendors the Right Questions (*Continued*)

- If the patron experiences a problem with self-checkout, how will the software prompt staff intervention?

Conversion

- How long in staff hours does it take a library of our size to convert its collection?
- Do you provide training?
- Does your system have the ability to process bar coded and RFID-tagged items?
- Do we have to buy conversion stations, or can we rent them?
- What exactly is needed for installation? Do we have to remove the old library circulation stations and old self-check kiosks ourselves?
- Have you installed on our ILS before? Are you a certified partner with our ILS? Can you demonstrate your interface with our library's circulation system?
- What if I change our ILS in the future? What happens with our RFID system?

Guarantee

- What happens if some of the tags you sell us do not work? Can we return them?
- What is the durability of the tag? Will it last the lifetime of the materials? Does it sustain functionality during a disaster (fire, flood, etc.)? How long will it last before it can no longer be read?
- For how long will you support and guarantee the correct operation of the technology and products?
- Can you provide an item-by-item service and maintenance contract that spells out what the buyer is entitled to in terms of service, turn-around time for response, consequences for the vendor if services are not provided according to the contract?

Technical Support

- Do you have a 24/7 technical service number? Is there centralized tech support only, or do you partner with local technicians to provide onsite support?
- Are there software and hardware upgrades? What is the cost, process, and time frame for repairs and upgrades?
- Can you ensure good installation and post-installation care?
- Will innovations in technology be backward-compatible?

ROI

- How long does it take to recover the initial investment through savings generated throughout the system? Do you have any framework for a payback period?
- Are there any hard figures for similar-size libraries, in terms of customer adoption rates, time savings, etc.?
- Can you prove this system will meet our needs in terms of weeding, inventory, shelf-reading, security, and item management for audiovisual materials and kits?
- Do your products do what they claim to do? Can you provide a list of other libraries using your

(*continued*)

Figure 7.5: Asking Vendors the Right Questions (*Continued*)

installed products? How many systems have you installed similar to our library?
- What kind of reports can be run using the RFID system and how can these reports make our operation more efficient?

Privacy and Security
- Explain your company's position and response to privacy rights issues
- What is the data structure and content of the chip?
- Is your information encrypted and is that encryption proprietary?
- Will your company continue to research ways to prevent the RFID tag from being defeated or hacked by third parties?
- Can the tag be easily pulled off?

Vendor
- Are you committed to ongoing research and development? Are you willing to think of additional library-related applications for RFID?
- Is the company viable? Are you financially solvent?
- Are you committed to serving my library's order and needs?

References

Ayre, Lori Bowen. 2006. "Wireless Tracking in the Library: Benefits, Threats, and Responsibilities." In *RFID: Applications, Security, and Privacy*, edited by Simson Garfinkel and Beth Rosenberg. Upper Saddle River, NJ: Addison-Wesley.

Berry, John N. III. 2005. "Five Steps to Excellence—Library of the Year 2005." *Library Journal* (June 15) Available: www.libraryjournal.com/article/CA606406.html

Infopeople and California Library Association's Information Technology Section. California Library Association. 2004. Available: http://infopeople.org/resources/rfid_survey

O'Connor, Mary Catherine. 2006. "New Orleans Library Reopens with RFID." RFID Journal (June 27). Available: www.rfidjournal.com/article/articleprint/2460/-1/1/

Schaper, Louise Levy. 2005. "How a Spark of Innovation in Fayetteville Changed the RFID and Self-Check Paradigm." *Computers in Libraries* 25, no. 1 (January): 6–8, 53–54, 56.

Thomas, Steven, Louise Schaper, and Robert Ford. 2004. "Fayetteville's Quest." *Library Journal* (October 15). Available: www.libraryjournal.com/article/CA456765.html

Ward, Diane Marie. 2004. "RFID Systems: The Helping You Buy Series." *Computers in Libraries* (March): 19–24.

Ward, Diane Marie, and Oleg Boyarsky, e-mail interview, July 9, 2006.

Ward, Diane Marie, and Vinod Chachra, e-mail interview August 26, 2006.

Ward, Diane Marie, and Emmett Erwin, e-mail interview, August 17, 2006.

Ward, Diane Marie, and Jacob Haas, e-mail interview, September 27, 2006.

Ward, Diane Marie, and Michael Jermyn, e-mail interview, September 2, 2006.

Ward, Diane Marie, and Gary Kirk, e-mail interview August 24, 2006.

Ward, Diane Marie, and Frank Mussche, e-mail interview August 23, 2006.

Ward, Diane Marie, and Shai Robkin, e-mail interview, May 14, 2006.

Ward, Diane Marie, and Pamela Rollo, e-mail interview, September 2, 2006.

Ward, Diane Marie, and Louise Schaper, e-mail interview, July 5, 2006.

8

Installing and Maintaining the Complete RFID System

Introduction

Researching and selecting the best RFID solution for your library is intensive, but the process is only half over. Installing the RFID system takes a lot of work, but luckily most of it is on the RFID vendor's shoulders. Although installation usually only takes a couple of days, it changes forever the way your library completes its work. This chapter describes the main points of the process in general terms as it will vary among vendors.

Anticipating the Top Five Vendor Needs and Expectations

It is advisable to ask prior to your installation date exactly what the vendor's installation crew expects and needs. In the early days of RFID, some libraries did not realize that the vendor expected that the existing circulation terminals would be removed prior to installation day. This can be awkward, so it is preferable to have a good line of communication about expectations and needs. The vendor should give you a firm commitment about the time needed for its crew to be onsite and when your tag shipment should arrive.

The way an RFID system functions is easier to grasp when you are able to see it in action. A committee might want to contact the RFID vendor and inquire if any of its previous installations would be willing to give a brief tour.

Site Survey

Ask your vendor if there are any concerns that your library might have about architecture that would cause it to be a complex deployment? As mentioned in Chapter 2, the size of the antenna is a determining factor as to what the read range will be between tag and reader. Read range is an important factor for library committees that are considering RFID. Library committees need to work with RFID vendors to strategically place the readers in order to get the best read rates. Vendors of RFID systems that can illustrate a proven record of successful implementations should be trusted by your planning committee to identify strategic obstacles to a 100 percent read capability.

Timetable

Design issues are especially important if you are looking at the prospect of moving into a new physical space. I asked Maureen Karl, Materials and Technology Management Division Chief at Arlington County Department of Libraries, about their recent decision to install an RFID solution. I asked how they are working out a timetable for installation. She replied: "Actually Tech Logic wishes we would hurry up and get along with this project! Repeated county building delays have slowed the process considerably, so all problems have been on our end to date. Tech Logic delivered our conversion stations and tags on schedule, and reminds us regularly of their eight- to ten-week order processing time frame. They seem anxious and ready to configure and ship our building equipment, and purchasing authority for the equipment orders for the new sites are in process as I write, with delivery and implementation planned for October." (Ward-Karl interview, 2006)

Placement of Circulation Desk and Self-Checkout Stations

Libraries in particular need to be sensitive about read range since circulation desk stations need to be placed far enough apart so that tags are not misread by a nearby reader. Libraries need to think about the distance between readers to avoid bleed-over from RF readers and objects. For example, if your checkout stations are two feet apart, you might introduce interference problems between patrons holding materials with RFID tags. You want to make sure that your manned-stations are at least three feet apart because otherwise there will be confusion between both readers trying to interrogate the RFID tags. You want to keep tags from the situation of being in both readers' field of read range. Vendors will work with a site survey of your library to find the right amount of space for installing multiple RFID circulation stations.

Sandra Collins of Northland Public Library in Pittsburgh, Pennsylvania, told me that although most RFID tags for libraries have a read range of less than one foot (30 cm), their reader antenna was so strong that it would sometimes pick up the materials of the second person in the queue. Their quick fix to this problem was to place a few sheets of standard aluminum foil underneath the staff desk, on the back board of the desk. This helped to keep those other materials out of the reader field. (Ward-Collins interview, 2006)

For more on this topic, see the accompanying DVD.

Security Gates

Security gates are usually 36 inches apart, which means that each coupler in the gate will read 18 inches. A library does not want a gate to issue false alarms, any more than it wants a gate to allow items out without detection. But you need to make sure the RF coupler in the gates detects materials that have the security bit turned on if the item is low to the ground or high above the gate.

Interference

A legitimate question to ask is how an RFID system impacts other wireless applications running in a library. Will librarians find that one system poses an inconvenient encumbrance upon the other? The RFID system should not have an impact upon the WiFi system, but it is best to work with your vendor on a site survey to ensure that your RFID system does not interfere with your WiFi and vice versa. Equally, traditional cell phones should not interfere with the RFID system. But, are there high power cables, many metal items or water near the gates that might interfere with the read accuracy? There are many factors that might affect successful RF reads. Library vendors are familiar with these factors and survey the site for its optimum RFID read ranges, but it is good for librarians to understand a little about things which might affect read range and read accuracy: metals can affect read rates by shielding or reflecting the radio signal; liquids absorb signals. The installers should have RF devices that measure the strength of the reader's antenna field.

This topic is discussed in depth in terms of retail installations in Chapter 8, "Case Analysis: Location Testing," of *RFID Labeling: Smart Labeling Concepts & Applications for the Consumer Packaged Goods Supply Chain* by Robert A Kleist et al. The chapter stresses the importance of location testing during pilot testing of RFID for CPG applications, yet the lessons learned from retail installation can prove applicable for libraries.

RFID-IN-ACTION INTERVIEW: INSTALLATION

On this topic, I interviewed, Jean Foster, the Director of Library Services at Windsor Public Library.

Q: What is the one thing you would change about your RFID system if you could?

A. Redesign circulation desk (to include internal book drop) and locate appropriately in relation to door gates. It worked much better at the new or newly renovated locations that were designed for the proper workflow for staff and customers.

Q: Were you satisfied with the read range of your RFID tags and readers?

A: When the first system was installed, the range seemed very limited. The system was sold so that a stack of books could be checked in with one pass, but the height of the staff, more often than not, was higher than reader range. After a while everyone adjusted their expectations. We found we had to mark the read area on the counter with tape to prevent customers from placing items in this area. (Ward-Foster interview, 2006)

Drafting the Conversion Plan

The most important aspect about converting your collection is to have a plan. What will be converted in the collection?

- all of your collection
- magazines
- audiovisuals
- storage materials
- reference materials and non-circulating material for in-house statistics
- will new materials come tagged from the book jobber?

Who will convert the collection?

- reallocating full- and part-time staff
- vendor's third-party option
- volunteers
- temporary staff

Figure 8.1: Ward's Survey Results: Library RFID Adopters	
What percentage of your collection are you converting to RFID?	Percentage of Responding Libraries
Tagging 100%	49%
Tagging 90–99%	15%
Tagging less than 89%	36%
Are you still using bar codes?	Percentage of Responding Libraries
Yes	85%
No	15%
Did you use this vendor option, or did you reallocate staff to complete this conversion?	
Reallocated Staff	78%
Mixture of volunteers and staff (temporary and/or FTE)	13%
Wanted to use vendor option, but was not feasible financially	6%
Only new items are tagged	3%

Has your vendor been accessible to help you troubleshoot any problems which arose after installation?		
Answer	Percentage	Number of Libraries
Yes	82%	29
No	3%	1
Yes and No	6%	2
Blank or no experience yet	9%	3

Did your vendor offer to convert your existing collection to RFID for your library using its staff rather than your library staff?	
Yes	24%
No	76%

What Will Be Covered in the Conversion?

Some libraries may have to use both RFID tags and bar codes for a period of time. Items that are in the process of circulating while the conversion is proceeding will have to be identified and tagged at some point. In order to make self-check more efficient, the self-check machines are able to read bar codes via line-of-sight, as well as use RF 13.56MHz to read the RFID tag.

Survey Results

I asked my surveyed libraries how many were still using bar codes on some or any part of their circulating collections. When I asked Lynne Jacobsen of Warren-Newport Public Library why the library decided to tag magazines and if she would suggest this as a good practice for other libraries, she offered: "We decided to tag magazines that we only keep for one year to enable seamless self-check for patrons and to enable automated checkin and sorting of magazines." (Ward-Jacobsen interview, 2006)

Gary Christopherson, Head of Circulation at Algonquin Area Public Library District, said at his library: "The only items in our collection that are not tagged with RFID are magazines. It is simple enough to keep track of one area of the collection. I would not recommend that libraries leave RFID tags off more than one or two areas of the collection." (Ward-Christopherson interview, 2006)

I asked Jean Foster, Director of Library Services at Windsor Public Library, whether they were tagging all their collection's items or just the new materials. She replied: "We are just tagging new materials. With the first installation an attempt was made at retrospective tagging, but was abandoned because of cost and amount of work for staff." (Ward-Foster interview, 2006)

Some libraries may continue to use bar codes on items. If a library has reciprocal borrowing privileges with a library that is not using RFID tags, this may pose a problem. Most RFID vendors have an optical reader on their self-checkout kiosks which allows the user to handle any non-RFID tagged items without staff intervention. Figure 8.1 shows that 85 percent of surveyed libraries use bar codes and RFID tags on some items.

Process of Tagging

A staff member takes a book and places an RFID tag on the inside rear cover. The placement of this tag will vary according to procedures followed at individual libraries, but it is advisable to place the tag a few inches from the bottom of the inside cover (front or back) of the book, near to the spine. Your staff should be consistent about the placement of these tags on the front or the back cover so that you do not create problems with on-shelf inventory. If the tags are flush against one another, they might cancel one another out. Some libraries stagger the placement during conversion so that tags on thin items are not flush against one another. Also, if the tags are too close to the metal shelf, the metal might affect the read rate.

For audiovisual items, there is a mechanism to help flatten the clear overlay booster label and the hub. Vendors may offer a tool that assists in the speedy application of these booster labels to the face of the CD or DVD. Since there is a little bit of an opaque area on the booster, one might want to think about how to position it on the disk so as to not cover up any important identifying information. For instance, on a video, it might be wise to avoid placing a label on the window that allows a clerk to see if the item was rewound.

Staffing the Collection Conversion

With any such monumental conversion, the need to physically handle each item is unavoidable and the cost in staff hours is high. The tagging of newly acquired materials is made easy with conversion stations, but it involves the physical handling of every item held by the library. This also necessitates a change in workflow for technical services people. If your tag has both item management and security on it, then your staff members no longer need to apply and link a bar code and add some type of security device. However, they need to get used to the routine of connecting an RFID tag and its item in the catalog. Fortunately, this procedure is as easy as one can imagine.

Library Employees

Your library needs to calculate how long it will take to convert the total number of items in your collection that you want tagged with RFID. To arrive at the number of tags you will need to buy for conversion, take the total number of items in the collection and subtract the number of physical volumes in sections identified for conversion to arrive at the total number of books to tag. Remember a bibliographic title may have multiple volumes associated with it, so if you are generating this number from an ILS report, be careful to look at total item records, and not just bibliographic records. It is always advisable to buy more tags than you think you will need to convert the existing collection in case some tags are defective.

It is advisable to work in teams, and divide up by class or decimal classification number in the print materials collection, and have another team specialize in audiovisual materials. Audiovisual materials will take longer because the hub label and perhaps a booster label will have to be placed on each CD and DVD that you convert, unless you choose to continue to use cases, then you have to apply the tag to the case. Books, multivolume sets, bound periodicals and magazines should be quick to convert. The committee should work with all stakeholders to determine:

- Will staff work in teams of two or alone?
- How long will shifts be?
- Will items be converted in the stacks on a portable cart, or in technical services?

- Are the team members going to stay focused converting the bar-coded items to RFID tagged items, or is this going to also involve weeding, inventory, and problem fixing as well, which will require additional procedures for identifying and fixing problems?

Let's conservatively assume a person can convert 100 tags per hour on a conversion machine and figure the work on a seven-hour day (taking into account breaks, lunch, and interruptions). Conversion systems work differently, so you may be able to convert more items per hour using system X rather than system Y. Some vendors feel that 200–300 items can be converted per hour. Having seen the process in action, this is definitely possible since the amount of work is minimal: the RFID tag and conversion station software do the majority of the work. Seventy-eight percent of the libraries I surveyed reallocated staff or used volunteers and temporary employees.

Volunteers

In my research, a trend I identified was the use of volunteers or temporary staff to supplement the work of reallocated staff. Louise Schaper, executive director of Fayetteville Public Library, told me about her library's ability to rally volunteer troops to convert the library's materials to RFID tagged materials: "This was easy. We have a capable manager of volunteer services who has a base of about 160 volunteers. She also reached out to Boy Scout troops, fraternities, etc. Our community is known for its volunteerism. We actually had more help than we could handle!" (Ward-Schaper interview, 2006)

RFID Success Story: Richland County Public Library

Richland County Public Library in Columbia, South Carolina (www.richland.lib.sc.us), has 1,170,000 volumes with nine branches and a large main library. Director of the Library, C. David Warren, oversees the operations of the 8th ranked library in the Hennen's American Public Library Ratings. Richland County Public Library's Web site notes that 2005 circulation was 3.1 million with 1.8 million visitors and the "Meet the Director" page explains that they have: "utilized new technology to serve these increased numbers of people and operate more efficiently. With special grant funds and support of the Friends, the library is implementing self-checkout. This system frees staff from time-consuming tasks like stamping date due cards and allows them to spend more time directly assisting library users." (Richland County Public Library Web page, 2006)

Helen Ann Rawlinson, Deputy Director for Youth and Support Services at Richland County Public Library, when asked about how they handled this conversion, having multiple branches to convert and install self-checkout readers at, said: "Staff from the Technical Services department have done most of the tagging at the branch libraries. A senior staff member in the department coordinates this, sets up a schedule, etc. We have found that working in pairs is the most productive. Branch staff also help as time permits. They work on returned items mostly. This, of course, takes time from regular tasks and some work has gotten a bit behind. We see this as a special one-time project, though, and feel that it will be worth the effort in the long run. We have also tried to pace ourselves and not push people. We have found that three-hour shifts seem to work best from a productivity and physical stamina standpoint. The project has been beneficial as staff from branches and Main have gotten to know each other. The branch staffs have been very welcoming, providing refreshments, etc., and while we are anxious to finish, staff have enjoyed the experience." (Ward-Rawlinson interview, 2006)

I asked Rawlinson how they handle the issue of returning items that were circulating during the conversion process. What happens to them? She believes: "it is necessary to address the issue of returns, because you certainly want to tag those before they get on the shelf. As I mentioned above, the branch staffs have handled those although Technical Services staff pitched in on that, too. This spring, we were able to hire some part-time helpers to begin tagging returns at the Main Library. It is amazing how much has been accomplished in this way. For about the last six weeks, we have also been tagging selected areas of the Main collection by using part-time helpers. Besides the thousands of returns that this group has tagged, they also completed the 100's, 200's, 400's, 500's, 600's, large print, and oversized collections. We are hoping that we will be able to continue this in the new fiscal year. In late August, we will return to the branches and we hope to be able to complete them by this time next year." (Ward-Rawlinson interview, 2006)

Training for Conversion

A major consideration with any new systems is how to train staff to adapt to the new workflow and processes that the new technology enables. Gretchen L. Freeman, Associate Director of Reference & Technology at Salt Lake County Library Services, was asked about her experience with this topic. The library has 320 full-time employees which would make it difficult to have a vendor train every one of them, hence they employed an increasingly popular training method called "train the trainer." Used by ILS vendors for years, the train the trainer method allows select people to be trained in problem solving and process application. They, in turn, train the remaining staff and serve as a knowledge base for the staff as a whole. I asked Freeman about the training: "The vendor trained our trainers and our trainers train each library before they go online with self-checkout. That usually requires at least two or more sessions in order to train all the library staff" (Ward-Freeman interview, 2006).

Some may find this method adequate, while others want large-scale onsite vendor-led training sessions, instructive videos, or printed manuals to help them. It is something that the committee responsible for bringing RFID to a library needs to

determine based on the stakeholders (the FTE and part-time workforce). The anecdotal findings from my research lead me to believe with confidence that the process
is straightforward and simple to grasp. I have not heard of library staff members having great difficulty adjusting to RFID. Of course, it is impossible to be exhaustive. It
is wise to ask vendors what the training packages are that they offer and base your
decisions on your staff's ability to adjust to new technology and altered workflows.

Vendor's Third-Party Option

Some vendors offer an additional convenience to make the conversion smoother
from bar code item management to RFID item management. Vendors may offer to
contract out to a third-party group to process the conversion of a library's existing
collection

The vendor will send a team of staffers to the library to go through the collection
and link each bar coded (or never previously bar coded) item to the new RFID tagged
system. I asked the surveyed libraries if the vendor offered to convert the existing
collection to RFID for them. The alternative to this option is to have library staff
reallocated to manually convert each item.

Although this appears to be a gracious offer, it is not a complementary service.
There is a fee associated, but it may be cost-effective since you will not have to rally
the staff around this task for months. The charge is on a per-item basis, but vendors
might adjust pricing based on the quantity to be tagged. Although it may be pricey,
the vendor's third-party staffed conversion of materials can be completed without
the reallocation of your staff, and this may be a cost that library committees will
want to figure into their RFID proposal. Allowing valuable library staff to continue
to outreach to the public and process new orders and catalog new materials may be
worth the vendor's price for tagging. My surveys of librarians and RFID vendors do
not show eagerness on the part of libraries to experiment with this option. If your
committee weighs the costs, it may be feasible to use this vendor option. The benefits of purchasing this service are that it:

- provides for an uninterrupted workflow for staff members
- conversion is done by trained professionals that are onsite and skilled in
  working through any technological problems which might arise

If there are attractive reasons for handing over the conversion process to the
vendor's professionals, why don't all libraries purchase this service? My research indicates the aversion to the vendor option is based on the cost of the conversion charged
by the vendor. In my 2006 survey of librarians, the question was asked: Did you use
this vendor option, or did you reallocate staff to complete the conversion? Respondents were prompted to choose one of the following options:

- used vendor option to convert RFID tags
- reallocated staff for conversion
- wanted to use the vendor option, but was not feasible financially

The results indicated an overwhelming trend for libraries to tag their own collections through a process of reallocating staff. Eighty-three percent of the surveyed libraries chose to reallocate their staff. Not one library chose the vendor option to have a third party tag the collection for the library. When I asked vendors if any libraries chose this option, 3M and Checkpoint Systems responded that a few had opted for this.

Managing Technical Services Workflow

At the point that your library commits to an RFID system, you will need to reengineer some system processes. The technical services department of your library needs to be kept in the loop about the change. All items need to be tagged and this may fall into the purview of technical services staff. A technical services worker needs to affix an RFID tag to each item before it moves to the stacks for potential circulation. It has been established by the libraries I have surveyed that this is a relatively easy procedure to train a worker to accomplish. Aiding in the processing of newly acquired materials is that some book jobbers will offer books with RFID tags, but this will only address your new purchases.

> Among the respondents, there was a 100-percent agreement that technical services departments were able to easily adapt to the tagging procedure for the RFID system.

I asked Manuel A. Paredes, Deputy Library Director of Cherry Hill Public Library, about RFID's impact on technical services procedures. He mentioned: "The effect to our technical services people on a daily or maintenance basis is minimal. It has added an extra step to place the tags and covers and then relate them to the record but we have been able to absorb the task without any additional personnel. We have a good staff." (Ward-Paredes interview, 2006)

Tagging Materials

Like a bar code, an RFID label is affixed to a book cover, dust jacket, or page. It is up to the library where to place the tag. RFID labels are usually placed on the inside of the front or back cover of the book. The science of finding the best location for a label is to be expected as part of your conversion. Books are made of paper and paper has translucence that will not interfere with UHF radio waves, but some libraries experience problems with accurate reads on thin books where tags are laying in the same place and have very little to separate them from one another. Due to possible interference during inventory, it is well-advised to test RFID placement with your vendor and spot check a group of books to ensure you are satisfied with the read rate speed and accuracy.

One of the many advantages that Edith Sutterlin, manager of Technical Services at Northland Public Library, noticed is that the RFID process allows them an opportunity to spot call number errors which might have otherwise gone unnoticed. Also, you might want to be alert to what type of desk you have and where you set a book you just tagged, specifically if you rest it on your legs. If you have a metal desk, it will shield any books on your lap, but if your desk is wooden and you put a recently tagged book on your lap, then it will be read through the desk and might cause the RFID conversion station to have an improper read. Therefore, be cognizant that a non-metal desk may pose problems if you have a tendency to rest books on your lap during conversion. You should also test your tagged items occasionally to make sure they read properly. (Ward-Sutterlin interview, 2006)

> Early adopter, Santa Clara City Library has a detailed guide through its entire RFID process from decision process to implementation with Checkpoint Systems found at: www.library.ci.santa-clara.ca.us/rfid/02_decision.html

Exploring RFID and Consortium Libraries

If your library is part of a consortium, you might experience more problems than a completely autonomous library. I spoke to Sandra Collins, Executive Director of Northland Public Library, about issues integrating with the ILS since her library is part of a large consortium: "Our issues came with migration from our independent SIRSI system to the III system used by the county consortium to which we belong — SIRSI supported a nice feature on the self-checkout which permitted customers to access their account to see what was checked out and permitted renewals without item in hand; III hasn't figured out how to allow that at this point. We were using SIRSI when we began with RFID and Bibliotheca had already tested its product with SIRSI and could guarantee that it worked. I had visited the Mastics-Moriches-Shirley Library in Long Island (Bibliotheca's first U.S. site): they use III so I did know prior to our migration that III would not be a major problem." (Ward-Collins interview, July 2006)

Additionally, Collins and Sutterlin showed me their in-house system to quickly identify books from their library as opposed to books belonging to their large consortium: The absence of a blue highlighter mark on the top of a book, or a pink dot on an audiovisual case, alert staff members that such an item is not from Northland Public Library and does not have RFID tags. Collins and Sutterlin showed me how as they converted their items they marked the upper edge of books with blue highlighter lines indicating the books are Northland's materials and have RFID tags. Their audiovisual materials have pink dots on the cover. This way any item that needs to be charged by bar code or from another consortium library in the consortium is easy to identify (Ward-Collins and Sutterlin interviews, 2006).

Likewise, Ellen Firer, Director of Merrick Library, noted that in their case: "We had many issues as part of a consortium. First of all, we still have an issue as to the self-checkout units. Items are stopped from self-check if there are holds on the item from any library in the system. We would not want our patrons to be prevented from taking out an item on hold for another library's patron, and we still have no fix for this. The ILS vendor has been notified, but to date, they do not see this as a priority. In addition, we have some items that are limited to our residents—we had to have the RFID vendor figure out a fix, and the only answer involved limiting self-check to our patrons only. Not the best solution, but the only way to prevent our new items from running off the shelf to neighboring library patrons, who limit their items to our patrons. As far as inventory purposes, we have not been able to make sense of the bibliographic records needed to use the inventory wand. We do not have control over these records, since they are centralized for the consortium, and as a result, we have to ask for the records to be formatted according to our needs. This also has not been totally successful yet. We have not been able to fully utilize the inventory aspect of RFID. Our issues are due to being part of a consortium, and not having full control over how we view our ILS circ records." (Ward-Firer interview, 2006)

Likewise, when I asked Gary Christopherson, Head of Circulation at Algonquin Area Public Library District, why they still need to bar code some items, he mentioned: "All of our items are bar coded. We are part of a large consortium, and all of the member libraries need to be able to check out the items. It is also helpful when the RFID tags fail. We are able to check the item in or out using the barcode." (Ward-Christopherson interview, 2006)

RFID-IN-ACTION INTERVIEW: SERVERS AND RFID

Jean Foster, Windsor Public Library, used Checkpoint Systems. Checkpoint's RFID system makes use of a server for its RFID events. For specifics, please see their Web site or Chapter 7 under the Checkpoint Systems heading.

Q: Did you have to buy a server for the RFID installation, and if so, did you have to buy one for each physical library branch?

A: The original version of the Checkpoint system we bought did require a separate server at each location. This was one of the first major issues I identified with the system as the servers were not set up to autoboot or recover after a power outage and we do not have IT staff at all locations. At the time, we only had one technician for ten locations. The last installation for a new library is now served from an existing server... we still have three servers. When they are replaced we are looking at consolidating all sites in one server... now possible with new version of software.

Q: Are there any reports generated by the RFID system that are useful for you and your staff?

A: We only use the reports to check on activities when alarm sounds. We use our ILS reports for circulation details. Mainly, it has been a lack of time to investigate whether the reports could have another use. (Ward-Foster interview, 2006)

Considering RFID and Integrated Library Systems

I contacted the major integrated library system vendors and received replies from three of those contacted: Ex Libris, Innovative Interfaces Incorporated, and Sirsi/Dynix. I was interested in the dialogue that occurs between RFID vendor, RFID customer, and the ILS technical support staff. All ILS vendors seemed comfortable and confident that RFID does not pose a huge amount of time and effort to integrate on the part of library systems staff, as the RFID vendors will oversee and work with library staff to get the RFID software functional.

RFID-IN-ACTION INTERVIEW: EX LIBRIS

www.exlibrisgroup.com

Ex Libris has installed its ILS in over 1,250 sites in 52 countries. Katriel Reichman of Ex Libris told me that the installations of RFID software with the ILS platform is easy and that the libraries don't seem to need a lot of technical support getting started. I asked her if she had requests from clients for specific types of reports or files in order to make use of the inventory control feature available with most RFID systems? Reichman noted: "Not beyond what is standard in ALEPH." Ex Libris does create formal partnerships or stamps of approval for RFID vendors that they have little or no problem with their RFID software being used on their ILS for circulation management. I asked if this was due to NCIP or SIP2, to which Reichman responded: "Yes." Reichman offers this advice to Ex Libris' Aleph 500 customers: "Make sure that the vendor uses standard protocol implementation." (Ward-Reichman interview, 2006)

RFID-IN-ACTION INTERVIEW: INNOVATIVE INTERFACES INCORPORATED

---

www.iii.com

Innovative Interfaces Incorporated was among the first ILS to experiment with RFID as the ILS provider of the early RFID adopter, UNLV.

James Boland is Innovative Interfaces Incorporated's Product Manager, Circulation.

Q: Have you had many requests from libraries about technical issues relating to their RFID system integration? Does it seem to be a fairly trouble-free experience for their systems people, or, do you field calls from your library or an RFID vendor to try and help troubleshoot? For the readers, what are the basic steps for integrating the RFID application with the ILS's circulation applications?

A: We have not received much from libraries in terms of the technical issues for RFID. For Innovative, there are two types of RFID development:

- There is RFID as a bar code reader. In this case, the RFID reader simply feeds the data to the Millennium system. There is no distinction that RFID was used versus a bar code reader, card swipe, or keyboard.
- There is RFID as an integrated part of the Millennium system. In this case, our server communicates with the RFID server via an interface.

While interface issues would be handled by our Help Desk staff, any issues with the RFID hardware/server would be addressed by the RFID vendor. To date, we have received no reports of problems regarding RFID after the implementation period—set up can be involved, but once it works, it works. RFID integration only applies to those RFID vendors with whom we have a business relationship. Presently, integration employs either SIP2 or XML (similar to NCIP) messaging depending on the application. Integration involves installing the appropriate protocol and testing that the messages are delivered correctly and the correct messages delivered. In the case of Millennium Self-Check and Millennium Circulation, we have updated the user interface for libraries to take full advantage of the RFID when checking out books.

Q: RFID systems communicate with the ILS's circulation system usually through SIP, SIP2 or NCIP protocol. Could you explain in layman's terms what this means? And if a library does not have SIP, how much does this cost in order to get them ready to install a RFID system?

A: The protocols mentioned are all forms of standard messaging used for communication between disparate systems. SIP and SIP2 work through TCP/IP and use a consistent set of fixed and variable length fields defined by 3M. NCIP is an XML based protocol that tags the data with appropriate labels. In both cases, the messaging is simply a means for the ILS server to talk with the RFID server. A common application is circulation as described in these sequential steps:

- Item is placed on an RFID pad.
- Data on the RFID chip in the item is transmitted to the RFID server.
- RFID server communicates (via SIP2/NCIP/other standard messaging) item barcode to ILS server.
- ILS server checks out item and informs RFID server (via same protocol) that transaction was successful.

- RFID server switches security bit in item RFID chip to allow the item to pass the security gate.

Whatever protocol is used for the ILS/RFID server communication, it must be installed on the library's ILS. III does charge for the installation and maintenance of the protocol, but I cannot report the cost.

Q: Do RFID vendors consult with you about their RFID systems and how best to load their application for smooth integration with the ILS? Do you certify any vendors—meaning that you are confident that their products are compliant with the protocols you support for communication interchange in the circulation module?

A: Our interaction with RFID and other vendors is customer-driven. We work with a vendor when we have a mutual library that will benefit from the collaboration. In this way, we ensure our development efforts are effective and produce real value for libraries. Typically, the same vendor has contracts with other III libraries who also want the same development. For the same reasons, III does not certify vendors. (Ward-Boland interview, 2006)

RFID-IN-ACTION INTERVIEW: SIRSIDYNIX

www.sirsidynix.com
Sirsi and Dynix merged to SirsiDynix in order to pull their strengths together to provide a solid integrated library solution. To this end, they have a list on their Web site of "partners": companies (including RFID vendors and tag makers) that meet SirsiDynix's interface standards for SIP2 and NCIP. Furthermore, they have a SIP2/NCIP Certification Program that provides proof that the RFID vendors passed SIP2 or NCIP product compliance tests. Included on the list: Bibliotheca-RFID, Checkpoint Systems, Integrated Technology Group, Libramation, Library Automation Technologies, Tech Logic, VTLS, and 3M.

> The SirsiDynix Vendors partner list is available at: www.sirsidynix.com/Partners/partners_alpha_list.php
> The SirsiDynix SIP/NCIP Partners list is available at: www.sirsidynix.com/Partners/partners_sip2ncip_list.php

I asked two SirsiDynix representatives about RFID. Chris Harris is Senior Market Consultant, RFID and Patron Self-Service for SirsiDynix. Brent Jensen is Senior Software Engineer and SIP/NCIP Manager for SirsiDynix.

Q: Have you had many requests from libraries about technical issues relating to their RFID system integration? Does it seem to be a fairly trouble-free experience for their systems people, or, do you field calls from your library or an RFID vendor to try and help troubleshoot? For the readers, what are the basic steps for integrating the RFID application with the ILS's circulation applications?

Harris: RFID integration with a library's ILS is designed to be fairly simple. In many cases, SIP, SIP2, or NCIP will be necessary when using RFID hardware, but this depends on the specific application. To be sure that a system will function appropriately, many RFID vendors will do remote testing with the library's database to ensure a smooth transition to this technology when the library is ready to install and go live.

Jensen: In my experience, the only RFID system integration that's troublesome is tied to how staff-intensive the process of replacing bar codes with RFID tags is. Most vendors offer tools to assist in this effort. So the basic steps would be to have any required protocol handler installed (SIP2, etc.), test with sample items with RFID tags, then replace the barcodes with RFID tags.

Q: Do you get requests from your library customers that have installed RFID to help them generate reports or files in a format that is usable by the RFID vendor's equipment/software in order to do shelf inventory, or take advantage of any other RFID-related application?

A: The design of these reports is something that SirsiDynix and our RFID partners can assist customers in doing. In most cases, the customers can perform these reports on their own after some basic training.

Q: Do RFID vendors consult with you about their RFID systems and how best to load their application for smooth integration with the ILS? Do you certify any vendors—meaning that you are confident that their products are compliant with the protocols you support for communication interchange in the circulation module?

Harris: RFID vendors often consult with SirsiDynix about how to best integrate their RFID systems with our products, and it is very common for our software engineers to work with RFID vendors on joint functionality projects. We work closely with our preferred RFID partners to make sure that customers purchasing those systems will have a system that will work with their ILS for years to come as both systems grow and change and the technology grows and evolves." (Ward-Harris and Ward-Jensen interviews, 2006)

Establishing Technical Support

Whatever your plan is though, you need a systems team that understands the machinery. But when serious issues arise with the equipment, you will need help from the RFID vendor. Technical support is a key element in the choice of a vendor. Librarians need to be confident that the vendor has a reliable team to offer support via telephone, online, or onsite. Eighty-two percent of surveyed libraries with RFID systems in place are happy with the amount of interaction with the technical support.

RFID Success Story: Kalamazoo College Library

An important consideration is to ascertain what your network of librarians will be in your region. Which libraries have the same installation that you do: Same RFID vendor, same ILS, and might you be able to network with informally? I asked Mary

Griswold, Circulation Supervisor at Kalamazoo College Library (www.kzoo.edu/is/ library), about her experience with RFID and technical support issues and how important networking is to help work out the technical bugs.

Q: Could you talk a little about your experience with technical support representatives to handle any hiccups with the system? What kind of issues have you encountered that you needed help with? You mentioned that much of your dealings with them have been over the phone. Has this been sufficient?

A: All of our support is done over the phone and by using a "netviewer tool." We have developed a good working relationship. The company assured us that we could have a technician in as we needed one in our setting up the system. We actually had one guy from Switzerland who came and installed the system. There was a second man who did the wiring connections. Recently, when I called in frustration about not being able to understand how the inventory wand was supposed to work, they did send someone who worked with tech support to walk through the process. As it was, there was some work to be done on the software to determine if books were actually in order by call number. We will receive an upgrade when that is complete. We have been pleased that (again working with technical support over the phone) we have been able to download files of items that have a status of "missing" or "paid" or are thought to be checked out. I had a student go to the stacks and she found over 100 books which fit these categories. We look forward to being able to do a complete inventory in the near future. Another frustration. . . . We learned (well into the project line) that we would have to purchase additional software from III to make the two systems work together. . . . It had not been budgeted. . . . It allows us to check out stacks of books out at our circ stations simultaneously; formerly we had to place one book on the RFID reader at a time and click on the "check out" button. Checking in books needed the same process. We opened the library in mid-December 2005 and are just now [June 2006] getting things as they really should be.

Q: Do you have any advice for other libraries in terms of technical support?

A: I would make sure you know thoroughly how technical support will be handled. Our way has been doable, but not everyone likes to work over the phone. Learn as much about the system you are choosing and talk to lots of folks who are currently using it. Find out the strengths and weaknesses of the support system. We had been corresponding with another library that had the same vendor and same ILS. They ran into similar problems. . . . He had additional issues since he belongs to a consortium of public libraries. . . . Now that things are working as they should, we're very pleased with the smooth processes. I'd probably make the same decision again. (Ward-Griswold interview, 2006)

Continuing Maintenance Procedures

The typical lifespan of a passive RFID tag designed for library usage is said to be the life of the item to which it is attached. But this may vary and time will tell us if this is correct in the next 20, 50, 100 years. It was reported that 3M tested the tags in preparation for their UNLV installation by leaving a tagged book in a car in the Nevada desert. Although the car reached 240°F, the tag was still operable. It would appear that a heavily circulated item will not have a shorter lifespan than a book which sits on the shelf unused for years. At this point, tags seems to have an unlimited amount of reads and they are durable.

In conclusion, the hard work associated with an RFID installation will be completed by the vendor; however, you need to work with the vendor's technical support for any problems that might arise. The tag is designed to be fairly indestructible under normal library conditions and is well-suited for a library item's typical lifespan. Since the tags are passive and powered by RF rather than an internal power source battery, the tags will only be functional while being read during borrowing, returning, shelf reading, or sorting. This assures a long lifespan for the tag and makes RFID a wise and enduring economic investment for item management and article security.

References

Kleist, Robert A., Theodore Chapman, David Sakai, and Brad Jarvis. 2005. *RFID Labeling: Smart Labeling Concepts & Applications for the Consumer Packaged Goods Supply Chain.* 2nd ed. Irvine, CA: Printronix.

Richland County Public Library. 2006. "Meet the Director" Web page. Available: www.richland.lib.sc.us/meet_director.htm.

Ward, Diane Marie, and James Boland, e-mail interview, August 16, 2006.

Ward, Diane Marie, and Gary Christopherson, e-mail interview, July 5, 2006.

Ward, Diane Marie, and Sandra Collins, e-mail interview, July 5, 2006.

Ward, Diane Marie, and Sandra Collins, interview, August 7, 2006.

Ward, Diane Marie, and Ellen Firer, e-mail interview, July 5, 2006.

Ward, Diane Marie, and Jean Foster, e-mail interview, July 4, 2006.

Ward, Diane Marie, and Gretchen Freeman, e-mail interview, July 4, 2006.

Ward, Diane Marie, and Mary Griswold, e-mail interview, July 5, 2006.

Ward, Diane Marie, and Chris Harris, e-mail interview, August 18, 2006.

Ward, Diane Marie, and Lynne Jacobsen, e-mail interview, July 11, 2006.

Ward, Diane Marie, and Brent Jensen, e-mail interview, August 18, 2006.

Ward, Diane Marie, and Maureen Karl, e-mail interview, July 12, 2006.

Ward, Diane Marie, and Manuel Paredes, e-mail interview, August 21, 2006.

Ward, Diane Marie, and Helen Rawlinson, e-mail interview, July 5, 2006.

Ward, Diane Marie, and Katriel Reichman, e-mail interview, August 15, 2006.
Ward, Diane Marie, and Louise Schaper, e-mail interview, July 3, 2006.
Ward, Diane Marie, and Edith Sutterlin, interview, August 7, 2006.

9

Protecting Staff and Patron Privacy within an RFID System

Introduction

When committees try to introduce RFID technology into the communal setting of a library, it can be a magnet for strong sentiment either for or against implementation. This chapter focuses on privacy rights. Privacy rights advocates have expressed concern about the potential for intrusion on First Amendment rights of citizens caused by potential third-party misuse of RFID systems in libraries. The conundrum: How does a library achieve the benefits of RFID and, at the same time, ensure patron privacy and reassure that RFID is not harmful? Librarians need to preserve library culture, the atmosphere of free inquiry, and patron privacy, while testing twenty-first-century technology to streamline work processes and enhance accurate access to information.

Guarding Privacy in Libraries

While manufacturers are selling products to an end user, libraries are the owners of the item that is loaned in confidence to a patron. Within this "handshake" is an important quotient of trust and privacy. As libraries do not allow patron borrowing records to be seen by outsiders, librarians take seriously the pledge to respect the rights of patrons to borrow materials in confidence, and to provide some environmental level of privacy within the library, such as not surveilling what people are reading. In a perfect world, one's library patronage activities would be anonymous and never pose a possible privacy invasion. Perhaps this has always been unrealistic, as all library circulation transactions (for example: borrowing, renewing, returning, billing overdue items) are linked to a patron's unique identification card. This identification card is tied to a user's name and address in the library's proprietary database, which is accessed by authenticated library staff. There is always a chance that a circulation staff member might call up a patron's borrowing record and see what he/she has charged. And the link between patron and circulating material may not be broken if a patron owes fines until the materials are returned. Why do we not lose sleep over this scenario, but do about RFID in libraries?

There should be no cloud of worry that librarians would welcome into the intellectual sanctuary a technology that would readily allow spying. People have a right to know what is tagged with RFID. There should be no hidden tags or readers. This is crucial information that librarians need to relate to the public: there will be no hidden tracking of library items within the walls of a library, and the RFID tags on materials will not carry a history of borrowing.

Realizing Technical Limitations of RFID

When privacy advocates charge that RFID poses a threat to patron privacy, librarians take this very seriously. However, the RFID tag used by library vendors is not a spy chip that will track a patron's whereabouts, and it has limited technical functionality specifically designed to protect patron privacy rights.

RFID tags on library materials are not designed to track a patron's movements inside or outside of the library's walls. To accomplish such a feat would take scores of RFID readers positioned throughout a town, all tied into a central network, and the assistance of a GPS (Global Positioning System). Just as a retailer does not care what a consumer does with a can of soup once it leaves the point-of-sale register, a librarian does not care what a patron does with a book after it is borrowed, but privacy advocates worry about who might be interested in borrowed items in the future.

Librarians have special needs that retailers do not have to consider. ILSs operate in a closed system, therefore, librarians have worked with RFID vendors to create tags that have a short read-range and only broadcast when they come into a reader's field. In no way would a patron have his/her privacy compromised since the tag does not contain any personal patron information, only a bar code or unique item identifier. Additionally, in order to correlate the data of the bar code to the actual title of the book, one would have to hack into the library's ILS to monitor the circulation module and borrowing records. Library OPACs have very good security because librarians have worked with vendors to ensure that this is done properly. The result is that we do not hear stories about library patron borrowing records being put up on the Web. This is a credit both to the vendors who provide secure networked information and also the librarians who demand a product that maintains their privacy rights standards.

There is no factual reason to postulate that the introduction of an RFID system would change the way circulation librarians act in regard to patron privacy. Furthermore, librarians supported by ALA and privacy rights advocacy organizations have vigilantly kept vendors to task about crafting RFID tags that are impervious to hacking, do not carry patron-related data, and that cannot be read by random readers. In an interview with Scott Carlson of the *Chronicle of Higher Education*, Peter E. Murray, Assistant to the Director of Technology Initiatives at the University of Connecticut's Libraries, was quoted as saying in regard to RFID's impact on patron privacy: "But it's a good point to start this discussion of the technology. If it is accepted in the library, it can be accepted anywhere, and if the library can serve as the instigator of that discussion, more power to us." (Carlson, 2004)

Mark Roberti, the editor of *RFID Journal*, was asked by Matthew Artz in 2005 about reading a bar code and privacy infractions: "The number is meaningless," Roberti said. "Unless you have access to the library database and know what book corresponds to the serial number, there is no privacy breach." (Artz, 2005a) Similarly, David Dorman wrote in his American Libraries column in December 2003: "Forgive me for being skeptical of all the hullabaloo, but I just can't get too worked up about a library book broadcasting its bar code for several feet to any and all who care to lug around portable RFID readers and eavesdrop on the reading habits of passersby carrying library books." (Dorman, 2003)

You might be apt to hear people refer to RFID as some type of super-snooping mechanism that uses GPS to triangulate the whereabouts of a person via his or her library book or that people will come into libraries and invade privacy with handheld readers. These scenarios are not realistic now. The RFID tags used by libraries are not that powerful and have a limited read range of about eight inches and the newest tags offer encryption and authentication aspects in order to prevent unauthorized reading of tags.

> The fact that librarians throughout North America are taking the issue of patron privacy seriously is reflected in the actions of the professional librarians' governing bodies in both the U.S. and Canada. Guidelines and principles for using such technology while remaining privacy-conscious were outlined in the American Library Association's 2005 "Resolution on Radio Frequency Identification (RFID) Technology and Privacy Principles," and most recently in Canada in the Ontario Information and Privacy Commissioner's 2006 "Privacy Guidelines for RFID Information Systems (RFID Privacy Guidelines)."

David Molnar and David Wagner in their paper, "Privacy and Security in Library RFID Issues, Practices, and Architecture," analyzed the state of RFID data privacy as it was in 2004. They suggested that "private authentication" was to be a key technical challenge for RFID: "We want tags to reveal their identity to authorized RFID readers (e.g., those owned by the library). However, for privacy, the tag must not disclose its identity until the reader has been authenticated; thus, the reader must authenticate itself to the tag before doing anything else." (Molnar and Wagner, 2004) The authors express their concern that if the technology advances, there is little motivation for a library to upgrade the tags which would be expensive and labor intensive. They forward several suggestions for tag architecture to enhance privacy.

Molnar and Wagner identify "hotlisting" as a means of possible nefarious track and trace. They posit that a person with a handheld reader could intercept RF transmissions or read the tags directly and later identify books from unauthorized third-party reads. This involves a person intent on identifying patron's reading habits using secretive reads of tags, gaining access to the bibliographic data and item records (even though most libraries do not allow users to call up records by bar code), and correlating the two. They experimented by reading the tag identification numbers at UNLV and the César Chávez branch of the Oakland Public Library using a standard Tagsys Medico S002 short-range reader: they saw the bar code identifier (Molnar and Wagner, 2004). It is good that title and author data was not on the tag.

In reality, if someone was that interested in obtaining someone's borrowing record, hacking into the ILS would probably be easier, or just looking over their shoulder. As Daniel McPherson and Vinod Chachra write in "Personal Privacy and Use of RFID Technology in Libraries," the fear of someone using a reader either in a car or the fear that a "satellite passing overhead is going to energize these tags is ignoring the reality that it would have to be within 18 inches of the item. At that distance, it would probably just be easier to read the title on the cover, rather than scan the item for its ID number!" (McPherson and Chachra, 2003)

> It is best to ask your vendor if the data transfer between tag and reader is authenticated and/or encrypted. For many committees, the public perception that RFID is a "spy technology" is an automatic deal breaker; however, with education about the true limits of the technology to send and receive data via authenticated and encrypted transmissions, this fear can be addressed.

Solutions

What do privacy rights activists offer as possible solutions? Working with scientists and engineers, the RFID industry responded with an option to deactivate or kill the retail RFID tag. Additionally, the option to provide individuals with devices that block the tag appears to be a feasible way to protect privacy. For example, a Danish RFID technology company, RFIDSec, has developed a privacy application for retail tags. Zeroleak™ uses "a zero-knowledge authentication protocol, which can verify that an RFID reader has the proper authority to read it but does not require the tag to reveal any identifying information during the authentication process." (Khan, 2005) Their product enables that when an RFID tag enters "privacy mode" no identifiable information is communicable, but EPC-related data that might relate to warranties, etc., will be transmitted to the consumers' personal digital assistant (PDA).

Claus Heinrich in *RFID and Beyond* challenges some of the more popular arguments about privacy rights associated with RFID installations. While he takes into account the arguments of privacy rights advocates, he reinforces: "The scanning range is extremely limited. Readers will not be ubiquitous. Tags can be encrypted or otherwise secured. Corporate databases are not shared by competitors or even non-competing companies in different industries." (Heinrich, 2005: 184) Researchers such as Heinrich, share with privacy right advocates and RFID proponents like EPCglobal that people need to be aware of RFID tags and should be allowed to discard them if they purchase an item. For library patrons, the ability to destroy the tag is not an option since the patron is borrowing the library's property. However, the former tenet is paramount: patrons need to know that their library uses RFID.

Exploring RFID in Real-World Libraries

- The best practice a library could have in terms of privacy rights and RFID is to have a privacy rights policy written and accessible to patrons. Examples are: Fresno County Public Library: www.fresnolibrary.org/about/rfid.html, and Santa Clara City Library: www.library.ci.santa-clara.ca.us/about-the-library/policies.html
- Prominently display that your library uses RFID.
- Tags should only contain a bar code or other unique identifier.
- Tags should carry no link to the patron.
- Data on the tag should be encrypted.
- The OPAC should not have a "search by bar code" query available to the public.
- With a privacy policy in place, a library committee can ask potential vendors how their system will ensure the upholding of their privacy rights policy.
- If your library is considering an RFID-enabled patron card, your committee might want to seriously consider having an opt-out card with a bar code

only just to assure any patrons that are trepidatious of RFID technology in their wallet that they can use their municipal or school library without stress. The opt-in and opt-out methodologies are supported by ALA in its "Choice & Consent" section of the "Guidelines for Developing a Library Privacy Policy." (ALA, 2006)

- Offer an open information session for your patrons with prospective vendors.

RFID Success Story: Berkeley Public Library

Berkeley Public Library (http://berkeleypubliclibrary.org) began a public discourse on RFID in August 2002, but had thought of it as a possible option when they were renovating the Central Library in 2000. They saw increased circulation with no companion increase in staffing. Berkeley Public Library saw opposition from staff and patrons about possible privacy rights, job security, and health issues associated with RFID implementation. Matthew Artz wrote of a protest in "Library Workers, Patrons Denounce RFID System." RFID installer, Checkpoint Systems, sent a representative, Paul Simon, to the information forum to answer community questions. Artz wrote that Simon was: "Addressing audience concerns" and conveyed that "Checkpoint RFID tags did not contain memory for additional information besides the book code and contained no heavy metals. Simon also insisted that Checkpoint was in sound fiscal health and would not go out of business, leaving the city stuck with no one to service the technology." (Artz, 2005b) Despite protests, Berkeley Public Library installed an RFID system and they provide an excellent model to follow on disseminating information to patrons using their Web site.

> The presence of vendors at informational forums is an excellent way to address questions of the public. To their credit, Berkeley Public Library and Checkpoint Systems worked together to try and reassure patrons about the technical nature of RFID.

Berkeley Public Library has a "Best Practices" page, an FAQ, a presentation on the health affects of RF available on their library Web page that are excellent models for other libraries to use to inform patrons about how RFID technology is used. In it the administration pledged that no library staff would be let go due to RFID and that there would be no linkages on the RFID tag linking it to the borrower. They are committed as all libraries to securing the database from unauthorized entry. Their main reason for RFID was an expectation that it would alleviate work-related stress injuries since workers compensation costs between 1998 and 2003 totaled $2 million. From the Library's Web page FAQ on RFID, administration addresses the financial details: "The RFID System, purchased in 2004, cost $650,000 including interest, to be paid over six years. The Board of Library Trustees approved RFID for an investment in long-term capability to promote public service while using efficiency measures to accommodate staffing constraints and reduce worker injury costs." (Berkeley Public Library, 2005).

Additionally, Berkeley Public Library's Elena Engel constructed a thorough docu-

> Berkeley Public Library information on RFID on their Web page includes: "A Best Practices for RFID Technology,"
> http://berkeleypubliclibrary.org/system/RFIDBEST.pdf,
> and an explanation of the health concerns about RFID,
> http://berkeleypubliclibrary.org/system/LibraryversionOct24.pdf
> There is also an FAQ at:
> http://berkeleypubliclibrary.org/system/RFIDFAQ3.pdf

ment titled "RFID Implementations in California Libraries: Costs and Benefits," which is discussed in more detail in Chapter 4. In many ways, Berkeley Public Library is a model for libraries to follow in being open to listening to critics, yet following through on the technology as long as all parties involved have all their concerns addressed.

Responding to Library Organizations, RFID, and Privacy Issues

American Library Association's (ALA) Position on RFID

As Howard Falk eloquently summarizes in his technology column titled "Privacy in Libraries," ALA "views privacy as essential to the exercise of free speech, free thought, and free association and believes that in a library, whether physical or virtual, the right to privacy is the right to open inquiry without having the subject of one's interest examined or scrutinized by others." (Falk, 2004: 281)

The American Library Association has responded to the call of its members to provide leadership and guidance on the topic of RFID, privacy, and libraries. Resources that are available on its Web site include:

- ALA has "An Interpretation of the Library Bill of Rights." Available at: www.ala.org/Template.cfm?Section=interpretations&Template=/ ContentManagement/ContentDisplay.cfm&ContentID=34182&CFID= 54426605&CFTOKEN=56681701
- ALA has a Web page on RFID with links to external data resources, privacy rights advocacy organizations, and news stories. Available at: www.ala.org/ Template.cfm?Section=ifissues&Template=/ContentManagement/ ContentDisplay.cfm&ContentID=77689

- The Council of the American Library Association issued a privacy policy statement on June 27, 2006, at ALA's Annual Conference in New Orleans, Louisiana titled: "RFID in Libraries: Privacy and Confidentiality Guidelines." Available at: www.ala.org/ala/oif/statementspols/otherpolicies/rfidguidelines.htm

- The Council had previously adopted a resolution on January 19, 2005, at ALA's Midwinter Meeting in Boston, Massachusetts, titled: "Resolution on Radio Frequency Identification (RFID) Technology and Privacy Principles." In it, ALA endorses the "BISG Policy Statement Policy #002: RFID Radio Frequency Identification Privacy Principles." Available at: www.bisg.org/docs/BISG_Policy_002.pdf ALA also affirms privacy norms that libraries using RFID should disclose its use to patrons, guard against having personal information recorded on tags, comply with relevant laws and best practices, and be able to verify these principles by independent audit. The full text of the Resolution is available at: www.ala.org/Template.cfm?Section=ifresolutions&Template=/ContentManagement/ContentDisplay.cfm& ContentID=85410

- ALA has a "Privacy Tool Kit" Web site for librarians who deal not just with RFID but with privacy as an issue for all aspects of librarianship and patron relations. It contains an overview of privacy in libraries, as well as procedures and a bibliography of other external resources. Available at: www.ala.org/ala/oif/iftoolkits/toolkitsprivacy/Default4517.htm

- The "Privacy Tool Kit" also features an extensive section titled: "Guidelines for Developing a Library Privacy Policy." The pages are essentially a best practices document which highlights privacy policies that are in place for academic and public libraries. This is something that should be of high interest to libraries pursuing RFID. Available at: www.ala.org/ala/oif/iftoolkits/toolkitsprivacy/guidelinesfordevelopingalibraryprivacypolicy/guidelinesprivacypolicy.htm

Canadian Library Association

The Canadian Library Association has issued position statements on the importance of patron privacy, the right to freely access information, and ethical behavior in library culture. "The Code of Ethics" is available at: www.cla.ca/about/ethics.htm and "The Citizenship Access to Information Data Banks—Right to Privacy" is available at: www.cla.ca/about/citizen.htm

Additional Canadian models exist, published by the Information and Privacy Commissioner of Ontario in 2004. Dr. Ann Cavoukian is the commissioner of this group and has played a large part in providing guidance to Ontario and Canada. Available via the Commission are:

- "Privacy Guidelines for RFID Information Systems (RFID Privacy Guidelines.)" Available: www.ipc.on.ca/docs/rfidgdlines.pdf
- "Practical Tips for Implementing RFID Privacy Guidelines." Available: www.ipc.on.ca/docs/rfidtips.pdf
- "Guidelines for Using RFID Tags in Ontario Public Libraries," published in 2004. Available: www.ipc.on.ca/docs/rfid-lib.pdf

Relating the History of Privacy Rights Issues to RFID Technology

RFID technology has quietly existed for decades without people taking exception to its existence or potential usage. The potential of RFID remained off the radar of most people for sixty years because it was not part of everyday life. Even today, the average person does not know what RFID is or what it can or cannot do.

Incrementally, our conception of consumer and patron privacy is eroded with every retail/grocery loyalty cards we sign up for and credit card purchase we make; however, the convergence of automatic identification technology and the largest retailers applying it on a potentially item-level basis was a touchstone for privacy rights advocates as intrusive. When news first broke that Wal-Mart chose RFID as a cost-effective supply chain application, it was common in 2002 and 2003 to locate articles that mentioned Orwell's *1984*, Huxley's *Brave New World*, or Spielberg's *Minority Report* in conjunction with an attempted scientific explanation of how RFID works. If an RFID tag was affixed to each item's packaging, then what happens when the product and the RFID tag go home with the consumer? Does the tag remain alive and will it continue to send out a signal like a beacon to anyone driving around with a RFID reader? Could your neighbor, armed with an RFID reader, know what you buy and from where you buy it? Most early web-based news reporting about RFID compared the tags to spy chips that would herald the genesis of a Big Brother society enabling the government to surveil citizens without their consent or knowledge.

> Most early Web-based news reporting about RFID compared the tags to spy chips that would herald the genesis of a Big Brother society enabling the government to surveil citizens without their consent or knowledge.

Web sites popped up alluding to RFID chips as the Revelations biblical "mark of the beast" passage. Also at this time, "war-driving" was becoming a new techno-geek-sport and some early articles claimed that tags would be transmitting from store shelf to the home garbage, people armed with a reader would "RFID-war-drive" through a neighborhood and "see" what you have in your home and where you purchased it.

> War-driving involves using a laptop, an antenna and some wireless-router sniffing software to inconspicuously drive around neighborhoods and see who has a wireless connection in their home, what company made the router, if it is named, and if there is WEP privacy protection associated with the wireless set up. Roaming people have the ability to hop onto your Internet connection and surf for free from your unique IP address—all without your knowledge or permission if your wireless network is not encrypted.

It is not of interest to librarians to monitor how books are used by patrons at home or in the library; however, it is valuable for a librarian to almost instantly be able to locate a misplaced book for an anxious patron. The tag for library applications is not designed to be read from one meter away; it is a considerably less powerful passive tag with a limited read range of about eight inches in optimum conditions operating on 13.56 MHz. There are indeed RFID tags in the market that are always transmitting their unique item data, that can be read through walls and from yards away by high-powered readers, but they are traditionally active tags designed specifically for use on government or military applications.

> The tag for library applications is not designed to be read from one meter away; it is a considerably less powerful passive tag with a limited read range of about eight inches in optimum conditions operating on 13.56 MHz.

The presence of the tag has only served to fulfill the store's contract with the manufacturer and will be designed to be cost-effective and, therefore, by default will not have a great read range and will not have GPS capabilities. As Claus Heinrich notes in *RFID and Beyond*, "The scanning range is extremely limited. Scenarios that depict criminals or FBI agents parked outside homes with RFID readers fail to take into account that EPCglobal tags are passive and operate at a UHF frequency that has difficulty interacting with metal and water. Tags next to human bodies (which are composed primarily of water) are often unreadable. Surreptitious scanning of someone's person or home would require that the spy in question get up very close and personal with a handheld scanner, and be very subtle about it. Readers will not be ubiquitous. Real World Awareness implementation projects are not built around the idea of implanting readers every few feet so that a pallet or individually tagged object is more or less continually scanned. Rather, readers would be placed only in strategic locations—warehouse floors and smart shelves, for example." (Heinrich, 2005: 184)

Legislating RFID

Many state senators have tried to introduce bills for legislation of RFID. California State Senator Deborah Bowen was one of the first to look into the privacy aspects of RFID and into restricting the ways businesses and libraries in California could use RFID tags. Claire Swedberg wrote in an article: "Opponents convinced the majority of the committee members that the timing for the bill (SB1834) was wrong and that the bill should not precede the actual installation of RFID in businesses and libraries" (Swedberg, 2004).

Many worry about the potential for third-party cloning of RFID cards without the card holder's consent. In February 2005, California Senator Joe Simitian introduced SB 682, "The Identity Information Protection Act of 2005," which would prevent identity documents (like a library card) from containing an identity chip and move to criminalize the unauthorized reading of RFID tags in California. The bill was passed by the California State Senate and was on the long process to enactment when it met with claims of trying to prevent RFID technology usage. The act was repeatedly revised and a recent version (August 15, 2005) suggested a three-year moratorium on using RFID in these types of cards and licenses. While in the Appropriations Committee the bill was put on hold for possible future action in the next two years, only to be resurrected in August 2006. Then, in October 2006, Senator Simitian's bill was approved by the California Senate (30 to 7 vote) but SB 768, "The Identity Information Protection Act of 2006," was eventually vetoed by Governor Arnold Schwarzenegger.

> The text of California Senator Joe Simitian's bill can be found at: www.leginfo.ca.gov/pub/bill/sen/sb_0651–0700/b_682_bill_20050815_amended_asm.html

U.S. Senators John Cornyn (R–Texas) and Byron Dorgan (D–North Dakota) called the first Senate RFID Caucus on July 13, 2006, in Washington, D.C. The meeting featured Mark Roberti, editor of *RFID Journal*, Patrick J. Sweeney, author and CEO of ODIN Technologies, and Daniels W. Engels, Director of the Texas Radio Frequency

Innovation and Technology Center at the University of Texas at Arlington, and formerly a leader of the MIT Auto-ID Center. Engels stated: "RFID technology is inherently neither good nor evil. The applications using RFID technologies will be overwhelmingly good and beneficial to society. Policies and laws exist to define the acceptable boundaries. . . . The new focus on RFID technologies is simply an opportunity to sharpen the boundaries that already exist." (Engels, 2006)

Understanding Privacy Rights Advocacy Groups

Consumers Against Supermarket Privacy Invasion and Numbering (CASPIAN)

An early lesson that was learned for all who plan to implement RFID was to be upfront with your patron base as to what the application is, and what are the technology's parameters and privacy rights safeguards. This is perhaps paramount for librarians to learn. European retailer Metro Group AG incorporated RFID on an item-level basis, but ran into a problem with consumers when privacy rights advocates discovered that the retailer embedded an RFID tag with customer-specific data into its loyalty card without informing consumers. Metro Group in Germany made a public relations faux-pas with not alerting customers about its RFID-enabled key fob and they had privacy rights advocates like CASPIAN to thank for pursuing the privacy issue in regard to their implementation.

The privacy rights group Consumers Against Supermarket Privacy and Numbering linked the ability for stores to "track" purchases to the omniscience they already possess over individual consumer shopping habits via the grocery loyalty cards and key fobs, and have likened it to an apocalyptic "Mark of the Beast" technology. Katherine Albrecht has championed the consumer's right to know when RFID is being used, and has criticized the efficacy of retailers to protect consumers privacy. Although the focus of the group has been on RFID's impact on consumers, the authors take libraries to task for using RFID at all. Albrecht, CASPIAN's founder, is the author of the *The Spychips Threat: Why Christians Should Resist RFID and Electronic Surveillance* (2005), and coauthor with Liz McIntyre of *Spychips: How Major Corporations and Government Plan to Track Your Every Move with RFID* (2005). Reporter Mark Baard notes: "Both books are published by the Christian publishing powerhouse Thomas Nelson. Both lay out the same totalitarian scenarios, based on documented plans by Philips, Procter and Gamble, Wal-Mart and other companies, along with the federal government, to track consumer goods and people individually." (Baard, 2006) Albrecht is also featured in a 2005 "RFID: The Battleground" video by Endtime Publishing discussing resistance to loyalty cards and RFID chips.

> Consumers Against Supermarket Privacy Invasion and Numbering
> Web site is: www.nocards.org/

Simson Garfinkel and Henry Holtzman deal more in depth with this issue in "Understanding RFID Technology" where they acknowledge how important it is to be sensitive to the views of groups: "Whether or not the Beast's mark is VeriChip or a credit card number is beyond the scope of this chapter. What's important, though, is that a number of individuals believe that RFID may be an instrument of [sic, the] Beast—that is, of the Devil—and have decided to fight against it for that reason." (Garfinkel, 2006: 35) Peter de Jager wrote in "Experimenting on Humans Using Alien Technology": "RFID technology treads dangerously close in some people's minds to the area of scripture, Revelations, and the 'Mark of the Beast.' There is a legitimate segment of the consumer base that believes in the mark of the beast. There is no point in disrespecting their perspective. We have to take them into account if we want RFID implementations to succeed." (De Jager, 2006: 446)

Privacy Rights Clearinghouse

Former librarian and current privacy rights advocate Beth Givens, directs the Privacy Rights Clearinghouse (PRC) (www.privacyrights.org). Givens offers in a presentation available on the PRC Web site a model for best practices for libraries to follow including the following paraphrased tenets: libraries should erect a privacy policy; make public its RFID system and policies; ensure that tag reading is not done in secret; users should know the purpose of RFID use; prevent any personal data on the tags; and have security and integrity in data transmission including encryption of the data packet (Givens, 2004).

Givens also gave testimony, "RFID and the Public Policy Void," to the California Legislature Joint Committee on Preparing California for the 21st Century in 2003. She made the case that there is no official body to investigate and regulate the potential for privacy rights infringements caused by RFID since the U.S. Office of Technology Assessment was closed in September 1995. On behalf of the Privacy Rights Clearinghouse (PRC) and other peer privacy rights advocacy groups, Givens suggests institutions should ensure privacy and continue consumer trust including full disclosure of the RFID system. The PRC Web site includes information about the potential for misuse of RFID tags.

Privacy Rights Clearinghouse
Privacy Rights Clearinghouse has information on RFID at:
www.privacyrights.org, including Beth Givens' and Lee Tien's "RFID
Implementation in Libraries," available at: www.privacy
rights.org/ar/RFID-ALA.htm, and the "RFID Position Statement of
Consumer Privacy and Civil Liberties Organizations," available at:
www.privacyrights.org/ar/RFIDposition.htm. Givens' testimony is
available at: http://privacyrights.org/ar/RFIDHearing.htm

Electronic Frontier Foundation

The Electronic Frontier Foundation (EFF) has lobbied for consumer and individual privacy rights since 1990. EFF is funded by private donors and does not receive corporate support. The organization questions the functional ability of RFID to erode privacy. In many respects the work of privacy groups such as EFF have kept RFID R&D teams attuned to the needs of libraries, which are different from the needs of manufacturers. It is their diligence that keeps RFID developers moving toward an impenetrable tag and system and reminds citizens about the dangers of living in a surveillance society.

For more information on the origins of EFF, see
www.eff.org/Misc/Publications/John_Perry_Barlow/HTML
not_too_brief_ history.html
Additionally, EFF has a campaign to "Keep RFIDs out of California
Public Libraries," available at:
www.eff.org/Privacy/Surveillance/RFID/libraries/

RFID-IN-ACTION INTERVIEW: PRIVACY RIGHTS

Lee Tien is the leading privacy rights advocate associated with RFID and has been a lawyer in the fields of information, free speech, and privacy for 15 years. Since 2000, he has worked as a lawyer with Electronic Frontier Foundation. I sought out his opinion on the current state of privacy, RFID, and libraries. He reminds us all how necessary it is to protect patron privacy now and in the future.

Q: What makes RFID right or wrong in a library setting, in your opinion? Do you think that a speedier checkout is worth potential privacy rights problems down the line?

A: IMHO [in my humble opinion] RFID is not ready for libraries today because of the lack of privacy protection. But it's not up to me. Public libraries are public institutions, and the decision should be made publicly after careful consideration.

Q: In your organization's opinion, is the current RFID architecture ready for libraries in terms of ensuring patron privacy? What is the chief problem with RFID and libraries?

A: In our view, RFID is not ready for prime time in libraries. The chief problem is really twofold: we don't think that library RFID systems are designed to protect patron privacy; we don't think libraries are taking the privacy issue seriously enough. In this sense the RFID and libraries issue isn't much different from RFID in most other contexts. Almost by definition, RFID usage poses privacy issues because of its dependence on open transmissions that are readily available to anyone with a compatible RFID reader. The development of RFID as a technology has been shaped by the goal of tracking things, particularly things (warehouse inventory, military equipment) that don't raise privacy concerns because the things do not belong to or aren't carried by individuals with a privacy interest (as opposed to soldiers or military personnel who are part of a more-or-less all-encompassing institution). As a result, it is not a very secure technology. It can be made more secure, but libraries have a long history of protecting patron privacy, recognizing that surveillance relating to "expressive goods" like books, movies, sound recordings, and so on raise free speech issues as well. What people read, watch, or listen to provide powerful clues about what they believe or think about politics, religion, and culture—matters that have always been magnets for government attention. That you are reading about Islam or Marxism or gay/lesbian culture is simply more sensitive than that you wear a particular size or brand of jeans. Unfortunately, there's a lot of very one-sided techno-cheerleading with respect to RFID right now.

Q: If patrons want more information about possible privacy rights infringements in libraries caused by RFID, do you offer an FAQ or Web page that gives information? How best can concerned patrons contact you for more information? Are you willing to help patrons organize and lobby against RFID?

A: We have some information on our Web site—letters to libraries about the risks of RFID as well as other public writings about RFID in other contexts. . . . I have been active in the Bay Area on library RFID, but I'm the only RFID specialist lawyer at EFF, and so our resources are very limited. The ACLU has also been active in this area, and I would recommend that patrons contact their local ACLU. Finally, there are library accountability groups in some communities who attend library trustee meetings and inform the public about important issues. In San Francisco, for instance, the Library Users Association has been a strong voice against library RFID.

Q: What happened in San Francisco with their attempt to introduce RFID? Could you provide highlights as to how EFF's campaign in San Francisco (in terms of grassroots organization) appears to have halted RFID installation?

A: In San Francisco, the library began to try to introduce RFID in an unfortunately stealthy manner. EFF and the ACLU of Northern California were alerted to the attempt by Library Users Association, a library accountability group led by Peter Warfield. EFF and ACLU-NC publicly criticized the library's attempt, first before the library board, and then before the board of supervisors. We were able to show that the library had not done its homework on RFID and convinced some of the supervisors that it was unwise to commit funds to RFID until the library had done a better job of justifying the expense in light of the privacy and "return on investment" issues. Over time, the library slowly backed away from the program, and funds were not appropriated. We believe the library is still interested, but will proceed much more cautiously. In this effort, we were greatly helped by library activists. There's quite a bit of information about our fight in San Francisco on the EFF Web site.

Q: Have there been other libraries that pulled back from RFID because of public outcry?

A: I'm not aware of any.

Q: Have you had reported to you any instances of privacy rights intrusions directly caused by RFID in any of the installed RFID libraries?

A: No, and I wouldn't expect to. It's almost intrinsic to most privacy violations that they are not directly perceptible to the victims. Victims of identity theft discover the problem long after the initial privacy violation. The only reason we know about most database breaches is because of California's law requiring notification when there's a security breach.

Q: Do RFID vendors for libraries seek out your counsel or opinions on RFID?

A: No.

Q: Would you patronize a library that had an RFID system? Why or why not?

A: My own public library, in Berkeley, has an RFID system. Like most library patrons, we have little choice about the library to use. (Ward-Tien interview, 2006)

It is this author's hope that when considering an RFID solution, library committees would open some RFID meetings to community members so that citizens could voice their opinions on the technology. The library is an integral part of a community and any members that feel uncomfortable about the privacy rights aspects of the technology should be encouraged to voice their opinion and have their questions addressed by experts and/or vendors.

Tabling RFID

San Francisco Public Library

www.sfpl.org

There are only a few instances when patron uproar has changed the way the library implemented RFID or delayed it. San Francisco Public Library is one such library. In 2004, San Francisco Public Library investigated using an RFID system for some of its library branches (including 19 renovations and new construction at five sites), and requested money to be reserved in the budget to craft an RFI for RFID. A sum of $300,000 for the first year of a six-year plan was written into the budget for 2004–2005. (San Francisco Public Library, 2005) In the spring of 2005, the Library Commission created the San Francisco Public Library Technology and Privacy Advisory Committee (LTPAC) to investigate and respond to privacy, job security, health-related and financial concerns expressed by citizens; however, San Francisco Board of Supervisor's Budget Committee voted four against one on reserving the funds on June 30, 2005, effectively tabling the forward progress of bringing RFID to San Francisco's Public Library system. LTPAC issued a 76-page summary report in October 2005 titled: Radio Frequency Identification and the San Francisco Public Library. The chief motivation for an interest in RFID for San Francisco Public Library was the potential for an RFID-based circulation system to increase efficiency in the circulation process and reduce the number of RSI reported by staff using the bar code scanner system.

San Francisco Public Library Technology and Privacy Advisory Committee (LTPAC) issued a 76-page summary report in October 2005 titled "Radio Frequency Identification and the San Francisco Public Library." It is available at: www.sfpl.org/librarylocations/libtechcomm/RFID-and-SFPL-summary-report-oct2005.pdf

---

Although San Francisco Public Library sought an RFID tag that would house the book's legacy bar code number and no patron-specific information, issues were raised. The public response to San Francisco Public Library's RFID implementation proposal was concentrated on the privacy rights aspects of the technology. At the time San Francisco Public Library was trying to implement, another Bay Area privacy rights organization was trying to educate library patrons about the potential for privacy rights infringements with RFID. Peter Warfield, Executive Director and co-founder of the Library Users Association, wrote "Industry's Gain, Library's Pain" with Lee Tien in 2005. In it, the authors compare the attractiveness of RFID to libraries as a "carrot and stick": "The stick is the thinly veiled, very real threat that RFID will usher in an age of ubiquitous surveillance in the near, if not immediate, future. The

Figure 9.1: Ward's Survey Results: Judging Patron Privacy and Staff Concerns

Did you encounter patrons who were worried about privacy rights infringements?

Response	Percentage of Libraries	Number of Libraries
Yes	91%	32
No	6%	2
No response	3%	1

How would you characterize the segment of your population that was concerned with privacy rights infringements caused by RFID?

Not applicable/not a problem	88%
Vocal Minority	6%
No response	6%

Did you encounter staff worried about the RFID system?

Response	Percentage of Respondents	Number of Respondents
Yes	51%	18
No	46%	16
No response	3%	1

carrot is the vain hope that libraries can save society from that dystopian future." (Warfield and Tien, 2005)

Judging Patron Privacy and Staff Concerns

The issue with privacy rights has not affected many libraries installing RFID. I asked in my 2006 survey of librarians who implemented RFID: Did you encounter patrons that were worried about privacy rights infringements? The results were interesting considering the amount of energy and public discourse that have surrounded RFID. Ninety-one percent or 32 library respondents did not experience any patron concerns. Only two respondents experienced patron concerns.

This low percentage of patrons concerned with RFID could be a result of several factors:

- an informed library patron base that trusts the library will only purchase a technology that protects their privacy rights
- an apathetic public that is not interested in the privacy aspect of a technology that promises to make life easier
- a successful library public relations information campaign that explains to patrons that their privacy is paramount
- patrons do not know that their library uses RFID
- patrons understand the library application will not affect them

In addition to the survey questions asking about privacy rights, I interviewed some libraries that had indicated that they had experienced some level of patron interest in the privacy rights aspect of RFID to see what worried patrons. Patrons that this author has surveyed informally over the years that express trepidation about RFID's role in twenty-first-century libraries are basically worried about having someone hidden with a reader spying on their reading choices.

RFID-IN-ACTION INTERVIEW: PATRON CONCERNS

I asked Marilyn Sheck of Seattle Public Library in an e-mail interview (July 3, 2006) about her patrons that expressed concerns about RFID.

Q: You experienced some patrons that were worried about privacy right infringements cause by the installation of an RFID system in the Library. You characterized this on my survey as "a vocal minority." Can you please elaborate on what were their concerns? Were they grassroots or backed by an organized privacy rights advocacy group? What did they do to voice their concerns?

A: They thought the government would spy on what they are reading using satellites. They were not part of an organized group. They called, e-mailed, or talked to staff. Their only concern seemed to be keeping the government out of their business. In addition to fearing government spying, they feared staff would lose their jobs, and they appreciate their staff and didn't want that to happen. (Ward-Sheck interview, 2006)

I asked Manuel Paredes, Director at Cherry Hill Public Library in Cherry Hill, New Jersey, about privacy and patron reaction to the RFID installation. He wrote to me: "At the time when we were considering and implementing RFID, there was a lot of press and ponderings regarding the technology. I think there was an article on Wal-Mart's efforts that was the genesis of most people's fears. That coupled with the Patriot Act made people nervous, I believe. The possibility that there would be a technology that could trace a person's buying habits by linking RFID, bar codes, credit cards and even GPS would be an invasion of privacy and an intrusion on individual rights. Since then, RFID has become more prevalent in everyday business and there hasn't been the technological links that everyone feared . . . at least that has been made public. The initial fears from the library community were from a small unorganized group of concerned patrons, who questioned whether or not we would be able to make the traces as they conjectured. At the time that we were implementing RFID, the library had not completed its other technology and using debit cards was a long way off. We were anticipating stand alone reports, let alone thinking about an integrated report system. Still, we received one or two letters and perhaps a handful of people came in individually to voice their concern. I think their fears were allayed once we explained the technology, its purpose and the larger concerns that we had in just getting the thing to work and the cost savings goal that we had. On the home front, the fact that there was no standard in RFID technology, coupled with various non-integrating proprietary systems, would soon lend support that we could not even consider how the technology could be used for anything else other than its intended purpose." (Ward-Paredes interview, 2006)

I was intrigued by the apparent division with privacy rights issues between the United States and Canada. It seems that those in the United States have had far more interest in the privacy aspect of RFID than those in Canada. I asked a library that recently purchased an RFID system about the atmosphere about privacy rights in Canada. Adrienne Canty, Manager of the Strathcona Branch of Edmonton Public Library in Edmonton, Alberta, Canada, responded: "I continue to be (happily) surprised at the lack of controversy there has been regarding the privacy/security issue and RFID. . . . A member of the public attending an event we held to acknowledge funding for the RFID project engaged one of our associate directors . . . in a discussion about security concerns, but that's really all that there has been in the way of public response to date. After every article in the paper I expect there to be letters to the editor about EPL's choice to move to RFID technology, and/or about RFID and privacy in general, but there's been nothing but silence so far. Why are we in Canada not experiencing the sorts of challenges that other libraries have faced regarding the protection of personal information? Two things, I believe: First, Canadians seem on the whole to be less concerned about the use of personal information than our counterparts south of the border (although there is growing concern about the use of personal information with increasing reports of identity theft, phishing, and other misuse). Perhaps it's because, with one-tenth of the population of the United States we have, accordingly, a lower overall incidence of identity/information misuse issues, so RFID/privacy/misuse are not as high on the public radar. Second, in Canada, we have legislation in place that protects the use of personal information. In Alberta, we have the Freedom of Information and Protection of Privacy Act (FOIP) that governs how personal information is collected, used, stored, and distributed. It's available online via the Alberta Queen's Printer Web site, at www.qp.gov.ab.ca/documents/Acts/F25.cfm?frm_isbn=0779746465. We also have a federal Privacy Act, available on the Justice Canada Web site, at http://laws.justice.gc.ca/en/P–21/index.html. There just doesn't seem to be the same concern amongst Canadians that there is in the States regarding the use of personal information, a result (perhaps) of the legal framework protecting privacy. . . . We at EPL have also been very clear throughout the project that only the bar code is programmed onto the RFID tag (no bibliographic information or personal information about the borrower). The public version of our catalog cannot be searched by item number, so any eavesdropper would not be able to search the database for identifying bibliographic information at any rate. At most, a determined eavesdropper accessing the bar code number on the chip could phone a library branch and renew the item for the customer who has borrowed it—any question like, 'What's the title associated with this bar code number?' would arouse suspicion and staff members would be alerted to something out-of-the-ordinary." (Ward-Canty interview, 2006)

Enhancing Patron Privacy with RFID

Electronic Article Surveillance is important for libraries to guard against theft. If something sets the electromagnetic system off, a circulation staff member needs to search the patron's bags and recheck the borrowed items to find out which item was not properly desensitized or which was being stolen. This can be very embarrassing for the patron and time-consuming and awkward for the staff member. RFID vendors that offer an EAS bit on the RFID chip remove the need for a second system for item security since item management and security are on one tag. This combination increases patron privacy because staff members will not have to go through a patron's bags to see what item set off the sensors: A staff person will know exactly which book was not desensitized because of the item identification information stored on the chip that trips the sensor gates will appear on a circulation desk screen.

Addressing Staff Concerns

It appears that the most concerned parties in RFID implementations are the library staff. When I asked in my librarian survey "Did you encounter staff that were worried about the RFID system?" Fifty-one percent of respondents said "yes." This may stem from a fear of technology making paraprofessionals obsolete. However, RFID offers paraprofessionals the opportunity to interact more with patrons in value-added conversations about the library and its holdings. From my research, I have not found any correlation to RFID causing the loss of library jobs. In fact, I generally hear anecdotal stories about how much improved the work environment and staff morale are after RFID installation.

Eric Ipsen wrote about the 2004 Public Library Association's annual convention and the 375 people who attended a presentation on RFID. From his experience he wrote that counter to what is in media reports: "RFID privacy issues were not a pressing concern for most librarians. . . . Most librarians understand the limitations of RFID read ranges in libraries—the government is unlikely to track what people are reading if it has to get within a foot of someone to scan a tag" (Ipsen, 2004). He goes on to mention that the records are stored in the library systems and that the potential for privacy intrusion is more possible from PATRIOT Act-sanctioned access to those records.

RFID-Enabled Patron Cards

I asked Camille Cleland, Assistant Director for Technical Services at Skokie Public Library, about the decision to use or not use patron cards. She responded "We do NOT use a patron card containing an RFID chip. We had sure thought about it, but due to expense, and maybe privacy issues, we decided to continue with the regular patron card" (Ward-Cleland interview, 2006). In my survey, I found that only a small percentage of RFID libraries have introduced or were interested in introducing a smart patron card. Some vendors offer this card with the potential for using it with other municipal applications. The RFID-enabled smart cards are not designed to track the owner's movements and will only be functional in the library setting; however, it is important for libraries to work with vendors and privacy rights advocates to ensure that this always remains the case.

In conclusion, each library committee needs to assess the value of RFID and how to address its patrons' right to privacy. With continual enhancements to the technology, RFID promises to be very useful to libraries, but librarians need to be vigilant and work with privacy rights advocates to ensure that RFID architects and vendors cherish the patron's right to privacy as much as the library profession.

References

American Library Association. 2006. "RFID: Radio Frequency Identification Chips and Systems." Available:
www.ala.org/Template.cfm?Section=ifissues&Template=/Content Management/ContentDisplay.cfm&ContentID=77689
Artz, Matthew. 2005a. "RFID: Library's New Technology Sparks Controversy." Mindfully.org: Technology (March 4). Available: http://mindfully.org/Technology/ 2005/RFID-Berkeley-Library4mar05.htm
Artz, Matthew. 2005b. "Library Workers, Patrons Denounce RFID System." Mindfully.org: Technology (August 5). Available: http://mindfully.org/Technology/ 2005/RFID-Patrons-Denounce5aug05.htm
Baard, Mark. 2006. "RFID: Sign of the (End) Times?" Wired (June 6). Available: www.wired.com/news/technology/1,70308–0.html

Berkeley Public Library. 2005. "Frequently Asked Questions on Radio Frequency Identification (RFID)" (September). Available: http://berkeley publiclibrary.org/system/RFIDFAQ3.pdf#search=%22berkeley%20public %20library%20faq%20rfid%22

Carlson, Scott. 2004. "Talking Tags: New High-Tech Labels Help Libraries Track Books, But Worry Privacy Advocates." *Chronicle of Higher Education* 50, no. 48 (August 6): A29. Available: http://chronicle.com/cgi2-bin/printable.cgi?article=http://chronicle.com/free/v50/i48/48a02901.htm

De Jager, Peter. 2006. "Experimenting on Humans Using Alien Technology." In *RFID: Applications, Security, and Privacy*, edited by Simson Garfinkel and Beth Rosenberg. Upper Saddle River, NJ: Addison-Wesley.

Dorman, David. 2003. "RFID Poses No Problem for Patron Privacy." American Libraries. *Technically Speaking* column (December). Available: www.ala.org/ala/alonline/techspeaking/2003columns2/december2003.htm

Engels, Daniel W. 2006. "Prepared Statement, U.S. Senate RFID Caucus Inaugural Meeting" (July 13). Available: www.rfidbusiness.org/news/files SenateRFIDCaucus EngelsStatement.pdf

Falk, Howard. 2004. "Technology Corner: Privacy in Libraries." *The Electronic Library* 22: 3: 281–284.

Garfinkel, Simson, and Henry Holtzman. 2006. "Understanding RFID Technology." In *RFID: Applications, Security, and Privacy*, edited by Simson Garfinkel and Beth Rosenberg. Upper Saddle River, NJ: Addison-Wesley.

Givens, Beth. 2004. "RFID Implementations in Libraries: Some Recommendations for 'Best Practices'." San Diego, CA: Privacy Rights Clearinghouse (January 10). Available: www.privacyrights.org/ar/RFID-ala.htm

Heinrich, Claus. 2005. *RFID and Beyond*. Indianapolis, IN: Wiley.

Ipsen, Eric. 2004. "Librarians Focus on RFID." *RFID Journal* (March 14). Available: www.rfidjournal.com/article/articleprint/829/–1/82/

Khan, Farhat. 2005. "Can Zero-Knowledge Tags Protect Privacy?" *RFID Journal* (September 27). Available: www.rfidjournal.com/article/articleprint/1891/–1/1/

McPherson, Daniel, and Vinod Chachra. 2003. "Personal Privacy and Use of RFID Technology in Libraries." VTLS Web site (October 31). Available: www.vtls.com/documents/privacy.pdf

Molnar, David, and David Wagner. 2004. "Privacy and Security in Library RFID Issues, Practices, and Architectures." Washington, DC: Computer and Communications Security 2004 Conference (October 27). Available: www.cs.berkeley.edu/~daw/papers/librfid-ccs04.pdf

San Francisco Public Library. 2005. "Radio Frequency Identification and the San Francisco Public Library." Technology and Privacy Advisory Committee. Available: www.sfpl.org/librarylocations/libtechcomm/RFID-and-SFPL-summary-report-oct2005.pdf

Swedberg, Claire. 2004. "California RFID Legislation Rejected." *RFID Journal* (July 5). Available: www.rfidjournal.com/article/articleview/1015/1/1/

Ward, Diane Marie, and Adrienne Canty, e-mail interview, August 16, 2006.
Ward, Diane Marie, and Camille Cleland, e-mail interview, July 5, 2006.
Ward, Diane Marie, and Manuel Paredes, e-mail interview, July 5, 2006.
Ward, Diane Marie, and Marilyn Sheck, e-mail interview, July 3, 2006.
Ward, Diane Marie, and Lee Tien, e-mail interview, July 10, 2006.
Warfield, Peter, and Lee Tien. 2005. "Industry's Gain, Library's Pain." Mindfully.org: Technology (May 10). Available: http://mindfully.org/Technology/2005/RFID-Industry-Gain10may05.htm

Additional Resources

American Library Association. 2005. "Resolution on Radio Frequency Identification (RFID) Technology and Privacy Principles." Available: www.ala.org/Template.cfm?Section=ifresolutions&Template=ContentManagement/ContentDisplay.cfm&ContentID=85331

American Library Association. 2007. "RFID: A Brief Bibliography. ALA Fact Sheet Number 25." Available: www.ala.org/ala/alalibrary/libraryfactsheet/alalibraryfactsheet25.htm

American Library Association. 2007. "Guidelines for Developing a Library Privacy Policy." Available: www.ala.org/ala/oif/iftoolkits/toolkitsprivacy/guidelinesfordevelopingalibraryprivacypolicy/guidelinesprivacypolicy.htm

Canadian Library Association. 1976. "The Code of Ethics." Available: www.cla.ca/about/ethics.htm

Canadian Library Association. 1987. "The Citizenship Access to Information Data Banks—Right to Privacy." Available: www.cla.ca/about/citizen.htm

Givens, Beth. 2006. "Activists: Communicating with Consumers, Speaking Truth to Policy Makers." In RFID: Applications, Security, and Privacy, edited by Simson Garfinkel and Beth Rosenberg. Upper Saddle River, NJ: Addison-Wesley.

Information and Privacy Commissioner of Ontario (Ann Cavoukian, Commissioner). 2004. "Guidelines for Using RFID Tags in Ontario Public Libraries." Available: www.ipc.on.ca/images/Resources/rfid-lib.pdf

Information and Privacy Commissioner of Ontario (Ann Cavoukian, Commissioner). 2006. "Practical Tips for Implementing RFID Privacy Guidelines." Available: www.ipc.on.ca/images/Resources/up-rfidtips.pdf

Information and Privacy Commissioner of Ontario (Ann Cavoukian, Commissioner). 2006. "Privacy Guidelines for RFID Information Systems (RFID Privacy Guidelines)." Available: www.ipc.on.ca/images/Resources/up-1rfidgdlines.pdf

10

Public Relations and
Patron Education

Introduction

Public and academic libraries have successfully achieved a balance implementing RFID while upholding their pledge of patron privacy. In this chapter, the positive public relations and patron education experiences of several libraries will be explored, as well as a candid discussion about the challenges of implementation. Interviews with librarians, project managers, and administrators involved with RFID library implementations serve as a guide to what a library committee may expect to encounter. Integrating an RFID system into an ILS is a challenge, but perhaps more challenging is allaying the public's skepticism or fear of RFID. Just as librarians strive to provide access to sound and accurate information through detailed bibliographic records in the online catalog, they need to provide accurate information about RFID to their patrons.

The best practice is to tell your patrons about your RFID system: let them know you are using RFID and have a sheet available that tells them what RFID can and cannot do. Libraries should learn from some retail missteps that if you are not up front with your patrons about the usage of RFID, it may set back your implementation and also cause your patrons to distrust you.

Successful Integration Starts with an RFID-Literacy Campaign

Successful integration of RFID is a tremendous accomplishment from a technical standpoint, but perhaps committees may overlook how crucial it is to be successful in explaining what RFID is to the patrons and the community at large. When asked what advice she would give to libraries of a similar size when they think about installing RFID, Seattle Public Library's Marilyn Sheck suggested: "Win over your customers and staff before you make the final decision. Decide whether it makes sense in your library. We had a definite business need, and RFID was our answer. Don't go with RFID just because it's cool technology or 'everyone else has it.' It is expensive and should be worth the investment." (Ward-Sheck interview, 2006)

As discussed in Chapter 1, popular culture contributes to a sense that this technology will invade privacy; however, these are not characteristics of RFID equipment used in libraries. Library-centric RFID vendors work closely with librarians to tailor systems that will not intrude upon the rights of the public. The most important component is to be open with the public from the start. Opening up informational sessions to patrons is a good step. For instance, Kansas City Public Library listed on its Web site that demonstrations by 3M and Checkpoint would occur over a two-month period in 2005. This allowed the library board trustees and interested community members an opportunity to explore RFID and to ask the experts about any issues that they might have concerns about.

The news posting about Kansas City Public Library's open meetings is available at: www.kclibrary.org/guides/central/index.cfm?news= read&newsID=3635

Some patrons may want answers to questions such as:

- Will RFID hurt me?
- Will someone know what book I am reading if I am in a study carrel?
- Will the RFID tag in my book affect my garage door opener?
- Will my cell phone make the library security gates sound an alarm?
- Is the RFID tag in the book tied to a GPS system so that my movements will be tracked everywhere when I am carrying this book?

One may think these questions are facetious and frivolous, but in fact they are all questions that I have been asked or that have been asked of people I know. These are in no way "dumb questions"; rather, they are fair questions because in some ways they are true to the nature of what RFID may potentially be able to do as a technology. These questions and more can be handled in an FAQ on RFID that your library can post in-house and on the Web.

A superb resource for information about setting up a library public relations campaign is Lisa A. Wolfe's *Library Public Relations, Promotions, and Communications,* published by Neal-Schuman Publishers, Inc. in 1997 in their "How-To-Do-It Manual" series.

Web Guides

An online guide explaining the implementation of your new RFID system will help to spread the true capabilities of RFID to your patrons. These guides need to present information in an approachable manner so as to educate the public about RFID without trying to give them a degree in engineering. There are a few guides currently available on the Internet that were produced by libraries.

- Fresno County Public Library offers a brief overview of what RFID is and what information library RFID tags have stored on them. For instance, a patron of Fresno County Public Library that is worried about the type of information housed on an RFID tag could access their web page about RFID and find answers to questions such as: "Is any personal information stored on the RFID tag? Can the RFID tag be read after I leave the library? Are there any health risks associated with RFID and radio waves?" Fresno County Public Library explains that no personal data is stored on a tag and that the only information on the tag (the bar code) is not searchable online by the catalog. Additionally, the library describes how the passive RFID tag is used in libraries. It is a good model for libraries interested in a brief Web page for information on RFID. It is available at www.fresnolibrary.org/about/rfid.html
- Santa Clara City Library produced a step-by-step guide for its Checkpoint System's Intelligent Library System implementation. Assistant City Librarian Karen Saunders provides an excellent example for other libraries to follow on disseminating information about the library's usage of RFID. The guide contains screenshots of work processes as well as a great deal of background information on why Santa Clara City Library decided on RFID. It is available at www.library.ci.santa-clara.ca.us/rfid/checkpoint.html
- Broward County Library produced a guide with a step-by-step approach to its implementation. It is available at Tech Logic's Web site: www.tech-logic.com/browardco/default.htm

Health Concerns Associated with RFID

Many patrons wonder about the safety of RFID since it is a new technology. Some readers may remember that when bar code scanners were first introduced into retail and grocery chains in the 1980s many worried about the long-term effects of being in close proximity to a laser beam UPC reader for long periods of time. Questions were raised about the possible effects of this technology on pregnant women. Decades have since passed, and we have seen the laser bar code reader become a piece of ubiquitous technology as has become the UPC code.

So now that the U.S. FDA determined it is legal to implant someone with a chip, what are the medical ramifications of this technology? There are no reports as yet, linking the implanted RFID tag to any adverse health conditions in humans, or in animals for that matter. While implanting in dogs and cats might serve a clear purpose, there are several companies that are trying to promote the implanting of microchips in humans; however, there needs to be more conclusive research and experimentation with the long-term effects of having a radio frequency transmit from one's body.

In my informal survey of library patrons, several raised questions about exposure to electromagnetic fields. To this date, the International Commission on Non-Ionizing Radiation Protection (ICNIRP) has issued findings on its research, including one abstract which mentions that: "All of these systems use electromagnetic fields to detect or communicate over a short distance (usually up to a few meters). For the general public, they involve brief exposure times of generally less than a few seconds. For occupational exposure, extended exposure times may occur." (ICNIRP, 2006)

Radio frequency waves used in libraries (13.56 MHz) are part of the High Frequency radio waves of the electromagnetic spectrum. Non-ionizing radiation is a result of radio frequency waves and is a low energy like radio, television, cellular phones, and Wi-Fi, and it is absorbed by the body which is composed of water and tissue. It is sometimes expressed that large amounts of this type of energy over a long period of time can heat tissue, but it is not like the type of ionizing radiation caused by X-raying body parts. RFID has been used for the last decade as an identifier in animals and is endorsed by many veterinarians and animal rights groups as a method to protect animals, so it is unlikely that these organizations would promote a technology that would cause long-term tissue damage to an animal or a human.

Information about the safety of non-ionizing radiation can be located at the following governmental resources:

- The International Commission on Non-Ionizing Radiation Protection (ICNIRP) publishes research findings at: www.icnirp.net. The group issued a report, ICNIRP Statement Related to the Use of Security and Similar Devices Utilizing Electromagnetic Fields, available at: www.icnirp.net/documents/EASD.pdf
- U.S. Department of Labor, Occupational Safety & Health Administration's Web page on Non-Ionizing Radiation: www.osha.gov/SLTC/radiation_nonionizing/index.html

- OSHA also has a page on "Radio Frequency and Microwave Radiation" and is available at: www.osha.gov/SLTC/radiofrequencyradiation/index.html
- The Federal Communications Commission also has a Web page devoted to Radio Frequency safety available at: www.fcc.gov/oet/rfsafety/ and an exhaustive FAQ at: www.fcc.gov/oet/rfsafety/rf-faqs.html
- The World Health Organization has a Web site devoted to electromagnetic research available at: www.who.int/peh-emf/research/en/, and Fact Sheet no. 304 about "Electromagnetic Fields and Public Health" at www.who.int/mediacentre/factsheets/fs304/en/index.html

Libraries should always make sure that the products they purchase meet all FCC requirements for electromagnetic devices. An additional step would be to measure the RF emissions from newly installed equipment to ensure that it is within the specified range necessitated by, and not exceeding what is required for optimum performance of the library applications.

Training the Patron on Self-Check

One important aspect to consider is how to attract a patron to a self-checkout kiosk that may seem foreign and intimidating at first to the uninitiated. Positioning a circulation staff member near the machine might be a good suggestion to help and pull the patrons out of borrowing lines at the circulation desk to take them to the self-check machine and guide them through the onscreen process. Posters advertising the new RFID self-checks might also be beneficial and cause interest and excitement to your patron base that is comfortable with ATMs and retail self-checkouts.

In Gollin and Pinder's study on self-check in the United Kingdom in 2003, the authors noted that many libraries experienced problems trying to get patrons to use the non-RFID self-check machines (48 percent) and also a reluctance from staff to promote the self-check machines (37 percent). (Gollin and Pinder, 2003: 49) They noted that self-check "significantly changes the experience of a user borrowing or returning library materials. Library users may require training and encouragement, and feel uncomfortable with the inevitable reduction in human contact. . . . Self-check might provide an improved service and another option for users, increase privacy, and reduce the amount of time spent queuing. . . . " (Gollin and Pinder, 2003: 44)

There is a segment of library patrons that would miss the interaction with circulation staff and may avoid the self-check units. Some patrons I have surveyed expressed comments such as:

- "I enjoy the service aspect of a library circulation desk. It is often where I find out about good books I might enjoy based on what I am checking out. The librarian tells me this, but a computer can't."

**Figure 10.1:   LAT's F5 Max RFID Self-Check
(Photo courtesy of LAT)**

**Figure 10.2:   Libramation's Self-Check Unit for the Whitby Public
Library
(Photo courtesy of Libramation)**

- "Why should I check myself out? Isn't that what they are paid to do as a service to the patron? That's why I pay taxes."
- "I prefer to have my children go to a circulation librarian. I want them to have the same type of library experience I had which included pleasant conversations with the attendants about what I'm reading and what I might like to read in the future. Without that human interaction, a trip to the library will be just as impersonal as a trip to the bookstore or shopping online."
- "I don't want to encourage self-checkout at the library any more than I want to at my local stores. I think self-check puts people out of work, maybe not now, but in the future. What will happen to the library staff?"

- "I am really not that comfortable with technology. What do I do if I make a mistake? I don't even like ATMs. I suppose if a librarian showed me how to use it, like stood beside me and guided me just once, I might feel comfortable with it."

The last two sentiments are echoed by many long-term library patrons: They don't want the library to lay off workers and they are afraid of making a mistake with the technology, perhaps not properly checking something in or out. The remedy for the legitimate fear of new technology is public awareness and training. The remedy for the first needs to be a realistic agreement from management that staff will not be let go if the popularity of self-check soars: existing circulation employees need to be retrained and repositioned to more value-added patron-based activities to continue the valuable work a library tries to accomplish.

The self-check machines will be able to report on how many transactions have occurred, thus enabling a library to have a firm idea on the adoption rate of using self-check. Northland Public Library went from 49 percent to 54 percent between 2005 and 2006, which indicates steady growth. (Ward-Collins interview, 2006) No staff were let go as a result of the integration of self-check.

I asked Manuel Paredes, director at Cherry Hill Public Library in Cherry Hill, New Jersey, about self-check adoption rates. He responded: "Our self-check we believe is about 40 percent. It is difficult to get a report when the gate recording activity fluctuates. On occasion the gates do not pick up the tag signal for an unknown reason. When the gate is adjusted, sometimes the result is an oversensitivity so that it goes off with double counts. Since we now have to change our gates and self-check stations, we are re-looking at and re-thinking our needs. Children need help with self-checkout so we'll probably scratch that. The gates need to be closer to the door so patron's don't side step the gate and if they try, the guard should stop them. But . . . if we have a guard at the door, do we need RFID for security? . . . We have not been able to free up our staff people as patrons seem to prefer the face to face and frequently run into questions when using self-check. If a person does not have any fines or holds overdue books then self-check works out ok but a large number of people generally have a question, reserve or issue concerning their account. So, reassign people. That's not really likely. Actually, Circ people are kind of specialized in their tasks and job classification, so moving them would be limited. If we made a change, it would most likely result in a reduction in force." (Ward-Paredes interview, 2006)

I asked Susan O'Neal, Director of Middletown Public Library, about patron adoption of self-check in an e-mail interview. She explained: "My staff thought the seniors wouldn't like it. Not! They are independent, have learned and love the self-checkout and not having to stand in line. This group in particular—when they are ready to go they are ready to go! The moms with 35 books and three kids in tow were probably the group that was the most dependent on staff assistance at the beginning, but most have "converted" to self-checkout, especially with the children helping. At present, about twenty-one months after implementation, 80 percent of all borrowing is done independently by our customers. One of our workstations is lower for ADA accessibility and we have observed no barriers to usage by individuals in wheelchairs. The touch screens are easy to use and text is minimal, large, and easy to read." (Ward-O'Neal interview, 2006)

An article by Mark Wolf of Farmington Public Library in New Mexico extols the virtue of self-check, "Self-Check Success." I believe it is a must-read as it is not only well written, but truly illustrates the way self-check can allow staff to interface on a deeper level with patrons. Wolf notes that they achieved 100 percent self-check routinely. He relates the story about a class of young children showing each other how to self-check materials and how circulation staff actually now have the time to interact with patrons on a level that goes beyond just exchanging quick pleasantries and moving onto the next customer in line. Wolf writes that circulation staff members were positioned "by the machines to encourage patrons to try the self-check. Part teachers, part librarians, and part salespeople, they circulated among the patrons to coach and chat with them. We discovered immediately that without the barrier of the circulation desk, patrons were much more open to talk and ask questions." (Wolf, 2006: 8–9)

Libraries do not want the introduction of self-checkout stations to give the appearance that library work is being shifted to the patron, as in retail stores, which might offend tax-paying patrons who look at the library as a service. It is the way in which a library promotes the self-check as a means of expedient self-service to those who simply want to charge items and not wait in line behind patrons with more involved questions. Karen Coyle once postulated: " . . . it could become the 'ATM' of the library world, the fast service with few lines that users come to prefer to old way of doing things." (Coyle, 2005: 488)

Best Practices

- Publicize RFID from the start: Do not hide the integration.
- Become knowledgeable about the technology. Make sure that your public services library staff has current, relevant, and scientific information about RFID.
- Have a privacy policy in place. Being armed with correct data will allow you to help the public with questions related to privacy.
- Identify the technology's benefits for both patrons and staff, and its drawbacks.
- Answer questions about the cost of the system.
- Refer patrons to well-respected sources of researched information.

- Demonstrate to patrons that RFID readers only work and read the tag within the specified short-range of the reader.
- Position self-check machines near the circulation desk so patrons have a clear option.
- Station a staff member near self-check machines to help guide patrons on use.
- Advertise your RFID self-check machines in posters and on the library's Web site.
- Make sure your self-check machines have clear onscreen instructions.
- Invite the public to open meetings showcasing RFID products with the opportunity for question and answer time with the vendors.

References

Coyle, Karen 2005. "Management of RFID in Libraries." *Journal of Academic Librarianship* 31, no. 5 (September): 486–489.

Fresno County Public Library. 2006. RFID at the Fresno County Public Library. Accessed January 30, 2006. Available: www.fresnolibrary.org/about/rfid.html

Gollin, Sarah, and Chris Pinder. 2003. "The Adoption of Self-Check Technology in UK Academic Libraries." *New Review of Academic Librarianship* 9, no. 1 (December): 42–58.

International Commission on Non-Ionizing Radiation Protection (ICNIRP). 2006. Available: www.icnirp.net/activities.htm

Ward, Diane Marie, and Sandra Collins, interview, August 7, 2006.

Ward, Diane Marie, and Susan O'Neal, e-mail interview, August 3, 2006.

Ward, Diane Marie, and Manuel Paredes, e-mail interview, August 21, 2006.

Ward, Diane Marie, and Marilyn Sheck, e-mail interview, July 3, 2006.

Wolf, Mark. 2006. "Self-Check Success." *Public Libraries* 45, no. 2 (March/April): 8–10.

RFID POCKET GUIDES

Pocket Guide A

Acronyms

Acronym	Explanation
ALA	American Library Association
AMH	Automated Material Handling
ASRS	Automated Storage and Retrieval System
BISG	Book Industry Study Group
CASPIAN	Consumers Against Supermarket Privacy Invasion and Numbering
CLA	Canadian Library Association
CPG	Consumer Packaged Goods
EAN	European Article Number
EAS	Electronic Article Surveillance
EFF	Electronic Frontier Foundation
EPC	Electronic Product Code
FTE	Full Time Employee
GPS	Global Positioning System

GUI	Graphical User Interface
HF	High Frequency
ICNIRP	International Commission on Non-Ionizing Radiation Protection
ILS	Integrated Library System
ISO	International Standards Organization
LF	Low Frequency
LITA	Library and Information Technology Association
MIT Auto-ID Center	Massachusetts Institute of Technology, Automatic Identification Technology Center
NCIP	NISO Circulation Interchange Protocol
NISO	National Information Standards Organization
OPAC	Online Product Access Catalog
PLA	Public Library Association
PRC	Privacy Rights Clearinghouse
RF	Radio Frequency
RFID	Radio Frequency Identification
RFI	Request for Information
RFP	Request for Proposal
RFQ	Request for Quotation
ROI	Return on Investment
RSI	Repetitive Stress Injury
SIP	Standard Interchange Protocol
UCC	Uniform Code Council
UHF	Ultra High Frequency
UPC	Universal Product Code

Pocket Guide B

Library of Congress Subject Headings for RFID and Related Topics

Radio frequency identification systems
Radio frequency identification systems | x Technological innovations
Radio frequency identification systems | x Security measures
Libraries | x Security measures
Electronic security systems
Electronic surveillance | x Social aspects
Privacy, Right of | z United States
Inventory control
Stack management (Libraries) | x Automation
Stack management (Libraries) | x Technological innovations
Charging systems (Libraries) | x Technological innovations
Book drops | x Technological innovations

Pocket Guide C

Ward's 2006 Survey of RFID Libraries and RFID Vendors, Survey Methodology

From late January to early April of 2006, I e-mailed 50 libraries that had completed RFID installation or were in the final stages of RFP contract-signing. Thirty-five North American (U.S. and Canadian) libraries responded and two British libraries that I had e-mailed separately (apart from the 50 North American). The surveys were completely filled for the most part. I promised not to attribute library information from the survey to libraries unless allowed. I further interviewed in person or via e-mail (a much more convenient and potentially error proof method) scores of librarians involved with RFID system purchase and installation. The results are based on quantitative analysis of the responses and are indicative of only the opinions and experiences of this sample.

I also surveyed from late May to early July of 2006 the top eight vendors of RFID solutions for libraries in North America. Again, I am not quoting their pricing directly. I used their figures to create an average cost, which in many ways reflects all of the estimates appearing in literature today. The results of the survey appear throughout the book and are easily located through figures and tables. I have no vested interest in any of the vendors, nor does my library (SUNY Buffalo) have or foresee an RFID system in its future. Blank copies of the surveys follow. Statistics for RFID library installations are based on responses supplied by vendors.

<u>Librarian Survey: RFID for Libraries 2006</u>
Diane Marie Ward

The responses you supply will be tallied and will not be attributed to you or your library. The responses are for pure statistical purposes for my book. I may call on you for a more in-depth interview in the future to speak to some of the points surrounding choosing and implementing an RFID-based library circulation and security system. Your participation is greatly appreciated and will help to further our profession and our outreach to our users. Please contact me with any questions you may have about this survey. Thank you for your time. Diane Marie Ward.

Please type in your answers to free-form questions after the question mark.
For yes and no questions, just place an "X" in the appropriate box.

===

Vendor used for your RFID system?

[   ]

Collection size (physical volumes):

[   ]

Did you tag all of these volumes?

	Yes
	No

If no, what percentage of your collection did you convert to RFID tags? %

[   ]

Staff size:

[   ]

Did your library form a committee to investigate the benefits of RFID?

	Yes
	No

How long was it from committee inception to RFID system purchase?

	Months

Does your library have more than one physical branch?

	Yes
	No

Did you implement the RFID circulation system at each branch?

	Yes
	No
	Does not apply

Did you encounter patrons that were worried about privacy rights infringements?

	Yes
	No

Did you encounter staff that were worried about the RFID system?

	Yes
	No

If yes, what were their worries: ____

How would you characterize the segment of your population that was concerned with privacy rights infringements caused by RFID?

	a vocal minority
	an overwhelming majority
	does not apply, we had no problem
	their concerns were enough to alter our original implementation plan

Did your vendor offer to convert your existing collection to RFID for your library using their staff rather than your library staff?

	Yes
	No

Did you use this vendor option, or did you reallocate staff to complete the conversion?

	Used vendor option to convert to RFID tags
	Reallocated staff for conversion
	Wanted to use the vendor option, but was not feasible financially

How long did it take to convert the materials in your collection?

	Months

How did your technical services adapt to the use of RFID tags:

	The tagging procedure was easy for our tech services staff to adapt to
	The tagging procedure was not easy for our tech services staff to adapt to

Are you still using bar codes?

	Yes, we use both bar codes and RFID tags for the present time
	No, we are strictly using the RFID tags for circulation

Did you select a tag which:

	is only for circulation, we continue to use 3M Tattle Tapes (TM) for item security
	is only for circulation, we continue to use another system other than 3M Tattle Tapes (TM) for item security
	has circulation and item security bit on one tag
	Other

Was the conversion to RFID:

	More expensive than originally budgeted for?
	Less expensive than originally budgeted for?
	About the same as originally budgeted for?

Do you consider your decision to switch to RFID:

	A success
	A failure
	No opinion at this point

Were you satisfied with the terms of the guarantee for your new RFID system?

	Yes
	No

Has your vendor been accessible to help you troubleshoot any problems which arose after installation?

	Yes
	No

Did you install RFID self-check-out kiosks?

	Yes
	No

Did you install RFID self-check-in kiosks?

	Yes
	No

Did you install RFID-enabled sorters and sorting bins for checked in materials?

	Yes
	No

Did you install mounted, stationary RFID readers in the library?

	Yes

	No

Did you purchase hand-held RFID readers?

	Yes
	No

Does your patron card contain an RFID chip:

	Yes
	No

Did your library circulation staff notice any decrease in repetitive stress related complaints after the implementation of the RFID system?

	Yes
	No

Have you recorded any time-related statistics that directly point to the RFID system as a time saver for staff and patrons?

	Yes
	No

Have you used your hand-held RFID reader to locate misplaced items in the stacks?

	Yes
	No

Has your staff used the hand-held RFID reader to inventory your collection:

	Yes
	No

Please choose the best range for the cost of your RFID system:

	$0-$150,000 (US)
	$150,001-$300,000
	$300,001-$500,000
	$500,001-$750,000
	$750,001-$1,000,000
	Over $1,000,000

What were the top three reasons you made the decision to purchase and install an RFID-based system:

1)
2)
3)

What are the top 3 questions you would encourage other libraries that are considering RFID to ask of themselves and of vendors before they make the change to RFID:
Ask of their library staff and committees

1)
2)
3)

Ask of vendors

1)
2)
3)

Any miscellaneous comments about your conversion to an RFID circulation and/or security system:

Thank you again!
Please email back to dianerfid@gmail.com

<u>**Vendor Survey: RFID for Libraries 2006**</u>
Diane Marie Ward

Your participation is greatly appreciated and will help to further the library profession's understanding of the real-world benefits of RFID and also serve to outreach to library users about the privacy issues associated with RFID. Please contact me with any questions you may have about this survey. Additionally, will you send me stock-digital images (.tiff format) of your products for my chapter on RFID equipment of hand held readers, wall-mounted and stationary readers, RFID tags for books and audio/visual materials, conversion stations?   Thank you for your time.   Diane Marie Ward.

For yes and no questions, just place an "X" in the appropriate box.

===

COMPANY SPECIFICS:

Company Name (as you would like it to appear in my book)

Address:

Phone:

Fax:

Web site:

Email contact:

Who is your Chief Executive Officer?

Do you have a Board of Directors?

	Yes
	No

If yes, do you have any librarians on your Board?

	Yes
	No

How many staff members do you have as of April 2006?

Year that your company began selling RFID solutions:

Are you a subsidiary of a parent company?

	Yes
	No
If yes, which company:	

Is providing RFID solutions for libraries the sole focus of your business?

	Yes
	No

<u>TECH RELATED:</u>

Do you have an in-house Research and Development team to engineer RFID applications for libraries, or do you outsource hardware design to a 3rd party vendor of tags, readers, etc?

	In-house research and design of hardware
	Outsource research and design of hardware

Who makes your tags?

How many bits are your tags

bits

Do you offer a tag that *HAS* a security bit for EAS (electronic article surveillance) on the tag?

Do you offer a tag that *DOES NOT HAVE* a security bit for EAS (electronic article surveillance) on the tag?

Do you supply on-site training for library staff members?

	Yes
	No

Do you offer on-site support for libraries after installation?

	Yes
	No

What are the basic points of your guarantee? (i.e. 10 years parts and labor on hardware, etc.)

Did you encounter clients that were initially unhappy with their RFID solution? (i.e. perhaps read rates fell short of their expectations).

	Yes
	No

If yes, what were common reasons for dissatisfaction:

<u>INTEGRATED LIBRARY SYSTEMS:</u>
Please list all the integrated library systems that you have worked with:

Are there any integrated library systems with which you cannot integrate RFID?

Are there any specific server requirements for an RFID system integration?

<u>CONVERSION PROCESS:</u>
Do you offer an option for customers that *your staff* will convert (RFID-tag) their existing collection?

	Yes
	No

How is this option priced? Per item or Per hour? Please give details.

How many libraries have selected this option?

[   ]

On average, how many items per hour may be converted to RFID using your conversion stations:

[   ]

CLIENTS:

Number of new clients with contracts for RFID implementation in 2004:

[   ]

Number of new clients with contracts for RFID implementation in 2005:

[   ]

Total number of RFID implementations completed by your company since company inception:

[   ]

Breakdown of that number (in real numbers, not percentages, please)

U.S.	
Canada	
Central & South America	
Australia	
Europe	
Asia	
Africa	

Is your current customer list located for prospective libraries to peruse? Please provide URL if on web.

[   ]

PRICE in US dollars.

Please list each model number with basic price. It is understood that prices will vary based on installation specifics. This section will be used primarily to give *general* information about the price range of readers and tags, etc. as a whole. Readers of the book will be directed to contact vendors for specific up-to-date quotes regarding pricing

Cost of a passive 13.56 MHz RFID tag for a book
1)

Cost of a passive 13.56 MHz RFID tag for audiovisual material:
1)

Cost of staff desk-stationary reader unit:
1)
2)

Cost of hand held reader:
1)
2)

Cost of wall-mounted reader:
1)
2)

Cost of conversion station for technical services staff:
1)

Cost of self check-out kiosk:
1)

Cost of self check-in kiosk station:
1)

Cost of sorting unit with bins:
1)

Cost of each additional bin for sorting unit:
1)

Cost of security gates for RFID-enabled EAS
1)

Cost of middleware software application for ILS:
1)

Estimated cost for an RFID system for a library with 500,000 books.

Top 3 questions asked by library clients:
1)
2)
3)

Top 3 misconceptions about RFID:
1)
2)
3)

How does your company handle the *privacy-related* questions regarding RFID systems? Has your company added security features to the package to secure privacy of patrons?
1)

Many worry about the potential for the RFID network to be vulnerable to hackers and third parties. What type of advice do you offer to your clients about making the network and database secure?
1)

One of the biggest concerns I have noticed in my research is that of library staff fearing that RFID will take their jobs. How do you address that question with your clients?
1)

Greatest benefit of RFID for libraries:
1)
2)
3)

What differentiates your company from the competition?
1)

Have your clients used the RFID system for inventorying their collection and if so, how many books per hour (on average) are they able to inventory?
1)

Thank you again.

Pocket Guide D

Recommended Resources: Books, Web Sites, Blogs, Discussion Boards, Organization News, and Vendors

Books

Banerjee, Ramanuj, et al. 1999. *The Case for Smart Cards 03*. London: UK Banking Technology.

Bhuptani, Manish, and Shahram Moradpour. 2005. *RFID Field Guide: Deploying Radio Frequency Identification Systems*. Upper Saddle River, NJ: Sun Microsystems Press, Prentice Hall Professional Technical Reference.

Coleman, Christopher. 2004. *An Introduction to Radio Frequency Engineering*. Cambridge, UK: Cambridge University Press.

Eskelinen, Pekka. 2004. *Introduction to RF Equipment and System Design*. Boston: Artech House.

Finkenzeller, Klaus. 2003. *RFID Handbook: Fundamentals and Applications in Contactless Smart Cards and Identification*. 2nd ed. Translated by Rachel Waddington. West Sussex, UK: John Wiley & Sons.

Garfinkel, Simson, and Beth Rosenberg, eds. 2006. *RFID: Applications, Security, and Privacy*. Upper Saddle River, NJ: Addison-Wesley.

Hawkes, P. L., D. W. Davies, and W. L. Price. 1990. *Integrated Circuit Cards, Tags and Tokens: New Technology and Applications*. Oxford: BSP Professional Books.

Heinrich, Claus. 2005. *RFID and Beyond*. Indianapolis, IN: Wiley.

Kleist, Robert A., et al. 2004. *RFID Labeling: Smart Labeling Concepts & Applications for the Consumer Packaged Goods Supply Chain*. Irvine, CA: Printronix.

Kleist, Robert A., et al. 2005. *RFID Labeling: Smart Labeling Concepts & Applications for the Consumer Packaged Goods Supply Chain*. 2nd ed. Irvine, CA: Printronix.

Paret, Dominique. 2005. *RFID and Contactless Smart Card Applications*. Translated by Roderick Riesco. West Sussex, UK: John Wiley & Sons.

Poirier, Charles, and Duncan McCollum. 2006. *RFID: Strategic Implementation and ROI: A Practical Roadmap to Success*. Fort Lauderdale, FL: J. Ross.

Shepard, Steven. 2005. *RFID: Radio Frequency Identification*. New York: McGraw-Hill.

Sweeney, Patrick J. II. 2005. *RFID for Dummies*. Hoboken, NJ: Wiley.

Web Sites

Inbox Robot
    www.inboxrobot.com/news/RadioFrequencyIdentificationRFID
More RFID
    www.morerfid.com
Network World: RFID
    www.networkworld.com/topics/rfid.htm
RFID International News
    www.rfidinternational.com
RFID Journal
    www.rfidjournal.com
RFID News
    www.rfidnews.com
RFID Update
    www.rfidupdate.com
RFIDExchange
    www.rfidexchange.com
Topix.Net: RFID News
    www.topix.net/tech/rfid
Tutorial Reports
    www.tutorial-reports.com/wireless/rfid/index.php
Using RFID
    www.usingrfid.com

Blogs, Discussion Boards, and News Compilers

RFID_LIB discussion list: Instructions for subscribing can be found at: http://slisweb.sjsu.edu/ecommunication/listsubscriptions.html

Klaus Finkenzeller's Home page
    http://rfid-handbook.de/index.html

RFID Buzz
  www.rfidbuzz.com
RFID Exchange
  www.rfidexchange.com
RFID Gazette
  www.rfidgazette.org
RFID in Libraries
  www.libraryrfid.net/wordpress
RFID Informationen
  www.rfid-informationen.de
RFID News: Doublecode News Network
  www.doublecode.com/rfid
RFID Society
  www.rfidsociety.org
RFID Talk
  www.rfidtalk.com
RFID Times
  http://rfidtimes.blogspot.com
RFID Update
  www.rfidupdate.com
RFID Weblog
  www.rfid-weblog.com
The RFID Weblog
  http://rfid.weblogsinc.com

Organization News

American Civil Liberties Union
  www.aclu.org
Association for Automatic Identification and Mobility
  www.aimglobal.org/technologies/rfid
CASPIAN Consumers Against Supermarket Privacy Invasion and Numbering
  www.nocards.org/AutoID
Electronic Frontier Foundation
  www.eff.org
Electronic Privacy Information Center: RFID
  www.epic.org/privacy/rfid
EPCglobal Inc.
  www.epcglobalinc.org
Eurotag
  www.eurotag.org
Near Field Communication Forum
  www.nfc-forum.org/home

Privacy Rights Clearinghouse
   www.privacyrights.org
RFID@WINMEC
   www.wireless.ucla.edu/rfid/index.asp
Smart Card Alliance
   www.smartcardalliance.org

RFID Vendors (North America)

Bibliotheca-RFID
   www.bibliotheca-rfid.com
Checkpoint Systems
   www.checkpointsystems.com
Integrated Library Technologies (ITG)
   www.integratedtek.com
Libramation
   www.libramation.com
Library Automation Technologies, Inc. (LAT)
   www.latcorp.com/latsite/index.html
Tech-Logic
   www.tech-logic.com
VTLS
   www.vtls.com
3M
   www.3m.com

RFID Vendors (Europe and Asia)

Intellident
   www.intellident.co.uk
LibBest
   www.libbest.com
ST LogiTrack
   www.stlogitrack.com
Wavex
   www.wavex-tech.com

RFID Tag Manufacturers

Lucatron
   www.lucatron.com
Philips Semiconductors
   www.semiconductors.philips.com
Tagsys
   www.tagsysrfid.com

UPM Rafsec & UPM Raflatec
  www.rafsec.com

Library Providers of Gates, AMS, Consultation

FKI Logistex
  www.fkilogistex.com
Sentry Technology Corporation
  www.sentrytechnology.com/librrfsys.htm

Index